GUIDE TO
THE USE OF LIBRARIES AND
INFORMATION SOURCES

Guide to the Use of Libraries and Information Sources

SIXTH EDITION

Jean Key Gates

Professor, School of Library and
Information Science,
University of South Florida

McGRAW-HILL BOOK COMPANY

New York St. Louis San Francisco Auckland Bogotá Caracas Colorado Springs
Hamburg Lisbon London Madrid Mexico Milan Montreal
New Delhi Oklahoma City Panama Paris San Juan
São Paulo Singapore Sydney Tokyo Toronto

1 2 3 4 5 6 7 8 9 0 D O C D O C 8 9 3 2 1 0 9 8

ISBN 0-07-022999-6

This book was set in Janson by Better Graphics, Inc. (CCU).
The editors were Judith R. Cornwell, Susan Hurtt and Bernadette Boylan;
the cover was designed by Carla Bauer; the production supervisor was Denise L. Puryear.
New drawings were done by Caliber Design Planning, Inc.
R. R. Donnelley & Sons Company was printer and binder.

Library of Congress Cataloging-in-Publication Data

Gates, Jean Key.
  Guide to the use of libraries and information sources/Jean Key
Gates.—6th ed.
    p.   cm.
    Includes index.
    ISBN 0-07-022999-6
    1. Libraries—Handbooks, manuals, etc. 2. Library resources—
Handbooks, manuals, etc. 3. Reference books—Bibliography—
Handbooks, manuals, etc. 4. Library science—Handbooks, manuals,
etc. I. Title
Z710.G27 1989
025.5'6—dc19   88-12700

About the Author

Jean Key Gates is Professor of Library and Information Science at the University of South Florida where she has designed and taught courses in basic information sources and in information sources in the subject fields. In addition, she designed and teaches the courses Foundations of Librarianship and Contemporary Publishing and Printing.

Her professional career has included administration, secondary school and university teaching, academic librarianship, research, publishing, and service to the profession–locally and nationally.

Professor Gates received her B.A. degree from Hendrix College, her M.S. degree in Library Science from the Catholic University of America, and continued her formal graduate study in special areas at the University of Arkansas, George Washington University, and the Catholic University of America. Her education, teaching, and research have been greatly enhanced by travel all over the world. She has visited many countries, libraries, and places which are important in the history of books and libraries, as well as places of outstanding historical and cultural interest.

The sixth edition of *Guide to the Use of Libraries and Information Sources* follows five highly successful editions which have been used in all English-speaking countries, translated into Spanish and Portuguese, and distributed by exclusive arrangement in Taiwan and in the Philippines.

Jean Key Gates is the author of *Introduction to Librarianship* and is the Consulting Editor of the prestigious McGraw-Hill Series in Library Education in which eighteen volumes have been published. Other publishing and research projects include making indexes for her own and other publications and serving as educational advisor for six filmstrips to accompany early editions of *Guide to the Use of Books and Libraries*.

Professor Gates has been honored by Hendrix College and the Catholic University of America for outstanding achievement in the field of library science and for distinguished service to her profession.

For Helena

Contents

Part 4
Information Sources in the Subject Fields

Part 5
Using Library Resources for a Research Paper

Preface

The purpose of *Guide to the Use of Libraries and Information Sources* is to provide a brief but comprehensive treatment of libraries, with emphasis upon the many kinds of library materials—their organization and arrangement, and their usefulness for specific purposes—and on the various services that libraries offer to their patrons. Particular attention is paid to academic libraries and to ways of using them most effectively.

The chapters are arranged in logical sequence, and reading straight through the text should give a full picture of the academic library and a reasonably clear picture of any library. Some repetition of ideas and information occurs. This repetition is by design: each chapter, while it is a necessary part of the whole, has been planned to stand alone, so that the instructor who has only a limited time in which to teach the use of the library can select the chapter or parts of chapters best suited to the requirements and purposes of a given situation.

Emphasis is placed on *how to use information sources*. The selection of titles to illustrate the several kinds of library materials was based on a critical study of the basic reference materials reviewed in a number of selective and evaluative bibliographies, including:

"Book Review," *Library Journal.* New York: R. R. Bowker Company, 1876– . (Semimonthly February—June, September—November; monthly January, July, August, December.)

Booklist. Chicago: American Library Association, 1905– . (Semimonthly; monthly in August.)

Choice. Chicago: American Library Association, 1964–   (Monthly except August.)

"Current Reference Books," *Wilson Library Bulletin*. New York: The H. W. Wilson Company, 1972– . (Monthly, except July and August.) Charles A. Bunge, editor, 1972–1981; James Rettig, editor, 1981–

RQ. Chicago: American Library Association, 1961– . (Quarterly.)

Sheehy, Eugene P. *Guide to Reference Books*. 10th ed. Chicago: American Library Association, 1986.

Also included are materials which I have used and evaluated in my own college teaching and reference work. The titles listed are only a selected sample of those now available, and each person will undoubtedly wish to add titles and to replace, with new editions and new titles, some of those which have been included. Listings of titles have been brought up to date by substituting new editions, adding titles omitted in the fifth edition, or adding titles published since 1983.

This book is not a manual for the study of a particular library. It is designed to serve as a textbook for college freshmen and other students who want or need instruction in the use of libraries and library materials. It will provide supplementary material for introductory courses in library science and can be used to advantage not only by reference librarians but by any person who is interested in learning what a library is and how to use it.

In general, each chapter includes (1) a definition of terms, (2) a brief statement of historical development, (3) discussion, and (4) appropriate examples.

Information sources are discussed as general or subject (specialized), according to kinds: dictionaries, indexes, handbooks, audiovisual materials, microforms, and others. Emphasis is placed on what they are, the purposes they serve, and the kinds of questions they are designed to answer.

Technical library terminology is used only when it seems to be essential. The language is, with few exceptions, that of the student and nonspecialist.

I am indebted to many authors, publishers, and holders of copyrights for permission to use their material. I should like to express my appreciation to my family and to my friends for their support; to my professional colleagues who answered questions or volunteered suggestions regarding this revision; to numerous users of the first, second, third, fourth and fifth editions, teachers, students, and others, who have made helpful comments; and to cooperative librarians in many libraries who helped locate needed materials.

Jean Key Gates

To the Student

In 1962, the first edition of *Guide to the Use of Books and Libraries* was published. The purpose of that book was to help students and other people use books and libraries more efficiently and effectively than they were then using them. In 1962, books were the major items in a library. There were some periodicals and newspapers, some audio, visual, and audiovisual materials, and some microforms; but the printed book received the greatest attention.

Though the library was considered a very important part of a college, it was not always the most inviting place on the campus. Some libraries were very severe and forbidding in appearance and some had rules and regulations that discouraged rather than encouraged their use by students. Even in 1962, there were librarians who seemed to be more interested in protecting books than in making them available to students.

Libraries are very different today. They have more books about many more subjects than they had in 1962, because there is more knowledge and information and therefore a greater variety of subjects which are of interest to people. Libraries also have more kinds and forms of materials—both book and nonbook—to provide the information that patrons want and need about the subjects that interest them and more means of access to that information: more indexes, catalogs, and bibliographies, as well as the computer and the CD-ROM; libraries also have access to numerous data bases—inside and outside the library—through on-line searching.

TO THE STUDENT

The appearance of the college library—and of other libraries—has changed. There are new buildings and remodeled buildings, all designed to be attractive and functional; they provide easier access to materials and they offer facilities which contribute to the user's comfort as well as to ease of use.

There are many more professional librarians now than there were when the first edition of *this book* was published; there is a consensus among them that the purpose of all library materials and resources is to contribute to the learning process; and they are generous with help and suggestions to persons who seek assistance.

One thing hasn't changed since 1962: *students still need help in using the library*. Perhaps they need it now more than ever before because of new materials, new forms of materials, and new subject matter. And in schools, colleges, and universities, in both formal classes and in day-by-day instruction in specific areas (the catalog, reference materials, microforms, equipment, etc.), librarians are aiding students in developing the skills they need to use the materials and services of the library advantageously.

Students learn how to locate information and utilize it for classwork, for recreation, and for special interests such as hobbies. What you learn while you are in college about the library and all the materials and services it offers will be helpful to you after college and throughout life. Information is a very important commodity in any career, and knowing how and where to find it is an asset in any position.

Other libraries—school, public, and special—provide services which are designed to meet the needs of their patrons. Many of these libraries have cooperative arrangements with college and university libraries in which they share certain materials and services. The librarians will explain these arrangements and how students can participate in them.

The purpose of *Guide to the Use of Libraries and Information Sources* continues to be to aid students—and other persons—in learning about the library and the materials and services it offers and to give suggestions about how to use all of them to the fullest possible extent.

Much attention is given to traditional materials, which all libraries have; but attention is given also to newer materials, equipment, and services which many libraries now have. All libraries will probably have some of the new technology and materials before the end of this decade.

Some attention is also given to the way libraries and library materials began, in the belief that a better understanding of what the library is *now* might be gained from a glimpse of how it started and how it has developed from the beginning to the present time.

Jean Key Gates

GUIDE TO
THE USE OF LIBRARIES AND
INFORMATION SOURCES

PART
1

The Library

CHAPTER

❧ 1 ❧

A Brief History
of Books and Libraries

The earliest system for storing information and transmitting it from one person to another was language. By the use of words, history, rituals, stories, prayers, and medical and other knowledge were passed on from one generation to another. When people realized that spoken words could be represented by visual symbols, they invented their second means for the preservation and transmission of knowledge: writing—the chief medium used for this purpose for more than 5000 years.

The first writings were crude pictures carved on rocks, stone, bark, metal, and clay, or whatever materials were at hand. They were of three kinds: (1) pictographic, representing an object; (2) ideographic, representing the idea suggested by the object; and (3) phonographic, representing the sound of the object or idea. Some of these ancient inscriptions can be interpreted. Crude picture writing was done on other materials which were at hand: vegetable fiber, cloth, wood, bark, animal skin, clay, and metal. However, only the writings on clay, metal, and stone have survived.

Most historians agree that all our systems of writing came from these crude carvings and picture writings.

The story of books and libraries from earliest times to the present is closely interwoven with the story of writing and other methods of preserving and transmitting information and knowledge, with the materials and the physical forms which have been used for these purposes, and with the methods of preserving them and of making them accessible for use. For with the first "book" came the necessity for a place to keep it, to make it accessible for use, and to pass it on to succeeding generations.

Writing, Books, and Libraries

ANTIQUITY

The Sumerians, Babylonians, and Assyrians

From about 3600 to 2357 B.C. the Sumerian civilization flourished in the Tigris-Euphrates Valley, and as early as 3100 B.C. Sumerian historians began to record their current history and to reconstruct the story of their past.

The system of writing of the Sumerians—perhaps their greatest contribution to human culture—is the oldest system known. The word "cuneiform," which describes their style of writing, is from *cuneus*, the Latin word for "wedge." The materials used were soft clay and a wedge-shaped stylus of metal, ivory, or wood. When the scribe had finished writing, the clay was baked until it was hard as stone. These pieces of baked clay, small enough to be held in the hand of the scribe, are called "tablets" and were the first books.

To the Sumerians, writing was first of all a tool of trade and commerce. In addition, it was an instrument for recording religious works: prayers, ritual procedure, sacred legends, and magic formulas. On these clay tablets are also preserved the records of the first schools, the first social reforms, the first tax levies, and the first political, social, and philosophical thinking. It was several hundred years before the Sumerians produced literature, but among the tons of tablets and cylinders removed from the ruins of Sumer's ancient cities are some containing literary works almost 1000 years older than the *Iliad*. They constitute the oldest known literature.

By 2700 B.C., the Sumerians had established private and religious, as well as government, libraries. Among these libraries was one at Telloh which had a collection of over 30,000 tablets.

Sumer's culture passed to Babylonia in Lower Mesopotamia, a civilization which lasted until 689 B.C. and which produced Hammurabi and his notable code of laws. In both Sumerian and Babylonian writing, the characters represented syllables rather than letters.

The Babylonians used writing in business transactions and in recording noteworthy events; thus their books were devoted to government, law, history, and religion. It is believed that there were many libraries in the temples and palaces of Babylonia. While none of these survives, the tablets of one of the most important ones, the library of Borsippa, were copied in their entirety by the scribes of Assurbanipal, king of Assyria (d. ca. 626 B.C.), who preserved them in his library at Nineveh. These duplicates of the tablets from Borsippa are the chief sources of our knowledge of Babylonian life.

The kingdom of Assyria, which existed at the same time as Babylonia, also inherited Sumeria's language and method of writing, but modified the written characters until they resembled those of the Babylonians. The most important library in Assyria was established at Nineveh by Assurbanipal. Tens of thousands of clay tablets were brought to this great royal library by the king's scribes, who traveled throughout Babylonia and Assyria to copy and translate the writings they found. The catalog of the Nineveh library was a listing of the contents of each cubicle or alcove, painted or carved on the entrance, where the clay tablets were arranged according to subject or type. Each tablet had an identification tag.

Among the most famous surviving specimens of cuneiform writing are the Code of Hammurabi,[1] now in the Louvre Museum in Paris, and the Gilgamesh Epic, part of which is the Babylonian story of the great flood. The key to this system of writing is the Behistun Inscription, which is located on the side of a mountain in Iran (Persia). Written in three languages (Persian, Babylonian, and Elamite), it was deciphered by Sir Henry Rawlinson when he was consul at Baghdad in 1844.

The Egyptians

The civilization of ancient Egypt flourished simultaneously with the Sumerian, Bablyonian, and Assyrian civilizations. The earliest known writings of the Egyptians date from ca. 3000 B.C. The writing material was the papyrus sheet,[2] and the instrument for writing was a brushlike pen made by fraying the edges of a reed.

Papyrus was far from satisfactory as a writing material, for there was constant danger of punching through it in the process of writing. Also, it was susceptible to damage from water and dampness, and when it was dry, it was very fragile and brittle. In spite of these limitations, however, papyrus was the accepted writing material throughout the ancient Mediterranean world and is known to have been used as late as A.D. 1022.

The form of the book in ancient Egypt was the roll, usually a little more than 12 inches high and about 20 feet long, made from papyrus sheets pasted end to end. The style of writing was hieroglyphic, a word derived from the Greek *hieros*, meaning "sacred," and *glyphein*, meaning "to carve." Hiero-

---

[1] The Code of Hammurabi was not written on clay but was carved on a diorite cylinder. Diorite is a granular, crystalline, igneous rock.

[2] To make a papyrus sheet, the marrow of papyrus stalks was cut into thin strips and laid flat, side by side, one layer crossways over the other. The two layers were treated with a gum solution, pressed, pounded, and smoothed until the surface was suitable for writing, and then sized to resist the ink.

glyphic writing, as old as the earliest Egyptian dynasty, was used as late as A.D. 394.

The Egyptians developed an alphabet of twenty-four consonants, but they did not adopt a completely alphabetic style of writing. They mixed pictographs, ideographs, and syllabic signs with their letters and developed a sketchy kind of writing for manuscripts, but the sacred carvings on their monuments were hieroglyphic.

Egyptian scribes were trained in the temple schools to learn to draw at least 700 different characters (hieroglyphs).

Writing was done in columns without spaces between words, without punctuation marks, and usually without titles; the text began at the extreme right and continued right to left. Egyptian rolls included religious, moral, and political subjects. The Prisse Papyrus in the Bibliothèque Nationale in Paris—the oldest Egyptian book known—is believed to have been written before the end of the third millennium (2880) B.C.; it contains the proverbial sayings of Ptahhotep. The longest Egyptian manuscript in existence, more than 130 feet long, is the Harris Papyrus, a chronicle of the reign of Rameses II.

The key to hieroglyphic writing is the Rosetta Stone, which was discovered near the mouth of the Nile in 1799 by a young officer of Napoleon's expeditionary force in Egypt. In 1821 this flat slab of slate, bearing an inscription in three styles of writing—hieroglyphic, demotic (popular), and Greek—gave to Jean François Champollion, the French Egyptologist, the clue needed to decipher the Egyptian hieroglyphics. It is now preserved in the British Museum in London.

Little is known about Egyptian libraries. There may have been private and temple libraries as well as government archives. Records indicate that a library existed at Gizeh in the 2500s B.C., and it is known that Rameses II founded one at Thebes about 1250 B.C. Rolls were kept in clay jars or in metal cylinders with an identifying key word on the outside or on the end, or they were stacked on shelves.

Other Semitic peoples

In addition to the Babylonians and the Assyrians, other Semitic peoples inhabited that part of the near east known as the "fertile crescent."[3] Among them were the Phoenicians. Phoenicia was the name given in ancient times to a narrow strip of land about 100 miles long and 10 miles wide between Syria and the sea.

[3] The region bounded by the Taurus and the mountains of Armenia and Iran, the Persian Gulf, the Indian Ocean and the Red Sea, Egypt and the Mediterranean (*Cambridge Ancient History*, I 1924, 182).

The Phoenicians were traders, and an important item in their wares was papyrus, which they imported from Egypt and exported to all the countries along the Mediterranean. It is believed that wherever the Phoenicians took papyrus, they also took the Egyptian alphabet. History gives them major credit for spreading the knowledge and use of the alphabetic characters which had been developed in Egypt, Crete, and Syria and which form the basis of Greek and of all European writing. The Phoenicians were not a literary people; writing and books were to them merely means of keeping their numerous commercial accounts, and in time they developed a cursive, flowing style of writing and replaced the cumbersome clay tablets with papyrus sheets.

The Chinese

The art of writing was known in China as early as the third millennium B.C. Materials on which the Chinese wrote included bone, tortoiseshell, bamboo stalks, wooden tablets, silk, and linen, and their writing instruments were the stylus, the quill, and the brush pen, depending upon the particular writing material used. The style of writing involved the use of characters, mainly ideographic, and book forms were the tablet and the roll. Little is known about their libraries.

The Greeks

In the early part of the second millennium B.C., Crete became the center of a highly developed civilization which spread to the mainland of Greece and, before the end of the fifteenth century B.C., throughout the entire Aegean area. The Cretans developed the art of writing from a pictographic system to a cursive form, now called "Linear A," and by the fifteenth century B.C. to a system now called "Linear B." Many scholars believe that the language of Linear B tablets is an early form of Greek which was spoken by the Mycenaeans who occupied Knossos about 1460 B.C. and eventually overthrew the Minoan kingdom. After 1200 B.C. the Mycenaean world ceased to exist and the script disappeared. A period of illiteracy is believed to have existed from this time until the Greeks adopted the consonantal twenty-two-letter alphabet of the Phoenicians in the eighth century B.C.

Of the seventh and sixth centuries B.C., only fragments of literature remain, but these fragments show the beginnings of new forms of poetry, notably the elegy and the choral lyric, and the birth of philosophy and scientific research. The fables of Aesop date from this period.

The fifth century was the golden age of Greek civilization, a period characterized by the highest form of literary creativity: the tragedies of Sophocles, Aeschylus, and Euripides; the lyric poetry of Pindar; the histories of Thucydides and Herodotus; the comedies of Aristophanes; and the philosophy of Socrates. This period, also referred to as the "Classical Age," extended through the fourth and into the third centuries B.C., finding expression in the works of Plato and Aristotle, as well as in drama, poetry, oration, and music.

During the Hellenistic period, which dated from the death of Alexander in 323 B.C. to the Roman conquest, the literary activities of the preceding century continued and there was a new emphasis on scientific knowledge (in the works of Euclid and Archimedes), on art, and on rhetoric.

In ancient Greece the materials used to receive writing were leaves or bark of trees, stone or bronze for inscriptions, and wax-coated wooden tablets for messages or notes. From the sixth century B.C., papyrus, which the Phoenicians brought from Egypt, was the usual writing material. In Hellenistic Greece, parchment and vellum came into use.[4]

The use of parchment and vellum made necessary the development of a new kind of writing instrument, the broad-pointed pen made from a reed or a quill. Parchment proved to be a better medium for writing than papyrus because it was smooth on both sides and was less likely to tear. Papyrus competed with it for three centuries, however, and only in the fourth century after Christ did parchment become dominant.

The forms of Greek books were the roll, the wax tablet, and the codex, in which the papyrus or parchment leaves of the manuscript were fastened together as in a modern book. The subject matter of Greek books included literature, history, science, mathematics, philosophy, religion, and politics.

Early Greek writing resembled that of the Phoenicians, who had brought them the alphabet, but gradually the Greeks changed the forms of the letters, added vowels, changed some consonants to vowels, developed lowercase letters, and began writing from left to right. The first books did not have spaces between words or punctuation marks of any kind. Change from one topic to another was indicated by a horizontal dividing stroke called the *paragraphos*, and if the roll had a title, it was located at the end. Before the conquest of Greece by the Romans, Greek grammarians had introduced some forms of punctuation.

Aristotle (384–322 B.C.) is said to have been the first person to collect, preserve, and use the culture of the past. The story of his library is told by Strabo. In Hellenistic Greece there were private, governmental, and royal libraries.

The greatest libraries were in Alexandria in Egypt. The Museion, founded by Ptolemy I (323–285 B.C.) as an essential part of the academy of scholars under his patronage, is reported to have reached a total of 200,000

---

[4] Parchment was the skin of animals, principally that of the sheep or the calf, prepared for writing. Vellum, which is made from the skin of calves, is heavier than parchment and more expensive. It is probably the most beautiful and the most lasting material ever used for books.

rolls within five years. It is said that foreigners were required, upon entering the Alexandria harbor, to surrender any books in their possession, later receiving copies in exchange for the originals. By the time of the Roman conquest, it contained 700,000 rolls, including manuscripts from all parts of the known world, written in Egyptian, Hebrew, Latin, and other languages. The second library, the Serapeum, founded by Ptolemy III (r. 246–221 B.C.) and located in the Temple of Serapis, grew to more than 100,000 volumes. Although there is not complete agreement regarding the fate of the Alexandrian libraries, many historians date the destruction of the Museion from Julius Caesar's campaign in Alexandria in 47 B.C. and that of the Serapeum from the reign of Theodosius the Great (A.D. 379–395), whose edicts against paganism resulted in the destruction of many pagan temples.

Second in importance to the libraries at Alexandria was the one at Pergamum, founded by Eumenes II (197–159 B.C.). Pergamum became outstanding for patronage of arts and letters, and book production was so intense that an embargo was placed by the Egyptians on the exportation of papyrus, with the hope of discouraging the copying of books. This act led to the increased production of parchment for use as a writing material.

According to Plutarch, Calvisius, a friend of Caesar, charged that Antony gave to Cleopatra the entire library at Pergamum, which contained 200,000 distinct volumes.[5]

The Romans

The Romans continued the Greek tradition in books. Through commerce with Greece, Rome had early adopted the Greek alphabet, and Greek culture became important in Rome following the first Punic war (264–241 B.C.). By the time of the Roman conquest of Greece, the Romans were under the influence of the Greeks to the extent that they read and studied their literature, philosophy, and science, sent their sons to Athens to be educated, and at times spoke Greek. Latin literature began in the second century B.C.

The materials which the Romans used for writing were papyrus, parchment, vellum, wood tablets coated with wax, the stylus, the split-point reed, and the split-feather quill.

The Romans developed a style of handwriting unlike the ordinary cursive writing for use in literary works. Much like the Greek, it consisted largely of capital letters. By the end of the fourth century after Christ, another style, called "uncial script," which involved the use of large, somewhat rounded letters, was the standard book script and continued as such until the end of the eighth century.

---

[5] *Plutarch's Lives of Illustrious Men*, corrected from the Greek and revised by A. H. Clough (Boston: Little, Brown & Company, 1930), p. 674.

The forms of the book in ancient Rome were the roll, the wax tablet, the diptych (two boards hinged together at one side with waxed surfaces on the inside for writing), and the codex.

Since the roll was relatively inconvenient to write upon and to read, it was superseded inevitably by the more usable form, the codex, which was used to some extent by the Greeks and which is known to have been in use among the Christians in the second century after Christ. From that time the codex generally was used for Christian works, even though the papyrus roll was continued in use for pagan works.

Roman books included all known fields of knowledge: law, science, mathematics, philosophy, politics, and religious and secular literature. The earliest known fragment of a manuscript book is the Papyrus Rylands, a tiny piece of a papyrus leaf of the Gospel according to St. John, dated (from the style of writing) in the first half of the second century after Christ. The Codex Vaticanus of the fourth century after Christ is the oldest extant manuscript of antiquity.

Roman generals brought back entire libraries from the campaigns in Greece, and these libraries, considered spoils of war, became their private collections.

Julius Caesar drew up plans for public libraries, but his plans were not carried out until the reign of Augustus, when Asinius Pollio established the first public library in Rome between 39 and 27 B.C. By the middle of the fourth century after Christ there were at least twenty-eight public libraries in Rome, and they were used by any person, slave or free, who could read.

The Ulpian Library, founded by Trajan—a scholarly collection housed in two structures, one for Latin and one for Greek works—was second in importance among ancient libraries only to those at Alexandria and Pergamum. In Roman libraries, Greek works were kept on one side of the library, and Latin works were placed on the other side; they were arranged according to subject on shelves or in bins. Except in rare cases, books had to be used in the reading rooms.

THE MIDDLE AGES

Monasteries

With the disintegration of the western Roman Empire[6] came the decline of classical literature, and all libraries, including Christian collections, suffered

---

[6] Emperor Diocletian (A.D. 284–305) had divided the Roman Empire into eastern and western spheres. In 330, Constantine, then emperor of both the east and the west, moved the capital from Rome to Constantinople. When the western part of the Roman Empire fell in 476, the eastern part (called the "Byzantine Empire") was entering upon a period of progress which was to last 1000 years.

at the hands of the barbarians. It was in the monasteries that literature was preserved and developed during the Middle Ages.

In the last half of the sixth century, under the leadership of Cassiodorus, the monastery became a center for all studies and for the preservation of all writings, both religious and secular. In southern Italy, Cassiodorus established the monastic community of Vivarium. He set up a great library which included manuscripts of the great literature of the past—Greek and Latin, pagan and Christian—and established a scriptorium (writing room) for the copying of Christian and secular literature, thus assuring the preservation of much ancient writing which would otherwise have been lost during those troubled times.

After Cassiodorus, intellectual activity came to a standstill in western Europe, except in Ireland. In the sixth century, numerous Irish monasteries came into existence and in their scriptoria a national script and a national art evolved and the first great development of manuscript books was begun—books which were characterized by superb calligraphy and illumination[7] and fine workmanship. Irish manuscript art reached its height in the *Book of Kells*, a manuscript of the Gospels, written in the eighth century and believed to be the most richly decorated manuscript ever produced in an Irish scriptorium.

Irish missionaries established monastic centers in Scotland, northern England, and continental Europe, including Lindisfarne in Northumbria, Luxeuil in France, and Bobbio in northern Italy.

During the eighth century, missionaries from the English church also established monasteries on the continent. Most notable of the English missionaries was St. Boniface, whose greatest monastery was at Fulda in Germany.

The reign of Charles the Great, or Charlemagne (768–814), marked by his efforts to raise the educational level of his subjects, brought to western Europe a period of educational and cultural growth. Alcuin, master of the school at York in Northumbria, was chosen by Charlemagne to direct his educational program. In 782, as head of the Palace School in Aachen, Alcuin began the task of establishing educational centers and disseminating learning throughout the Frankish Empire. Scriptoria were established in monasteries and a carefully planned system of selecting, collecting, and copying religious and secular literature was begun. When Alcuin retired from the Palace School to the monastery of St. Martin at Tours, he made the monastery a center of learning, and the works copied in the scriptorium served as models for copyists for many generations. This revival of learning during the time of Charlemagne is called the "Carolingian Renaissance."

In the scriptoria of countless monasteries in continental Europe, Ireland, and England, as well as in the Byzantine Empire and the Moslem world,

---

[7] Decorations of ornamental letters, scrolls, and miniatures—small paintings in color.

manuscripts were copied and recopied by the monks and by secular scribes who were often brought in for special tasks. These manuscripts tell us much of what we know of the ancient world. In these institutions were preserved the books of the Bible; the epics of Homer; the poetry of Virgil; the Greek dramas; and the scientific, legal, and philosophical works of the great minds of antiquity.

The chief materials used by the monks for writing were plain or dyed parchment or vellum, quill pens, and many kinds of colored inks. The forms of the book were the roll and the codex.

Early monastic libraries were small. Manuscripts were expensive: a large Bible was bought for 10 talents (about $10,000), and a missal was exchanged for a vineyard. A monastery library would have many copies of the Bible, the service books of the church, lives of the saints, early Christian writings, law, poetry, and some classical works.

Books were kept in chests or cupboards, or they were brought out and chained to desks for safety. Most of the reading was done standing up. In general, books were arranged by subject or kind—religious or secular, Greek or Latin. At first, catalogs were rough checklists. Later, a fuller and more precise description of a book and its contents was given in the listing.

Universities

From the fall of Rome to the twelfth century, education was in the hands of the monastery, and instruction was chiefly theological. Some instruction was given to sons of noblemen and, in some cases, to promising children of the poor. In trading centers there were schools to train clerks.

By the middle of the twelfth century, men were going to school to study Latin grammar and other basic subjects. The rise of cathedral schools, the study of Latin grammar, the appearance of writing in the vernacular (the language of the masses), and the increasingly favorable social and economic conditions gave rise to the universities.

The university of this period was a group of teachers organized as a kind of guild and empowered by either religious or civil government to grant degrees. The outstanding universities of the Middle Ages were the universities of Bologna, Paris, Prague, Heidelberg, Oxford, and Cambridge.

Book dealers (*stationarii*) and their scribes were an important part of every medieval university. They were appointed or controlled by the university to guarantee the authenticity of texts. They kept in stock correct editions of books used for instruction and rented them to the students. Dealers in parchment and vellum were licensed by the university. Since the universities constituted both the chief supply of books and the chief demand for them, they became the main centers of the book trade and of the publishing (copying) business. Book forms were the roll and the codex.

There was little need for libraries as long as the students could rent the texts they needed. However, as the number of students increased, the universities were forced to establish libraries. In time, books were given by individuals to the universities for the use of students.

Each college within a university had its own library. Arrangement and organization were similar to those of the larger monastery libraries except that books were divided according to the subject taught. They were arranged according to size or accession, sometimes on shelves rather than in chests. The more important books were still chained to the desks.

The Renaissance

In Italy during the fourteenth century, Petrarch and Boccaccio were laying the foundations for a new revival of learning. They searched medieval monasteries for old manuscripts, and many long-lost Latin works were recovered. The fall of Constantinople in 1453 aided the revival of learning by dispersing to Europe many works of ancient Greek and Latin literature. This period, the Renaissance (also called the "age of humanism"), was characterized by the unceasing search for missing ancient Greek and Latin works and the intense effort to read and understand them and to imitate their style and form. Florence became the center of the Italian Renaissance, and under the Medici saw the most brilliant development of culture since the Golden Age of Greece.

Printing with movable types

The zeal for learning which characterized the Renaissance brought a demand for books which could no longer be satisfied by handwritten copies. The need for a new and faster medium for transmitting knowledge was urgent. In northern Europe by the middle of the fifteenth century, this medium had been developed: printing with movable types.

The success of printing depended upon a cheap substance on which to print, an ink which would adhere to type, a press which could apply heavy pressure over a larger frame, and a general knowledge of metal technology.

By the second quarter of the fifteenth century, these needs had been met. Paper was a cheap and plentiful material on which to print. Discovered in China in the second century but used little by the Chinese, paper had traveled west along the trade routes. It was brought to Persia in the eighth century; it was displacing papyrus in Egypt in the ninth century; the Moslems used it in Spain in the eleventh and twelfth centuries; it was manufactured in southern Italy in 1270; and by the end of the fourteenth century, it was manufactured in France and Germany. The material used in making paper was linen rags.[8]

A suitable ink was developed by adapting the oil paints which the artists of the time were using.

The screw presses which were used for pressing olives and grapes and in binding manuscript books were used to apply pressure over a large frame.

The general knowledge of metal technology, which was essential to the success of printing, was borrowed from the goldsmiths and silversmiths. Carving of woodblocks for wood-block printing and engraving on metal by goldsmiths and silversmiths had reached a high degree of perfection. This knowledge was easily transferred to the process of making metal types.

Perhaps no event in human cultural history exceeds in importance the invention of printing with movable types.[9] Learning, which was formerly confined to monasteries or available only to the student, particularly the wealthy student, was now within reach of any person who wished to pursue it.

Movable word types made of clay originated in China but were used very little. It is to Johann Gutenberg, born in Mainz, Germany, about 1400, that credit is given for the development of printing with movable types. His creative genius combined the available materials and supplied the remaining essentials which made possible the printing of the famous 42-line Bible, commonly called the "Gutenberg Bible," between 1450 and 1456. This was the first book printed with movable types.

The printed book was new only in the way it was made; it was not new in appearance. The types were similar to manuscript writing. Space was left for illumination and rubrication,[10] which were done by hand. The first illustrations were woodcuts. This similarity to the handwritten book continued for more than a hundred years.

---

[8] The linen rags were softened to a pulp and molded into sheets on a wooden frame. The sheets were drained, pressed and pressed again, hung to dry completely, and then sized to make them impervious to ink.

[9] The Babylonians and the Egyptians had used metal or wooden seals to print on soft clay or on wax; the Romans printed symbols on coins and stamped official documents with a carved seal; as early as the fifth and sixth centuries, the Chinese used carved seals to print short mottoes and charms. The full-page woodcut, printed from a wooden block on which the text and illustrations had been carved, was the next step in printing. By the ninth century, the Chinese produced a complete book printed in this manner. This kind of book was called a block book. The *Diamond Sutra*, a block book printed in A.D. 868, has survived. By the tenth century, printing in this manner was common in China. In Europe there were woodcut prints by the fourteenth century.

[10] Rubrication was writing or underlining in a color (e.g., red) a heading or a part of a book or a manuscript.

The first printed works are called "incunabula" (from the Latin *incunabulum*, meaning "cradle"), indicating that printing was in its infancy. The subject matter of early printed books included the Bible and other religious works, textbooks, histories, travel books, and literature of all kinds.

During the last quarter of the fifteenth century, printing spread to all major cities of Europe. More than 20,000 different works and editions of this period survive. The first book printed in the English language was the *Recuyell of the Histories of Troy*, printed between 1474 and 1476 by William Caxton, who learned the art of printing in order to be able to print his own translation of this work.

The sixteenth century is notable for the rise of a large number of printing families, each with its own specialty. The House of Estienne, for example, printed Greek and Latin classics. The French printer Geoffroy Tory was responsible for introducing the accent, the apostrophe, and the cedilla into the French language; and in Venice, Aldus Manutius developed a system of punctuation marks. By 1700 the printed book had reached its present form, with a title page, illustrations, a table of contents, and even a kind of index.

The invention of printing provided an unparalleled and effective impetus to the rebirth of learning. Precious manuscripts of the past, formerly copied one at a time by hand, could be reproduced in multiple copies and passed on to those who eagerly sought them. By making written works quickly available, the printing press also encouraged the production of new literature, and in this way it helped to create the "professional literati." The printing press and the increased dissemination of printed materials contributed significantly to the spread of the Reformation, and the stimulus which it gave to mapmaking hastened the era of discovery and exploration.

1500 TO 1900

Europe

Books after 1500 varied widely both in format and in content. There were many large volumes, many very small ones. Bookbindings ranged from ornate, bejewelled, gold-tooled leather to plain vellum and, eventually, paper. Printing types ceased to be copies of manuscript writing and assumed an identity all their own. In the sixteenth and seventeenth centuries periodicals were published; in the late seventeenth century newspapers appeared.

The contents of books during these centuries included religious and classical subjects, as well as science, superstition, travel, and romance.

The nineteenth century brought new mechanical developments, including stereotyping and the cylinder press. The first successful effort to set type mechanically and thus speed up printing was the invention of the linotype machine by Ottmar Mergenthaler in 1866. Other inventions followed.

In the nineteenth century there was much fine printing, especially in England. Wood came into use as a material for paper, books were bound with cloth, and copyright legislation was enacted.

In Europe, libraries flourished during the period from 1500 to 1900. Italy was outstanding for the number and quality of libraries in the sixteenth century. The Laurentian Library in Florence, the Ambrosian Library in Milan, and the Vatican Library in Rome were the most important.

In France, the Bibliothèque Nationale (which had its origins in the collections formed by the kings of France and dates from Francis I) was moved to Paris by Charles IX (1560–1574) and was greatly expanded and enlarged by Louis XIV (1643–1715).

Germany had the finest libraries of the nineteenth century. State librar-ies and university libraries were outstanding for size, content, and organiza-tion. There were also circulating libraries with catalogs, popular reading rooms, and children's collections.

The libraries of Oxford University, Cambridge University, and the British Museum (the National Library) were the most important in England.

The Austrian Royal Library, the royal library at Brussels, and the university libraries at Ghent and Louvain were other important libraries founded between 1500 and 1900.

America

Among the valued possessions which the early settlers brought to America or imported as necessities as soon as they were settled were books. Even though a printing press was in operation in Massachusetts as early as 1639, books had to be imported from England and the Continent for many generations. The earliest book known to have been printed in colonial America was *The Bay Psalm Book*, printed in 1640.

Important private libraries of the early colonial period were those of Elder Brewster of the Plymouth Colony (about 400 different works), John Winthrop (over 1000 volumes), and John Harvard (more than 300 volumes). Outstanding eighteenth-century libraries were those of Cotton Mather of Boston (between 3000 and 4000 volumes), James Logan of Philadelphia (more than 2000 volumes), and William Byrd II of Virginia (3600 titles).

In 1731, Benjamin Franklin and a group of his friends in Philadelphia established the first subscription library, a voluntary association of individ-uals who contributed to a common fund to be used for the purchase of books, which every member had the right to use but whose ownership was retained by the group. Subscription libraries (also called "social libraries") of several forms and names flourished for more than a century. Their collections, at first largely moral and theological in content, in time included history, biography, literature, travel, and scientific materials.

The first colleges in the American colonies—Harvard (1638), William and Mary (1695), Yale (1700), and Princeton (1746)—began with, or were accompanied by, gifts of books. Although the Massachusetts General Court voted in 1636 to set aside £400 for the establishment of a "schoole or colledge," Harvard was not opened until 1638, when John Harvard bequeathed to the new college one-half of his estate and his entire library of 320 volumes. Yale College began with forty books. Each of the eleven clergymen who met in 1700 for the purpose of forming a college brought a number of books which he gave "for the founding of a college in this colony" (Connecticut). Most of the volumes in the early college libraries were books on theology, but there were also copies of the classics and of philosophical and literary works. By 1725 the Harvard Library had 3000 books, and was the largest college library in the colonies.

Before the Revolution nine colleges were formed in the colonies, and by the time of the Civil War more than 500 colleges and twenty-one state universities had been established.

In the early college libraries there was no effort to make books available to students; rather, it seemed, books were protected from the students. This protective attitude continued throughout the nineteenth century, and as late as the 1850s, some college libraries were open only one hour every two weeks, others one hour twice a week, and a few one hour a day. In some libraries, attempts were made to classify books into three groups: memory, judgment, and imagination; or history, philosophy, and poetry. In others, books were arranged according to appearance, accession, or donor. The location symbol for books gave the physical location only and did not indicate the subject class to which the book belonged. Catalogs were printed lists, with little information about the books.

Following the Revolution, historical societies were formed to collect materials important in the history of the state or territory and a library was an essential part of each society. The Library of Congress (LC) was established in 1800 to serve the needs of the Congress,[11] and in the following decades state and territorial libraries were organized to collect and preserve publications of the state or territory and to serve the needs of the state or territorial government.

The first tax-supported town library in the United States was established in Peterborough, New Hampshire, in 1833. But it was not until 1854, when the Boston Public Library was opened to the public, that the free, public, tax-supported library became a part of American life.

By 1890 the public library had become an established institution in America, and the organization and development of libraries was given added

[11] See pp. 51–52.

impetus after that time by the state library commissions, which were established to aid in founding libraries and in improving and extending their services.

In 1876 the American Library Association was organized to promote libraries and librarianship throughout the United States. That same year Melvil Dewey published the first edition of his *Decimal Classification*, and eleven years later organized—at Columbia University—the first library school for the training of professional librarians, which he served as director.

MODERN ERA: THE TWENTIETH CENTURY

At the close of the nineteenth century in the United States, there was a developing interest in all libraries and in the training of persons for library positions. Financial aid during the last quarter of the nineteenth century and into the first quarter of the twentieth century came from gifts of private philanthropy. The greatest individual benefactor of libraries was Andrew Carnegie, whose gifts totaled over $41 million. Other benefactors included the Rockefeller Foundation, the Ford Foundation, and individual philanthropists who have opened their collections of rare books to the public. Examples of rare-book libraries are the Pierpont Morgan Library in New York City and the Folger Shakespeare Library in Washington, D.C.

From 1956 through 1965, Congress passed a succession of acts which provided financial aid to public, school, and academic libraries for improvement and expansion of facilities and services; libraries entered a period of rapid and enormous growth in size, number, and importance.

Each state has made legal provision for public library service and the state library commission is authorized to aid in founding local, county, and multicounty libraries. The state library provides consultants for all aspects of library service and administers state and federal grants-in-aid.

In an effort to provide more and better library services, state library commissions are developing library systems. These are cooperative endeavors in which a number of local libraries join together and, under the direction of a separate board, form a system. The resources of all libraries in a system are available to member libraries. Access is by means of telephone, teletypewriter, photocopying, or interlibrary loan. In a network of libraries, access to resources of member libraries is by means of computers, telefacsimile, and other forms of communications technology.

The public library is now recognized as a valuable complement to the public school in education for democratic living. In carrying out this function, the public library provides special services for children and young people; promotes educational, civic, and cultural programs; makes special materials available to the handicapped; supplements school library collections; and carries library materials to rural and isolated areas via the book-mobile.

The Library Services Act, enacted in 1956, promoted the extension of public library services to rural areas only and included funds for materials and services, but not for buildings. This act, amended in 1964 and thereafter called the Library Services and Construction Act (LSCA), extended federal aid to urban as well as to rural public libraries for materials, equipment, salaries, and also for construction. It provided funds for interlibrary cooperation, state institutional library service, and library services to the physically handicapped. Under this act, during the twenty-five-year period from 1956 to 1981, federal funds brought public library service for the first time to more than 17 million people and improved library service to 100 million people. Two thousand public library buildings were built, remodeled, or expanded, and 171 million books were purchased with a combination of LSCA, state, and local funds.[12] Public library building has continued, and 187 new buildings, additions, and renovations were completed in 1986.[13]

The first legislative act providing for federal aid to public education, the Elementary and Secondary Education Act of 1965, included a five-year program of grants to be used for the acquisition of library resources and other instructional materials, for setting up model school library programs, and for strengthening school library supervision. The act has aided more than 60,000 public and private elementary and secondary schools. In 1985, 93 percent of public schools had school library media centers.[14]

The American academic library has grown tremendously—not only in terms of number of volumes, but also in terms of its importance in the instructional program. The Higher Education Facilities Act of 1963 authorized federal grants and loans to institutions of higher education for the construction of various facilities, including libraries. From 1969 to 1985, more than 850 separate academic library buildings were completed and more than 640 other buildings housing libraries were constructed, remodeled, or renovated.[15]

---

[12] "25 Years of Achievement with the Library Services Act and the Library Services and Construction Act, 1956–1981" (Washington, D.C.: Washington Office American Library Association, 1981), *passim*.

[13] Bette-Lee Fox and others, "Library Buildings—1986," *Library Journal*, CXI (December 1986), 49–59.

[14] Mary Jo Lynch, *Libraries in an Information Society* (Chicago: American Library Association, 1987), p. 10; used with permission of the American Library Association.

[15] "Academic Libraries, 1969–1979," *Library Journal*, CIV (December 1, 1979), 2526; "Academic Library Buildings," *Library Journal*, CVI (December 1981), 2278, and Bette-Lee Fox, *op. cit.*, pp. 42–45.

The increasing emphasis on research since World War II has resulted in greatly expanded research facilities in universities, government agencies, large public library systems, and existing research libraries and has also brought about the development of an increasing number of independent private research libraries and centers. Examples of privately endowed research libraries are the John Crerar Library in Chicago, the Henry F. Huntington Library in San Marino, California, and the Linda Hall Library in Kansas City, Missouri.

Special libraries, which provide information resources vital to the parent organization's specialized clientele, are developments of the twentieth century. The special library may serve an industry, a business firm, a newspaper, a church, an art museum, or an association. Depending on the nature of the group it serves, the special library's collection may be varied, containing books, pamphlets, reports, periodical publications, translations, research and laboratory notebooks, patents, sheet music, audiovisual materials, microforms, or other materials—whatever is required to meet the needs of its clientele. There are more than 10,000 special libraries in the United States.

Today there are more than 115,000 libraries in the United States—public, school, academic, and special—with collections ranging in size from under 2000 items in small school library media centers to more than 1 million in large public and academic libraries and 80 million in the Library of Congress. From 1984 to 1986, academic, public, and school libraries spent more than $5½ billion for operating expenses, including salaries, print and nonprint materials, equipment, computer hardware and software, maintenance, and supplies.[16]

In 1987, 471 new buildings, renovations, and additions were in progress,[17] and new buildings continue to be built.

At the present time, the physical forms used for storing information and transmitting it from one person to another include books and other printed forms as well as nonbook forms such as films, filmstrips, slides, transparencies, disk and tape recordings, microforms,[18] videotapes, videodiscs, videotex, teletext, sound tracks, computer programs, and data bases. Many libraries use computer technology for various functions in the library: administration, cataloging, acquisitions, circulation, and others. Some libraries have on-line catalogs,[19] which supplement or have replaced card and book catalogs. Many others are planning to have on-line catalogs available in the near future.

---

[16] Mary Jo Lynch, *op. cit.*, pp. 9, 12, 18, 27, 29, *passim.*

[17] Bette-Lee Fox, *op. cit.*, p. 60.

[18] Microforms include microfilm, microfiche, and other forms of microphotography. See pp. 161–164.

[19] See Chapter 5, Library Catalogs, for a discussion of the on-line catalog.

In the expanding field of librarianship there are still the traditional, essential positions of library director, reference librarian, catalog librarian, acquisitions librarian, and circulation librarian. But there are many new positions: medical cataloger, rare-book librarian, systems analyst, minority services librarian, editor of publications, preservation specialist, archivist, project manager, and information manager.

Summary

Highlights in the history of books and libraries (based on Chapter 1) are shown in Table 1.1 on pages 22–23.

Review Questions

CHAPTER 1. A BRIEF HISTORY OF BOOKS AND LIBRARIES

1. Trace the ways information has been preserved and transmitted from the earliest times to the present, giving specific examples of the various methods.
2. With what people or peoples has each of the forms in Question 1 been identified?
3. Trace the kinds of technology which libraries have used from the earliest times to the present. Discuss the styles of writing and the various materials used for storing and transmitting information.
4. Name some friends (patrons) of libraries from the earliest times to the present. How did they contribute to books, libraries, or both?
5. What new skills have been needed with each change in the way information is collected, recorded, and transmitted?
6. How have economic, societal, and educational conditions influenced books and libraries? Give examples.
7. Suggest some topics from Chapter 1 that you might use for a term paper.

Bibliography

Bieler, Ludwig. *Ireland, Harbinger of the Middle Ages*. London: Oxford University Press, 1963.

Bury, J. B., Cook, S. A., and Adcock, F. E. (eds.). *The Cambridge Ancient History*. 2d ed. Vol. I: *Egypt and Babylonia to 1580 B.C.* New York: Cambridge University Press, 1924.

TABLE 1.1
Highlights in the history of books and libraries.

People or period	Approximate dates	Kind of writing; materials used	Forms of the book	Kinds of libraries	Examples of libraries	Examples of writing
Prehistory		Pictographs Landmarks Word of mouth				Cave paintings
ANTIQUITY Sumerians Babylonians Assyrians	3600 B.C. 626 B.C.	Cuneiform Clay Stylus	Clay tablet Clay cylinder	Temple Government Private Royal	Telloh Borsippa Nineveh	Code of Hammurabi
Egyptians	3000 B.C.	Hieroglyphic writing Papyrus sheets Reed brush, inks Alphabet of 24 consonants	Roll	Temple Government Private	Gizeh Thebes	Prisse Papyrus Harris Papyrus Inscriptions
Phoenicians	2756 B.C.	Alphabet of 22 consonants Papyrus	Roll Sheet			
Chinese	3d millenium B.C.	Ideographic characters Bone, bamboo, silk, linen	Tablet Roll	Temple		
Greeks (Crete) Greeks	2d millenium B.C. 6th century B.C. – 146 B.C.	Linear A Linear B Phoenician alphabet; added vowels Papyrus, vellum, parchment, wax-coated boards	Tablet Roll Wax tablet Codex	Private Royal Government	Alexandrian library Library at Pergamum Aristotle's library	
Romans	753 B.C. – 476 A.D.	Greek alphabet Papyrus, vellum, parchment, wax-coated boards, quill	Roll Codex Diptych Wax tablet	Private Government Public Christian Pagan	Ulpian library	
MIDDLE AGES Monasteries Western Europe	400 A.D. 12th century after Christ	Alphabet Handwriting: different styles at each monastery	Roll Codex	Church Monastery Royal Private		Book of Kells

		Plain and dyed vellum, parchment; illumination				
Ireland England	12th century to 15th century Renaissance	Handwritten books; Parchment, vellum	Roll; Codex	Private; Royal; Church; Monastery; University	University of Paris	Book of Hours; Greek and Latin works
Invention of printing with movable types	15th century	Printing with movable types; Parchment; Paper	Handwritten books; printed books; printed leaflets; calendars	Public; Private; Government; Royal		Gutenberg Bible
1500–1900 Europe		Printing; Paper	Handwritten books; printed books; periodicals; maps; pamphlets; newspapers	National; Private; Public; University; Royal	Vatican library; Oxford; Cambridge; British Museum; Bibliothèque Nationale	
America	1607–1776	Printing with movable types (1639); Paper	Printed books; Almanacs; Magazines; Government publications; Pamphlets; Broadsides	College; University; Private; Subscription	Harvard; Yale; William and Mary; Princeton	Bay Psalm Book
America	18th and 19th centuries	Printing; Paper	Printed book; Paperbacks; Broadsides; Pamphlets; Almanacs; Magazines; Maps; Government publications	College; University; Private; Public; Government		Library of Congress; Boston Public Library
America	20th century	Printing; Paper; Film; Tapes; Disks; Computer printing; Microforms; Magnetic tape	Printed books; Periodicals; Audio, visual, audiovisual forms; Microforms; Databases; Videoforms	Academic; Special; Public; School; Research; Private; Government; Rare-book archives		New York Public Library; Folger Shakespeare; Major university libraries; Major public libraries; Library of Congress

Brooke, Christopher. *The Monastic World 1000–1300*. New York: Random House, 1974.

Chiera, Edward. *They Wrote on Clay*. Chicago: University of Chicago Press, 1938.

Durant, Will. *The Story of Civilization*. Vols. I–V. New York: Simon and Schuster, 1944–1966.

Evans, Joan (ed.). *The Flowering of the Middle Ages*. New York: McGraw-Hill Book Company, 1966.

Gates, Jean Key. *Introduction to Librarianship*. 2d ed. (McGraw-Hill Series in Library Education). New York: McGraw-Hill Book Company, 1976.

Goodrum, Charles A. *Treasures of the Library of Congress*. New York: Harry N. Abrams Company, Publishers, 1980.

Grant, Michael (ed.). *The Birth of Western Civilization: Greece and Rome*. New York: McGraw-Hill Book Company, 1964.

Grun, Bernard. *The Timetables of History: A Horizontal Linkage of People and Events*. New York: Simon and Schuster, 1979.

Harris, Michael H. *History of Libraries in the Western World*. Metuchen, N.J.: Scarecrow Press, 1984.

Herodotus. *The History of Herodotus*. Translated by George Rawlinson. New York: Tudor Publishing Company, 1941.

Hessel, Alfred. *History of Libraries*. 2d ed. Translated by Reuben Peiss. New York: Scarecrow Press, 1955.

Hobson, Anthony. *Great Libraries*. New York: G. P. Putnam's Sons, 1970.

Jackson, Sidney L. *Libraries and Librarianship in the West: A Brief History* (McGraw-Hill Series in Library Education). New York: McGraw-Hill Book Company, 1974.

Johnson, Elmer D. *A History of Libraries in the Western World*. New York: Scarecrow Press, 1965.

Kramer, Samuel Noah. *From the Tablets of Sumer*. Indian Hills, Colo.: Falcon Wing's Press, 1956.

McMurtrie, Douglas C. *The Book: The Story of Printing and Bookmaking*. New York: Oxford University Press, 1943.

Piggott, Stuart (ed.). *The Dawn of Civilization*. New York: McGraw-Hill Book Company, 1961.

Platt, Colin. *The Atlas of Medieval Man*. New York: St. Martin's Press, 1980.

Plutarch's Lives of Illustrious Men. Corrected from the Greek and revised by A. H. Clough. Boston: Little, Brown & Company, 1930.

Posner, Ernst. *Archives in the Ancient World*. Cambridge, Mass.: Harvard University Press, 1972.

Rice, David Talbot (ed.). *Dawn of European Civilization.* New York: McGraw-Hill Book Company, 1966.

Shera, Jesse H. *Foundations of the Public Library: Origins of the Public Library Movement in New England from 1629–1855.* Chicago: University of Chicago Press, 1949.

Strayer, Joseph R. (ed.). *Dictionary of the Middle Ages.* New York: Charles Scribner's Sons, 1982– . 12 vols. (In progress.)

Thompson, James Westfall. *Ancient Libraries.* Berkeley: University of California Press, 1940.

———. *The Medieval Library.* New York: Hafner Publishing Company, 1957.

Ver Steeg, Clarence L. *The Formative Years: 1607–1763* (The Making of America Series). New York: Hill and Wang, 1964.

Vervliet, Hendrik D. L. (ed.). *The Book through Five Thousand Years.* London: Phaidon Publishers, Inc., 1972.

Wright, Louis Booker. *The Cultural Life of the American Colonies* (The New American Nation Series). New York: Harper & Brothers, 1957.

CHAPTER
2

The Parts of the Book

In order to understand and appreciate the importance, significance, and usefulness of each of the physical parts of a book, one needs only to recall the lack of aids to the reader in the early forms of the book.[1] Each of the parts of the book has been added because it contributes to the usefulness of the book and to the ease of use by the reader.

Physical Divisions of the Book

The physical divisions of the book can be grouped as follows: (1) the binding, (2) the preliminary pages, (3) the text, and (4) the auxiliary or reference material.

BINDING

The binding holds the leaves of the book together, protects them, and makes them easy to handle. It may be plain or decorated, and it may bear the author's name and the title. It has two important parts, the spine and the endpapers.

The spine is the binding edge of the book and carries the title or a brief form of it, the author's name, the publisher, and the call number if it is a library book.

The endpapers are pasted to the covers to make them stronger; they may carry useful information, such as tables, maps, graphs, and rules.

[1] See Chapter 1.

26

PRELIMINARY PAGES

The preliminary pages precede the body of the book and include the flyleaves, the half-title page, the frontispiece, the title page, the copyright page, the dedication, the preface, the table of contents, lists of illustrative material, and the introduction.

The flyleaves are blank pages next to the endpapers; they are the first and last leaves in the book.

The half-title page precedes the title page and serves as protection for it; it gives the brief title of the book and the series title if the book belongs to a series.[2] The series is important because it is included in the description of a work in a bibliography,[3] e.g.;

Lunt, William Edward. *History of England.* 4th ed. (Harper's Historical Series). New York: Harper & Brothers. 1957.

The frontispiece is an illustration relating to the subject matter of the book; it precedes the title page. Not all books have a frontispiece; it is most commonly found in a biographical work in which it is usually a picture of the biographee. A frontispiece is frequently found in an art book; it may be a reproduction of a painting or other work or a painting or photograph of an artist.

The title page is the first important printed page in the book; it includes the following items:

1. Title; that is, the name of the work
2. Subtitle, a descriptive phrase which clarifies or explains the main title
3. Author's name and, usually, facts concerning his or her status, such as academic position, academic degrees, or the titles of other works by the same author
4. Name of the editor, if there is one
5. Name of the illustrator or translator, if there is one
6. Name of the person who wrote the introduction, if other than the author
7. Edition,[4] if it is other than the first

---

[2] A series is a number of separate works issued successively and related to each other in subject, form, authorship, or publication.

[3] A bibliography is a list of works used in writing a book, a paper, or an article, or a list of works recommended for further reading. See also pp. 151–153 and the section on bibliography in Chapter 25.

[4] An edition is the total number of copies of a book or other publication printed from one set of type. A revised edition is a new edition in which the text of the original work has been changed or new material has been added. A revised edition will have a new copyright.

8. Imprint, which includes the place of publication, the publisher, and the date of publication

The title page is the authoritative source of information which is used in listing a source in a bibliography. If the title page is destroyed, facts of authorship, publication, etc., must be arrived at by tedious scientific processes such as a study of the kind of paper used and the watermark.[5]

Nonprint and nonbook sources do not have title pages in the same form that books have them, but they do have comparable sources of authoritative information. On a disk, descriptive (bibliographical) information is found on the label or the slipcase: title, performer, recording company, copyright date, contents, and production facts such as length in minutes, number of revolutions per minute (rpms), etc. On a filmstrip or film, it is found in the title frames at the beginning which give the title, subtitle, producer, photographer, place, publisher or distributor, and date. The label on a cassette gives title, performer(s), producer, place, date, and a contents note. On a microfilm or microfiche, the opening frames give author, title, producer or publisher, place, and date.

The back (verso) of the title page gives the date of the copyright,[6] the names of the copyright owners, and other information, including restrictions on photocopying.

The dedication page follows the title page and bears the name or names of the person or persons to whom the author dedicates the book.

The preface introduces the author to the reader and gives his or her reasons for writing the book; it indicates those for whom the book is intended, acknowledges indebtedness for services and assistance, and explains the arrangement, symbols and abbreviations used, and any special features.

The table of contents is a list of the chapters of the book with page numbers; it may be so detailed that it serves as an outline of the book.

The lists of illustrative material may include illustrations, maps, or tables.

---

[5] A watermark is a marking in paper made by pressure of a design in the paper when it is molded into sheets, and visible when the paper is held up to the light.

[6] Copyright is the exclusive right to publish, reproduce, and sell a literary or an artistic work. The new copyright law, which took effect January 1, 1978, provides that for works already under statutory protection (created before January 1, 1978) the copyright term is twenty-eight years, renewable for forty-seven years. For works created after January 1, 1978, the new law provides a term lasting for the author's life and an additional fifty years after the author's death. (See Public Law 94-553 for additional information about copyright. See also p. 33.)

The introduction describes the general subject matter and plan of the book.[7]

TEXT

The text is made up of the numbered chapters and constitutes the main body of the book.

AUXILIARY OR REFERENCE MATERIAL

The auxiliary or reference material follows the text and may include an appendix or appendixes, a bibliography, a glossary, notes, and one or more indexes.

An appendix may contain material referred to, but not explained, in the text (such as biographical or geographical information), or it may contain the text of a statement referred to in the text (such as the Library Bill of Rights).

A bibliography may be a list of the books, articles, and other materials which the author has used in writing the book, or it may be a list of materials recommended for further reading. A bibliography at the end of an article or a book, or as a separate publication, is an invaluable aid in research. It directs the user to additional sources which will be useful and points out different types of sources, such as books, journals, newspapers, and nonbook material, which might provide needed information.

The glossary is a section which lists and explains or defines all technical terms or foreign words not explained in the body of the book.

All footnotes, if they are not placed at the bottom of each page, may be placed in a section for notes. This section may contain explanations of certain passages in the text and descriptive information about the sources listed.

An index is a list of topics discussed in the text, arranged alphabetically with page references. An index may have subdivisions of the topics and cross references. The detailed subdivisions of the index are useful in limiting a subject or in suggesting headings under which to search in other sources such as the library catalog, indexes, and reference books for additional information on a topic.

Not all books have all the parts which have been discussed in the preceding paragraphs, nor do the parts always follow the order given in this chapter.

---

[7] The introduction may be written by the author, by a person of importance who has encouraged the author to write the book, or by one who considers the book an important contribution. It may be an elaboration of the preface, or it may be the first chapter in the book.

Care of Materials

Care in opening a book when it is new and careful handling of the book at all times will add to its years of usefulness. Care in handling nonbook materials such as films, slides, tapes, microforms, records, and disks will help to prevent scratches, smudges, tearing of film or tape, and scratching and warping of records, thus adding to their usefulness and to the user's enjoyment of them.

Summary

Some of the parts of the book are useful from the standpoint of the book, such as the binding which holds it together. From the user's point of view, the binding is useful also because it usually gives brief information about the book which makes it easy to locate on the shelf.

By reading the preface and introduction, the researcher may be able to tell whether the book will be useful for a particular purpose. The table of contents will give the scope of the book and the items covered, and the reader can see whether or not the topic under study is included. The index also helps on this point, especially if it gives subdivisions of a topic as well as broad topics.

On the title page—and only on the title page—the user will find the correct bibliographical information about the book. One item, the copyright date, is found on the verso of the title page. If this page should be lost, it would be very difficult to establish and verify a book's identity (see p. 154).

Other parts of the book provide additional sources for study (the bibliography) or explain, clarify, or expand upon items in the text (the glossary, notes, maps, and illustrations). The habit of looking at these parts before beginning to read a book can be both useful and timesaving.

Review Questions

CHAPTER 2. THE PARTS OF THE BOOK

1. Examine your textbooks to see which of the parts of the book named in this chapter each one has. How many of these parts of the book have you used? In what ways have they been helpful?

2. Read the prefaces and introductions to your textbooks (if they have them). Would it have been helpful to read them before beginning your classes? Why?

CHAPTER

3

Academic Libraries

Libraries in institutions of higher learning—academic libraries—are as varied and distinctive as the institutions which they serve. There are the libraries in community colleges and in four-year colleges, and there are the central libraries in the universities and the more specialized libraries in colleges within the universities. In each kind of institution, the purposes, staff, buildings, program of services, equipment, and physical facilities of the library are determined by the extent and nature of the curriculum, the size of the faculty and student body, the methods of instruction, the variety of graduate offerings, the needs of faculty and graduate students for advanced research materials, the amount of financial support, and whether or not the library is a part of an area, state, or regional cooperative system in which certain materials, equipment, and services may be shared.[1]

Function and Organization

Academic libraries differ from each other in many respects but they all have the same basic function, which is to aid the parent institution in carrying out its objectives. The library contributes to the realization of these objectives and supports the total program by acquiring and making available the books, materials, and services which are needed.

In carrying out its responsibility in the academic program effectively, the library[2] performs certain activities and offers certain services.

[1] See p. 18.

[2] "The library" refers to the professional staff and the personnel under its direction.

1 It selects and acquires books and materials through purchases and gifts.
2 It prepares these materials for the use of students, faculty, and others who require them. This preparation includes:
   a Classifying materials according to the classification system in use by the library[3]
   b Cataloging these materials, that is, providing descriptive information about each one as to author, title, facts of publication, number of pages, illustrative material, and subject matter
   c Stamping, pasting, typing, and lettering
3 It makes these materials easily accessible physically through open shelves or other efficient means and bibliographically through catalogs, bibliographies, indexes, and thesauri.[4]
4 It circulates materials from the general collection and from the reserve collection. (Reserve materials are those in which class assignments have been made; they are kept together in one place and administered under special rules and regulations.)
5 It gives reference service. The reference staff answers questions that range from simple questions requiring only simple answers to questions that require lengthy searches of a number of different sources. The reference librarians assist the user in locating materials; give guidance in choosing materials for given purposes; aid the user in learning to use the various library materials: the catalog, the indexes, reference materials, microforms and other nonbook materials and the equipment they require; suggest additional sources which might answer a question or provide additional information; provide assistance in defining a question or limiting a topic for a term paper and suggest sources which are helpful in the research for and the preparation of the term paper; and prepare bibliographies and reading lists on various subjects and make them available to library users.
6 It offers both formal and informal instruction in the use of the library. A daily activity of the reference librarians is helping users learn how to use the various materials and equipment in the library. Regularly scheduled classes in the use of the library which are taught by the reference staff may be required or the courses may be electives. They usually carry one or two hours of college credit. The reference staff also gives lectures on specific topics and on special types of materials.
7 It borrows and lends materials on interlibrary loan. An interlibrary loan is a transaction in which library material, or a copy of the material, is made available by one library to another upon request. Since a library

---

[3] See Chapter 4.
[4] A thesaurus (plural, "thesauri") is a detailed list of subject headings.

cannot own all materials, interlibrary loan (ILL) is a means of borrowing materials which users need for research and serious study from local, state, or regional libraries. The reference department is responsible for this service to users; it borrows materials from another library for the use of students or faculty members. Each library has a borrowing policy and a lending policy. This policy governs the kinds of materials a library will lend and the conditions under which it will be borrowed or loaned; the amount of charges the library makes for lending materials; the length of time the materials may be kept; the responsibility of the borrower regarding compliance with the copyright law; photocopying of material;[5] the form of the request; etc. Each library provides information to library users regarding the purpose of ILL and the library's ILL policies.

8 It provides adequate and comfortable physical facilities for study, including carrels for private study and such aids as typing facilities and photocopying devices which are operated by users or by the library staff. In some libraries, especially in community college libraries, facilities for graphic, photographic, audio, and video production are provided.

9 It may make bibliographical searches by computer. In many libraries terminals are provided so that students can make their own searches. (See pp. 164–165.)

10 It administers the total library program, including the budget, the organization and supervision of the various library activities, the maintenance of the building and equipment, and the public relations activities.

In most libraries, these activities are divided into departments such as the acquisitions department, the cataloging department, the circulation department, and the reference department, all of which are under the administrative head of the library. These departments may be subdivided according to specific activities, such as technical processes, or according to

---

[5] The copyright law which became effective January 1, 1978, established the conditions under which photocopies or reproductions of copyrighted works may be made. One specified condition is that the photocopy or reproduction is not to be "used for any purpose other than private study, scholarship, or research." If a user makes a request for or uses a photocopy or reproduction for any other purpose, that user may be liable for copyright infringement. Libraries are required by law to place a notice to this effect on photocopying machines, at places where orders for copies are accepted by libraries, and on all printed forms supplied by libraries for ordering copies. Other conditions of copyright are found in Section 107 and Section 108 of PL 94-553. The librarian will be able to explain the user's responsibility as well as the library's responsibilities in the matter of photocopying.

specific materials, such as audiovisual and other nonbook materials; they may be combined; and they may be given different names. Many academic libraries have departmental branches in the respective departments, such as a collection of materials in the history department. Others, especially university libraries, are organized departmentally according to subject areas, such as the education library or the engineering library, each with its own staff, collection, catalog, and services. In this type of organization, materials in each departmental catalog are also entered in the main catalog of the university library. Academic libraries may have other special departments or divisions, such as the rare-book room, the periodicals department, the government documents room, the curriculum laboratory, and so on.[6]

Kinds of Materials Provided

The quantity and diversity of library materials will vary according to the size, purpose, and the program of the college, but in most college libraries materials will include:

1 Reference sources of a general nature and reference sources in the subject fields, with emphasis upon the subject areas included in the instructional program.[7] These reference sources include dictionaries, encyclopedias, indexes, yearbooks, handbooks, atlases, gazetteers, bibliographies, reference histories like the *Cambridge Ancient History* and the *Cambridge History of American Literature*, and nonbook sources such as microforms.
2 A collection of materials containing:
   a Book and nonbook materials which relate to and supplement each curriculum offered, such as history, education, foreign languages, and mathematics
   b Important general materials not relating to a specific subject area and important sources in subject fields not included in the college curriculums
   c Books and nonbook materials for voluntary and recreational reading, viewing, and listening

[6] In some institutions, the library is a department of a larger learning resources division which has, in addition, a language laboratory, classrooms, audiovisual department, and television studios.

[7] The academic library must support not only the traditional programs, but also such programs as independent study, tutorial, honors and seminar-type experiences, programs of study abroad, residence-hall libraries, year-round study, off-campus courses, and advanced research.

3   Periodicals and newspapers—current issues, bound volumes, and issues on microfilm and microfiche.
4   Pamphlets and clippings.
5   Audiovisual materials, which include pictures, motion picture films, slides, filmstrips, music, phonograph records, tape and disk recordings, maps, globes, cassettes, videotapes, and videocassettes.
6   Microfilm, microcards, microfiche, and other microforms.
7   Government publications.
8   Programmed materials.
9   Archival materials pertaining to the institution.
10 Equipment for the use of these materials, such as microreaders and listening and viewing equipment.
11 Terminals for on-line catalog and other searches—computer or CD-ROM.

Staff

The academic library is administered and staffed by professional librarians who have a broad, general education and the specializations which are required in each area of service offered by the library, such as specialties in the subject fields, in languages, in audiovisual and other nonbook materials, in guidance of readers, and in computer and other technologies. They have an understanding of the educational philosophy and teaching methods of the institution and work with the faculty in selecting and evaluating materials to support the instructional program. They keep up with trends in higher education, curriculum development, methods of teaching, and new materials and new sources of materials. They may teach a course in their specialty and they may participate in team teaching.

Types of Academic Libraries

Each kind of academic library—the community college, the college, and the university—in addition to the characteristics which it shares with all other academic libraries, serves certain purposes and has certain features peculiarly its own which grow out of the particular character and scope of the institution of which it is a part.

COMMUNITY COLLEGE LIBRARY

The public community college is designed to meet the needs of the high school graduate who may not choose to go to a four-year college but must have additional education and training to prepare for a vocation, to update occupational skills, or to acquire new skills. It also provides for the needs of the student who will continue formal education at a four-year institution.

The community (junior) college library must provide the materials and services to support each of the programs offered—general education, vocational, technical, semiprofessional, and adult education—and to serve the needs of the widely different students who enroll in these courses and the faculty members who teach them. The community college library may provide cultural activities for the entire community and often serves as a center for community affairs.

COLLEGE LIBRARY

The name "college" is given to any institution of higher learning that is not divided into separate schools and faculties, that offers a four-year curriculum leading to a bachelor's degree in arts and sciences, and that requires for admission graduation from an accredited secondary school or its equivalent. The name, however, does not indicate the wide variation among colleges in purposes, programs, and size. There are liberal arts colleges, colleges for the preparation of teachers, technical colleges, professional colleges, agricultural colleges, and so on.

Since it is the basic function of the college library—as it is of all academic libraries—to support the program of the parent institution, each college library is in some ways different, but basically they all strive to meet the needs of all their patrons, from the professor engaged in advanced research to the first-year student.

UNIVERSITY LIBRARY

A university has a liberal arts college; it offers a program of graduate study; usually it has two or more professional schools or faculties; and it is empowered to confer degrees in various fields of study.

The program of the university library ranges from the needs of the first-year student to those of the doctoral candidate engaged in scholarly research and the research professors. For the undergraduate students, the university library provides materials and services specifically designed to meet their requirements. The university library may be a central library which serves all students—undergraduate as well as graduate. Some universities provide a library for undergraduates in a separate building with all the materials, facilities, and services necessary to meet their basic needs. In other universities the undergraduate library is not in a separate building but occupies one or more floors of the central library; in still other universities, the central library makes special provisions for undergraduates, such as reading rooms with special reserve and reference collections. In any case, the central library and the undergraduate collection are open to all students.

Rules and Regulations

In order that all students will have an equal opportunity to use the library materials, certain rules and regulations are established in all libraries. These rules govern the kinds of materials which are circulated, the length of time they can be borrowed, the fines charged for overdue books, the use of library facilities—reading rooms, listening rooms, conference rooms, and other special areas—interlibrary loans, photocopiers, computer searches, and the hours of service.

Orientation Visit

A part of the first-year orientation program in most colleges and universities is a visit to the library. In many libraries students are given a handbook which includes information about the physical arrangement of the library, the kinds of materials it provides, the classification system in use, the nature of the library catalog, the rules governing the use of the library, and the schedule of the hours the library is open.

Summary

The size of the academic library varies from the small community college or college library with a centralized collection of 60,000 to 100,000 volumes and two professional librarians to the large university library with a central library of more than a million volumes, a research library, an undergraduate library, departmental libraries, and learning laboratories and a staff large enough to operate all these facilities.

Most libraries make available handbooks which give basic information about the library, such as physical layout, materials and services offered, the hours it is open, rules and regulations, and availability of computer searches.

The basic activities of administering the library, building the collection of materials, organizing the materials for easy use, and assisting patrons in using them are common to all libraries—public, school, academic, and special— and an understanding of what a library is, how it is organized, and the many materials and services it offers is essential for anyone who is preparing for a career as a librarian.

Review Questions

CHAPTER 3. ACADEMIC LIBRARIES

1. What kind of college are you attending? In what ways does the library of your college differ from other academic libraries?
2. The basic purpose of the academic library is to support the curriculum. State the ways in which the following activities help accomplish that purpose:
   a Selection and acquisition of materials
   b Classification of materials
   c Cataloging of materials
   d Reference service
   e Circulation
   f Instruction in the use of the library
   g Interlibrary loan
   h On-line searches
3. How is your library arranged? What classification system does it use? What kind of catalog or catalogs are in use? Are there departmental libraries?
4. Why are rules and regulations important? List the most important rules of your library.

PART

2

The Organization and Arrangement of Library Materials

CHAPTER

4

Classification

Classification is the systematic arrangement of objects, ideas, books, or other items which have like qualities or characteristics into groups or classes. The like characteristics may be size, color, type, form, content, or some other feature.

Historical Development of the Classification of Books

Ever since there have been books, there has been the problem of organizing and arranging them so that they can be used easily and conveniently. Clay tablets were arranged on narrow shelves according to subject or type. Papyrus rolls were placed in clay jars or metal cylinders which were labeled with a few key words describing their content. Parchment rolls were divided by author or title or by major subject or form groups and were placed in bins or on shelves. In medieval monasteries, manuscripts were classified as religious or secular, Latin or Greek; or they were divided according to subject matter, and all books on a subject were kept in the same chest. Books in medieval university libraries were divided according to the subjects taught and were arranged by size and the date acquired on shelves or in chests. After the advent of printing, books were classified as manuscript books or printed books or as Latin, Greek, or Hebrew. In the college libraries of colonial America, the organization was by location symbol—alcove 1, shelf A, book 6—with subject or language divisions within the alcoves.

    Since the time of Aristotle, philosophers and nonphilosophers alike have been devising schemes for the classification of knowledge. In his *Advancement*

41

of Learning, published in 1605, Sir Francis Bacon developed a plan for classifying knowledge into three large divisions: history, poetry, and philosophy. These large divisions were then subdivided into specific classes, with further subdivisions within the classes.

Thomas Jefferson adapted Bacon's plan for the classification of knowledge for use in his personal library at Monticello; and when he sold his library of 6700 volumes to the United States to replace the Library of Congress which had been destroyed by the British in 1814,[1] his classification system went along with it and was used by the Library of Congress until 1864—and, with modifications, until the end of the nineteenth century, when the development of a new classification system was begun.[2]

When Melvil Dewey, a student library assistant at Amherst College in 1872, decided to organize the contents of the college library, his first step was to develop a classification system. After studying the schemes for classifying knowledge which had been devised by Aristotle, Bacon, Locke, and other philosophers, as well as some more recently published library classification schemes, he decided to group books according to subject matter. Like his predecessors, Dewey divided all knowledge into main classes which he subdivided into specific classes and into further subdivisions within each class, always proceeding from the general to the specific.

Purposes and Characteristics of Library Classification Systems

The chief purpose of a classification system in a library is to provide a basis for organizing books and materials so that they can be found quickly and easily by those persons who use the library; it is also a means of bringing materials on the same subject together so that they can be used easily and conveniently. Since ease of use is the basic concern, library classification schemes place materials in those categories from which they are most likely to be called for by those who need them. In addition, such schemes provide for the form of the material as well as for the subject matter; for example, dictionaries, encyclopedias, handbooks, periodicals, and other book forms have specified numbers.

---

[1] The Library of Congress was housed in the Capitol building when it was burned by the British in 1814.

[2] See p. 51.

The first step in classifying according to subject is to arrange all knowledge into major classes, bringing together into one class the parts which are related and arranging the parts in some logical order, usually from the general to the particular. The several classes so formed constitute the classification scheme.

To be used, these classes must follow a definite and established plan so that they can be referred to again and again. Such a plan is called a "schedule." Classes and subdivisions within the classes are arranged in logical order.

Each class of the schedule and each subdivision within each class must be given a symbol so that all the materials in which a particular subject is discussed can have the same number. The symbols used are letters of the alphabet, Arabic numerals, or a combination of these.

Library classification systems follow the generally accepted ideas of what major classes of knowledge are: philosophy, religion, science, history, language, literature, art, and so on. A general class number or letter is assigned to these large classes; for example, in the Dewey Decimal Classification System, 900 is General Geography and History; 973 is History of the United States; and 975 is History of the Southeastern United States. The smallest numbers belong to the largest subjects, and the longest numbers are assigned to the smallest or most specialized areas. For example, 780 is Music; 789.9 is Music Recordings; and 789.9122 is Electronic Music Recordings.

In addition to a definite and established schedule of classes, there must be an index to all materials which are classified according to this schedule so that these materials can be found quickly and easily. The index to all the classified materials in a library is the catalog,[3] which gives the location symbol for each publication. This location symbol is the call number, composed of the classification number and the book number (see pp. 49–51, 55–56).

Theoretically, a classification system should be so organized that material on any one subject can be found in only one place. Some subjects, however, have so many aspects, so many phases, so many contributing factors that it may not be possible to place all material relating to such a subject in only one class. For example, on a given subject, such as the great depression, historical information may be found in the History class, economic data in Economics, sociological facts in Sociology, cultural information in Literature.

[3] The catalog may be a card catalog, a book catalog, a computer printout, a microfiche catalog, an on-line catalog (to a data base) or some other form, and it is supplemented by files, bibliographies, and indexes.

It is important to remember that even though books are classified according to the subject which is given the greatest emphasis, they may, to some extent, treat other subjects.[4]

Dewey Decimal Classification System[5]
HOW THE DEWEY DECIMAL SYSTEM WORKS

In the Dewey Decimal Classification System, Arabic numerals are used decimally to signify the various classes of subjects.

Dewey divided all knowledge, as represented by books and other materials, into nine classes which he numbered 100 to 900. Materials too general to belong to a specific group—encyclopedias, newspapers, magazines, and the like—he placed in a tenth class, which preceded the others as the 000 class. Each of the nine subject classes was organized as follows: the first of the ten divisions of every subject was given to the general books in that subject.

700 CLASS: The Arts (general divisions)[6]

700 The arts

701 Philosophy and theory

702 Miscellany

703 Dictionaries and encyclopedias

704 Special topics of general applicability

705 Serial publications

706 Organizations and management

707 Study and teaching

708 Galleries, museums, art collections

709 Historical and geographical treatment

The remaining nine classes were assigned to specific subject areas, within each class moving from the general to the specific. The 700 class and selected subdivisions illustrate the general-to-specific organization:[7]

---

[4] See Figure 5-6.

[5] Certain selections in this section have been reproduced from *Dewey Decimal Classification and Relative Index*. Devised by Melvil Dewey, Edition 19. Edited under the direction of Benjamin A. Custer (Albany, N.Y.: Forest Press. A Division of Lake Placid Education Foundation, 1979), 3 vols. Each quoted selection is documented.

[6] *Ibid.*, 700 Class, The Third Summary, Vol. 1, p. 480. Reprinted from *Dewey Decimal Classification and Relative Index*, Edition 19, 1979, by permission of Forest Press Division, Lake Placid Education Foundation, owner of copyright.

[7] *Ibid.*, Vol. 2: Schedules, pp. 709–799, *passim.*

710 Civic and landscape art

712 Landscape design
    712.5 Public parks and grounds
    712.6 Private parks and grounds

720 Architecture

721 Architectural construction
    721.042 Skyscrapers
    721.0462 Architectural construction for use by the handicapped

725 Public structures
    725.16 Post office
    725.19 Fire station

730 Plastic arts   Sculpture

736 Carving and carvings
    736.2 Precious and semiprecious stones
    736.25 Sapphires

740 Drawing, decorative and minor arts

745 Folk arts
    745.1 Antiques
    745.5 Handicrafts
    745.582 Beads
    745.592 Toys

750 Painting and paintings
    751.422 Watercolor painting
    751.425 Ink painting
    751.45 Oil painting

760 Graphic arts   Prints

769 Prints
    769.17 Techniques of reproduction
    769.172 Reproduction and copies
    769.174 Forgeries and alterations

770 Photography and photographs

778 Specific fields of photography
    778.55 Motion picture projection
    778.59 Television photography

780 Music

782 Dramatic music and production of musical drama
    782.1 Opera
    782.8 Theater music

784 Voice and vocal music
    784.4 Folk songs

784.5 Popular songs
784.52 Country music
784.54 Rock (Rock 'n' roll)
790 Recreational and performing arts
796 Athletic and outdoor sports and games
    796.3 Ball games
    796.332 American football
    796.3322 Strategy and tactics
    796.33222 Formations, e.g., Split T
    796.33223 Line play
    796.33224 Backfield play
    796.33225 Passing
    796.33226 Blocking and tackling
    796.33227 Kicking
    796.3323 Refereeing
    796.3326 Specific types of American football
    796.33263 College
    796.33264 Professional
    796.33272 Bowl games

In 1876 Dewey's *A Classification and Subject Index for Cataloging and Arranging the Books and Pamphlets of a Library* was published as an anonymous 44-page pamphlet. Today a substantial majority of all libraries in the United States, including most school libraries, many public libraries, and many academic libraries, follow Dewey's system. It has been translated wholly or partly into scores of languages and is now in the nineteenth edition.[8]

The Dewey Decimal Classification System provides for the form (periodicals, dictionaries, encyclopedias, etc.) as well as for the subject matter of the materials to be classified. The standard subdivisions for all classes are:[9]

—01 Philosophy and theory

—02 Miscellany

—03 Dictionaries, encyclopedias, concordances

—04 Topics of special applicability

—05 Serial publications

—06 Organizations and management

—07 Study and teaching

[8] *Ibid.*, Vol. 1, pp. xi, xxii.
[9] *Ibid.*, p. 2. See also Class 700 (general divisions), p. 44.

—08 History and description of the subject among groups of persons

—09 Historical and geographical treatment

The ten classes of the Dewey Decimal Classification System, as listed in the Second Summary, The 100 Divisions, are:

Second Summary: *The 100 Divisions*[10]

000 Generalities
    010 Bibliography
    020 Library and information sciences
    030 General encyclopedic works
    040
    050 General serial publications
    060 General organizations and museology
    070 Journalism, publishing, newspapers
    080 General collections
    090 Manuscripts and book rarities

100 Philosophy and related disciplines
    110 Metaphysics
    120 Epistemology, causation, humankind
    130 Paranormal phenomena and arts
    140 Specific philosophical viewpoints
    150 Psychology
    160 Logic
    170 Ethics (Moral philosophy)
    180 Ancient, medieval, Oriental
    190 Modern Western philosophy

200 Religion
    210 Natural religion
    220 Bible
    230 Christian theology
    240 Christian moral and devotional
    250 Local church and religious orders
    260 Social and ecclesiastical theology
    270 History and geography of church
    280 Christian denominations and sects
    290 Other and comparative religions

300 Social sciences
    310 Statistics

[10] *Ibid.*, p. 472.

320 Political science
330 Economics
340 Law
350 Public administration
360 Social problems and services
370 Education
380 Commerce (Trade)
390 Customs, etiquette, folklore

400 Language
    410 Linguistics
    420 English and Anglo-Saxon languages
    430 Germanic languages   German
    440 Romance languages   French
    450 Italian, Romanian, Rhaeto-Romanic
    460 Spanish and Portuguese languages
    470 Italic languages   Latin
    480 Hellenic   Classical Greek
    490 Other languages

500 Pure sciences
    510 Mathematics
    520 Astronomy and allied sciences
    530 Physics
    540 Chemistry and allied sciences
    550 Sciences of earth and other worlds
    560 Paleontology
    570 Life sciences
    580 Botanical sciences
    590 Zoological sciences

600 Technology (Applied sciences)
    610 Medical sciences
    620 Engineering and allied operations
    630 Agriculture and related technologies
    640 Home economics and family living
    650 Management and auxiliary services
    660 Chemical and related technologies
    670 Manufactures
    680 Manufacture for specific uses
    690 Buildings

700 The arts
    710 Civic and landscape art

720 Architecture
730 Plastic arts   Sculpture
740 Drawing, decorative, and minor arts
750 Painting and paintings
760 Graphic arts   Prints
770 Photography and photographs
780 Music
790 Recreational and performing arts
800 Literature (Belles-lettres)
810 American literature in English
820 English and Anglo-Saxon literatures
830 Literatures of Germanic languages
840 Literatures of Romance languages
850 Italian, Romanian, Rhaeto-Romanic
860 Spanish and Portuguese literatures
870 Italic literatures   Latin
880 Hellenic literatures   Greek
890 Literatures of other languages
900 General geography and history
910 General geography   Travel
920 General biography and genealogy
930 General history of ancient world
940 General history of Europe
950 General history of Asia
960 General history of Africa
970 General history of North America
980 General history of South America
990 General history of other areas

CALL NUMBER IN THE DEWEY DECIMAL SYSTEM

The class number and the book or author number make up the call number of a book or other type of material. A book (or any other type of information source) is classified according to the subject matter it covers and is given the number in the classification schedule which stands for the subject. The class number for a dictionary of music is 780.3; since there are many dictionaries of music and since all of them will be placed in the 780.3 number, it is necessary to have a means of distinguishing one from another. This distinction is made by assigning a book number (or author number) as well as a class number, using the initial of the author's last name plus Arabic numerals.

Author numbers are usually taken from a table called the Cutter table[11] in which numerals, used decimally, are assigned to letters of the alphabet in the order of the alphabet, thus providing for alphabetical arrangement by author. Examples of names and numbers they would be given from the Cutter table are:[12]

Bane	B215	Bond	B711
Bartholomew	B287	Borg	B732
Beard	B368	Boyle	B792
Best	B561	Brunswick	B911
Bing	B613	Burdett	B951
Blake	B636	Butler	B986
Bloomfield	B655	Byron	B996

The title of a publication may be represented in the call number by the first letter of the title, excluding articles. This letter, in lowercase, is placed immediately following the book number and serves to distinguish between books on the same subject written by the same author. Thus the call number for *A Dictionary of Music* by Beard is 780.3 B368d, whereas the call number for *A Concise Dictionary of Music* by Beard is 780.3 B368c.

The arrangement of classified materials on the shelves follows the outline of the classification system. They will appear on the shelves in this order:

745.4	745.4441	745.5	745.537	745.54
H883n	F352d	V882a	P359w	N134b
745.674	745.7	810	810.9	810.903
L152g	B121f	D191s	Ar658a	L181t
810.91	810.917	810.93	810.95073	810.974
B582c	D193s	C111a	N564r	F692h

In some libraries, fiction and biography are not classified. Books of fiction may be given the designation F or Fic plus an author number and arranged alphabetically on the shelves by author. An example is Fic M621 for *The Covenant* by James Michener.

[11] Many libraries use the table which was developed by C. A. Cutter about the time Dewey was devising his classification system. This accounts for the fact that the author or book number is also referred to as the "Cutter number." Adaptations of this and other tables are in use. All are used for the purpose of arranging books within a class alphabetically by author.

[12] *C. A. Cutter's Cutter-Sanborn Three-Figure Author Table.* (Chicopee, Mass.: H. R. Huntting Company, n.d.). Some libraries use a two-figure table.

Biography, instead of being given a class number, may be marked B and arranged in alphabetical order by the subject of the biography—for example, B R781 for a biography of Franklin Delano Roosevelt.

Special symbols are sometimes added to the call number to indicate that the book is shelved in a particular location or that it is a particular kind of material. For example, the symbol R or Ref with the call number signifies that the book is a reference book and that it is located in the reference collection. J or C above or below the call number might mean that the book is in the children's collection. H.H. or a similar symbol with the call number may indicate that the book is one of a memorial gift collection which is kept together in one place. For nonbook materials, the words Kit, Video, Transparency, Filmstrip, or Phonodisc may be added to the call number.[13]

Library of Congress Classification System

The Library of Congress was founded in 1800 by and for the Congress of the United States. The earliest classification of books in the library—as in many other libraries of the time—was by size. When Congress purchased Thomas Jefferson's private library in 1815,[14] his classification system and catalog were included. Jefferson's classification, based on a modification of Francis Bacon's division of knowledge, was used by the Library of Congress until 1864, and with some adaptations until the end of the century.

In 1897, when the Library of Congress was moved from the Capitol building to its own building, the collections contained more than 1½ million items and the library was receiving more than 100,000 items each year. It was then that a new system of classification was begun, designed specifically for the Library of Congress.[15] This system of classification is still being developed; it is under constant study, classes are revised whenever it is necessary, and new classes are added.

The functions of the Library of Congress, the nature of its collections at that time and its expected acquisitions, and the ways the collections were to be used, determined the organization and the details of the classification system. Since the library was to serve the Congress, it was assumed that the holdings in the branches of knowledge most used by lawmakers—the social sciences—would be very large and diverse, and adquate provision had to be

---

[13] See also Figure 14-1.

[14] See p. 42.

[15] See L. E. La Montagne, *American Library Classification with Special Reference to the Library of Congress* (Hamden, Conn.: The Shoe String Press, 1961).

made for these fields. It was also expected that the library would receive, through purchase, national and international exchange, gifts, copyright deposit, and other sources, much material which university and other scholarly libraries would not ordinarily acquire. Therefore, because of the range and diversity of materials, a comprehensive and minute classification system was needed. The primary concern in devising the new system was that it should meet the requirements of Congress. In addition, it must provide for the organization of large amounts of diverse material, both scholarly and popular.

In spite of the fact that it was designed specifically for the Library of Congress collections and is particularly suited to very large collections, the Library of Congress Classification System is used widely in America and in other countries, and increasingly, academic and public libraries are adopting it.

HOW THE LIBRARY OF CONGRESS SYSTEM WORKS

The Library of Congress Classification System combines letters of the alphabet and Arabic numerals. Starting from a base of twenty-six letters, it offers, in theory, 676 subject divisions—compared with 100 divisions (from a base of 10) in the Dewey Decimal Classification System. At the present time, the letters I, O, W, X, and Y are not used but are reserved for further expansion.[16]

Unlike the Dewey Decimal Classification System, in which each class follows the same form, no two classes of the Library of Congress Classification System are identical in their divisions. Each subject class has been given individual treatment and has been developed according to the kind of material which the Library of Congress had or expected to acquire in that subject area. There are no memory devices or constant form numbers because not all classes have all forms of materials. Each class is, in fact, a separate classification. There are, however, some basic features which are characteristic of all classes.

1. In the Library of Congress classification, general materials, such as periodicals, dictionaries, directories, and so on, appear early in the class, for example:[17]

---

[16] See pp. 56–59 for a listing of the main classes and selected subdivisions.

[17] Subject Cataloging Division, Processing Department, *Library of Congress Classification, Class M: Music and Books on Music*, 3d ed. (Washington, D.C.: Library of Congress, 1978), *passim*.

ML   Literature of Music
ML 1   Periodicals
ML 12   Directories
ML 25   Societies
ML 29   Foundations
ML 32   Institutions
ML 100   Dictionaries, Encyclopedias
ML 111   Bibliographies

2. The classes in the Library of Congress classification, like those in other classification systems, proceed from general to particular:[18]

M   Music
M1627   National music
M1628   National music—United States
M1629.3   Music for national holidays
M1629.3.F5   Fourth of July
M1629.3.T4   Thanksgiving Day
M1629.3.W3   Washington's Birthday
M1630.3   Special songs
M1630.3.A5   America
M1630.3.S68   Star-Spangled Banner
M1630.4.Y2   Yankee Doodle

3. Main classes are marked with a single letter:[19]

P   Language and literature

4. Principal subdivisions are denoted by an added letter:

PN   Literary history and collections (General)
PR   English literature
PS   American literature

[18] *Ibid.*

[19] Subject Cataloging Division, Processing Department, *Library of Congress Classification, Class P, Subclasses PN, PR, PS, PZ, General Literature, English and American Literature, Fiction in English, Juvenile Belles Lettres*, 2d ed. (Washington, D.C.: Library of Congress, 1979), *passim.*

5. Further subdivision is by use of Arabic numerals in ordinary sequence, beginning at 1 in each of the main divisions and going as high as 9999 in some classes.[20]

PN 1   International periodicals
PN 2   American and English periodicals
PN 3   French periodicals
PN 1560   The performing arts
PN 1992   Television broadcasts
PN 6109.9   Collections of poetry by women authors
PN 6700   Collections of comic books

6. Decimal letters and numbers may also be used in the class number to subdivide a subject alphabetically by subject or form or by state or country:

PN 6110   Special collections of poetry
PN 6110.C7   Collections of college verse
PN 6110.H8   Humor
PN 6110.S6   Sonnets
PN 6511   Oriental proverbs
PN 6519.A7   Arabic
PN 6519.C5   Chinese
PN 6519.J3   Japanese

A class number may have both a decimal number and a decimal letter and numeral:

PN 1993.5   History of motion pictures
PN 1993.5.A1   General history of motion pictures
PN 1993.5.U65   History of motion pictures in Hollywood, California

7. The decimal letter and Arabic numeral combinations are used for persons as subjects and authors as well as for subjects which are not persons:

PS 708.B7   William Bradford (author of the colonial period)
PS 595.C6   Collection of cowboy verse

[20] Numbering may not be continuous, since one or more numbers are frequently left for expansion.

In no other classification is alphabetical suborder within the class so commonly used. But the alphabetical designation is not uniform in every class; for example, C7 in another class is not college verse, and in another class J3 is not Japanese proverbs.

Usually two letters and four figures are the limit of the length of a class number, but the class number may be expanded by the use of decimal letters and numbers, as has been noted.

Through the combination of letters and numerals, the Library of Congress classification provides for the most minute grouping of subjects. In general, because of the specificity of the class number, only a brief author number is used. It is taken from a modified Cutter table[21] and allows for alphabetical arrangement by author within a subject class. Author numbers, used decimally, may be made up of a letter and one numeral or a letter and two or three numerals.

CALL NUMBER IN THE LIBRARY OF CONGRESS SYSTEM

The Library of Congress classification numbers range in length from one letter and one numeral (P 1) to two letters, four numerals, one decimal number, and a decimal letter and number combination (PN 1993.5.U65). The classification proceeds from general to specific, and the longest numbers belong to the most specialized subjects.

All numbers before the decimal are read in ordinary sequence; all those following the decimal are read decimally. Therefore, PN1993.5.U65S4 will come before PN1994.C5. Class number and author number make the call number. The last letter-and-numeral combination is the author number. Examples of class numbers and author numbers are:

PN1	PN86	PN86	PN1993.5.U65	(class number)
A86	K57	K7	S4	(author number)
PN1994	PN6099	PN6099	PN6110.C7	(class number)
C5	L27	L4	T47	(author number)

Books are arranged on the shelf according to the classification and, within each class, alphabetically by author. The following examples show the way the call number looks on the spine of a book and how the books would be arranged on the shelf:

[21] See p. 50.

PN	PN	PN	PN	PN	PN	PN
1	56.5	56.5	86	86	1990.4	1991.3
A86	.C48	.C5	K57	K7	.D5	.U6
	W39	W16			V57	B78

PN	PN	PN	PN	PN
1992	1993	1994	6099	6110
T4	.5.U65	C5	L4	.C7
	S4			A86

Because of the length and the complexity of Library of Congress classification numbers, and because collections in which the system is used are
generally quite large, the researcher can save time by beginning a search for
materials with the library catalog. In fact, as library collections increase and
become more diversified and as all classification systems become more complicated, the necessity for using the catalog increases. However, if library
users will learn the letter designations and the range of numbers for the fields
in which they are working and will remember the general to specific arrangement, they can soon be able to go directly to those sections and browse. In all
literatures, a large number of the subdivisions are devoted to individual
authors; for example, the subclasses in English literature (PR) from PR1509
through PR6076 are devoted to individual authors from the beginning to
about the middle of the twentieth century.

A listing of the classes and a selected list of subclasses from the Library
of Congress Classification System follows.[22]

A			General Works
	AE	1–90	Encyclopedias (General)
	AI	1–21	Indexes (General)
	AY	10–2001	Yearbooks. Almanacs. Directories
B			Philosophy. Psychology. Religion
	B	1–5739	Philosophy (General)
	BF	1–940	Psychology
	BL	1–2790	Religions. Mythology. Rationalism
	BM	1–990	Judaism
	BP	1–610	Islam. Bahaism. Theosophy, etc.
	BR	1–1725	Christianity (General)
C			Auxiliary sciences of history
	C	1–51	Auxiliary sciences of history (General)

[22] From the Library of Congress, Subject Cataloging Division, Processing Services, *LC Classification Outline*, 5th ed. (Washington, D.C.: Library of Congress, 1986).

	CB	3–481	History of civilization
	CC	1–960	Archaeology (General)
	CT	21–9999	Biography
D			History: General and Old World
	D	1–1075	History (General)
	DA	1–995	Great Britain
	DC	1–947	France
	DD	1–905	Germany
	DE	1–100	The Mediterranean region. Greco-Roman world
	DK	1–973	Soviet Union
	DS	1–937	Asia
	DT	1–995	Africa
	DU	1–950	Oceania (South Seas)
E–F			History: America
	E	11–29	America (General)
		51–99	Indians. Indians of North America
		186–199	Colonial history
		456–655	Civil War
G			Geography. Anthropology. Recreation
	G	1–9980	Geography (General)
	GB	3–5030	Physical geography
	GN	1–890	Anthropology
	GR	1–7070	Manners and customs (General)
	GV	1–1860	Recreation. Leisure
H			Social Sciences
	H	1–99	Social sciences (General)
	HC	10–1085	Economic history and conditions
	HG	1–9999	Finance
	HJ	9–9995	Public finance
	HM	1–299	Sociology (General and theoretical)
	HQ	1–2039	The family. Marriage. Woman
	HX	1–970.7	Socialism. Communism. Anarchism
J			Political science
	JA	1–98	Collections and general works
	JF	8–2112	General works. Comparative works on Constitutional history and administration
	JK	1–9993	United States
K			Law
	KF	1–9827	Federal law. Common and collective state law

L			Education
	L	7–991	Education (General)
	LB	5–3640	Theory and practice of education
M			Music
	M	1–5000	Music
	ML	1–3930	Literature of music
N			Fine Arts
	N	1–9165	Visual arts (General)
	NA	1–9428	Architecture
	ND	23–3416	Painting
	NX	1–820	Arts in general
P			Language and literature
	P	1–1091	Philology and linguistics (General)
	PA	1–8595	Classical languages and literature
	PC	1–5498	Romance languages
	PD	1001–1350	Germanic languages
	PJ		Oriental languages and literatures
	PN	1–6790	Literary history and collections (General)
	PQ		Romance literatures
	PR	1–9680	English literature
	PS	1–3576	American literature
	PT		Germanic literatures
	PZ	5–90	Fiction and juvenile belles lettres
Q			Science
	Q	1–385	Science (General)
	QA	1–939	Mathematics
	QB	1–991	Astronomy
	QC	1–999	Physics
	QD	1–999	Chemistry
	QE	1–996.5	Geology
	QH	1–278.5	Natural history (General)
	QK	1–989	Botany
	QL	1–991	Zoology
	QM	1–695	Human anatomy
	QP	1–981	Physiology
	QR	1–500	Microbiology
R			Medicine
	R	5–920	Medicine (General)
	RB	1–214	Pathology
	RK	1–715	Dentistry
	RT	1–120	Nursing

S			Agriculture
	S	1–954	Agriculture (General)
	SB	1–1110	Plant culture
	SD	1–668	Forestry
	SF	1–1100	Animal culture
	SK	1–579	Hunting
T			Technology
	T	1–995	Technology (General)
	TA	1–2040	Engineering (General)
			Civil engineering (General)
	TK	1–9971	Electrical engineering. Electronics
			Nuclear engineering
	TP	1–1185	Chemical technology
	TS	1–2301	Manufactures
	TX	1–1107.4	Home economics
U			Military Science
	U	1–900	Military Science (General)
	UA	10–997	Armies: Organization, description, facilities, etc.
	UD	1–495	Infantry
V			Naval Science
	V	1–995	Naval science (General)
	VA	10–750	Navies: Organization, description, facilities, etc.
	VD	7–430	Naval seamen
	VE	7–500	Marines
	VK	1–1661	Navigation. Merchant marine
Z			Bibliography and Library Science
		4–8	History of books and bookmaking
		40–115.5	Writing
		116–265	Printing
		662–1000.5	Libraries and library science
		719–871	Libraries
		1001–8999	Bibliography

The library user should keep in mind that some types of materials may be arranged by some method other than subject. In depository libraries, where government publications are housed, the publications are usually arranged according to the Superintendent of Documents Classification System, which is an arrangement by publishing agency (see Chapter 15). In the Educational Resources Information Center (ERIC) files—which contain educational research reports on microfiche—the fiche are filed by Educational

Documents number, e.g., ED 191022, ED 191023, ED 191024, ED 191025. The library user may need to look into several kinds of catalogs, indexes, bibliographies, or files in order to locate all the materials in the library on a given subject.

Summary

An understanding of library classification systems in general, and of the ones used in a particular library, aids in using that library efficiently.

The user should remember that a class number does not embrace all the materials on a given subject, that books and other materials are classified according to the subject which is given the greatest emphasis, and that additional material on a subject may be found in some or in all the major classes of the classification system.

The classification system provides an introduction to the generally accepted divisions of knowledge, and the classification schedule is an illustration of the process of limiting a subject, of proceeding from a large general subject to smaller specialized areas of that subject.

An understanding of the classification system helps the user locate quickly the books and materials in any reference room or in an open-shelf library. It makes it easier to locate the general books—encyclopedias, periodical indexes, etc.—and to go directly to those sections of the library where books on given subjects are shelved.

Review Questions

CHAPTER 4. CLASSIFICATION

1. What is meant by classification? Give some examples of classification other than library classification.
2. Using the Dewey Decimal Classification on pp. 47–49, find the large class number for each of the subjects you are taking. Find these same subjects in the Library of Congress Classification System outline on pp. 56–59.
3. Using the Cutter numbers on p. 50, give the approximate Cutter number for any of your classmates whose names begin with B.
4. Following the examples given on pp. 45, 46, 53, 54, take each of the subjects you are studying and subdivide it, going from general to partic-

ular. Subdivide the following subjects, going from general to particular: recreation, aviation, computers, planets, sports, music.

5. Name several ways in which the two major classification systems differ.
6. In what ways can you benefit from an understanding of the classification system in use in your library?

CHAPTER

 5

Library Catalogs

Originally, the word "catalog" meant a list or an enumeration. It has come to mean a systematic or methodical arrangement of items in alphabetical or other logical order, with the addition of brief descriptive information such as price, size, and color. A library catalog, then, is a systematic listing of the books and materials in a library with descriptive information about each one: author, title, edition, publisher, date, physical appearance, subject matter, special features, and location. It is an index to the library materials which it includes just as the index of a book is the key to the contents of that particular book.

Not all the materials in a library are listed in the library catalog; for example, individual articles in periodicals are not listed in the catalog but are located by using indexes,[1] periodicals may not be listed in the catalog but may be in a special file called the "serials file";[2] government documents, pamphlets, clippings, audiovisual materials, microforms, and other special types of materials are sometimes not included in the catalog but are located by means of bibliographies, lists, or special catalogs and files.[3]

The function of all these bibliographical tools—card catalogs, other forms of catalogs, indexes, bibliographies, and special catalogs, lists, and files—is to make the total resources of the library fully and easily accessible to the users.

[1] See pp. 112–122.

[2] A serial is a publication issued in successive parts, usually at regular intervals, and, as a rule, intended to be continued indefinitely. Examples are periodicals, newspapers, yearbooks and annual reports, and so on.

[3] See Chapter 14, Nonbook Information Sources, and Chapter 15, Government Publications.

Forms of Library Catalogs

All library catalogs provide the same kinds of information: about the item cataloged, author, title, facts of publication, number of pages, special features such as illustrations and bibliographies, and subject matter. They differ in the way the information is presented. (See Figures 5.1 and 5.9). The library catalog may be a book catalog, a computer output microform (COM) catalog, a card catalog, an on-line catalog accessed by computer, or a CD-ROM (compact disk–read only memory) catalog.[4]

BOOK CATALOGS

Some library catalogs are in the form of printed books. This form of catalog has always been in use to some extent and was at one time the generally accepted form. It was discarded because, as libraries grew in size, the printed catalog was soon out of date since cards for new materials could not be interfiled alphabetically. Photocopying devices, modern photographic equipment and microphotography, and the computer have made book catalogs easily and economically available again and many libraries use this form of catalog.

Book catalogs may be used for books, for nonbook materials, or for both. They may be divided—author, title, or subject—or all entries may be filed in one alphabet. Some libraries use a book catalog for only one kind of material, e.g., periodicals.

In a book catalog which is reproduced photographically, the entries are simply photographic reproductions of printed or typed catalog cards displayed in page format. In computer-produced catalogs, the entries may consist of full information or of only two lines, depending upon the amount of information which was fed into the computer. The computer not only can make multiple copies of a catalog but can also interfile new entries in the old alphabet with each printing.

Advantages claimed for the book catalog are that it is easier to use; a large number of entries can be seen at a glance (e.g., all books by an author follow each other on one or more pages); duplicate copies of the catalog can be made and put in every room of the library; and so on. Disadvantages are the difficulties in keeping it up to date and the necessity for consulting more than one volume.

---

[4] See pp. 65–78 for a discussion of the card catalog; pp. 79–81 for a discussion of the on-line catalog; p. 80 for a discussion of the CD-ROM catalog.

COM CATALOGS

A large number of academic libraries—as well as public and other kinds of libraries—have COM catalogs. A COM catalog (or COMcat) is produced directly from machine-readable records. In this process, the catalog card which is in digital form on a computer-generated tape is converted into print on a microform, either microfilm or microfiche.[5]

In the COM (microfiche) catalog, the information on a catalog card is reduced 42 times or 48 times. At a reduction of 42 times, a fiche contains 207 frames, and each frame can contain twelve or thirteen catalog cards (more or less, depending on the amount of information on a card), or approximately 1035 titles. If the catalog card information is reduced 48 times, a fiche can contain approximately 1350 titles. A library collection of 200,000 titles could be stored on about 160 fiche. Access to the microfiche is by means of a reader especially designed for that purpose. The reader has a large screen on which the cards are displayed. A COM reader (terminal) takes up little space (about 20 by 19 by 15 inches with a 12- by 14-inch screen). The fiche are stored outside the reader—usually in slots on each side and in numerical order, arranged alphabetically.

Some COM catalogs are on microfilm—16-mm or 35-mm—onto which the catalog cards are photographed in microimages. Each frame can contain up to 100 lines of print, and up to 174,000 titles can fit on a 6-inch roll of microfilm.[6] In a COM catalog which uses microfilm, the film roll is inside the reader; an index on the outside of the reader cabinet provides access to the contents. An entire library catalog can be contained in one COM (microfilm) catalog. Like the microfiche catalog, the microfilm catalog must be read with a reader especially designed for it.

The COM catalog may be an author catalog, having only author cards; a title catalog, having only title cards; a subject catalog, having only subject cards, or a dictionary catalog, with all kinds of cards in one alphabetical arrangement.[7] In some libraries, the total holdings of the library are in the COM catalog. In other libraries, the COM catalog supplements the card— or other—catalog. In libraries which are changing to a COM catalog and in libraries in which the COM catalog supplements the card catalog, it is often necessary to look in both catalogs to complete a search for information.

All COM catalogs have the same advantages: they require small space; they are easy and economical to duplicate, and a library can have a COMcat in every department and on every floor; they are easy to use.

[5] See pp. 161–164.
[6] See pp. 161–163.
[7] See pp. 66, 74–78.

CARD CATALOGS

Card catalogs are made up of 3- by 5-inch cards on which the cataloging information is printed, typewritten, or photocopied. The cards are filed alphabetically in trays or drawers.[8]

Common Characteristics of Library Catalogs

All library catalogs, regardless of form, have some things in common:

1. They provide aids for the user: labels on the outside and guide cards on the inside of the trays in the card catalogs, an index on the cabinet of the COM reader, and printed instructions and illustrations to aid in using the on-line catalog and the CD-ROM catalog.

2. They have many cross references: a *see* reference refers from a heading that *is not* used to one that *is* used; a *see also* reference refers from a heading that *is* used to another that *is also* used.

Highway law	Music festivals
see	see also
Highways	Concerts
Modern languages	Middle Ages
see	see also
Languages, Modern	Chivalry
Computers	Hurricanes
see	see also
Computing machines (Computers)	Typhoons
Clemens, Samuel Langhorne 1835–1900	Folk-songs
see	see also
Twain, Mark 1835–1900	Ballads

3. The catalog cards in all library catalogs give the same kinds of information about the items they describe: author, title, imprint,[9] collation,[10]

---

[8] In 1987, most library catalogs are still in card form; however, many libraries are converting to on-line or to CD-ROM catalogs (see pp. 79–81) or are making plans to change to one of those forms.

[9] Publisher, place of publication, date of publication.

[10] The collation indicates the number of volumes or pages, the number and kinds of illustrations, and the size of the book.

notes, subject headings, and other information.[11] At the present time catalog cards are available from several sources: Library of Congress, commercial firms, Ohio Computer Library Center (which prints cards by computer) and local processing centers. Most libraries make some of their own cards. Therefore, catalog cards do not always look alike, but they do give the same kinds of information. (See Figures 5.1 and 5.9.)[12] The library catalog is the reader's chief means of discovering and locating material in the library.

1. It points out the location of the books and other types of materials the library holds by giving the location symbol or call number.
2. It lists in one place, in alphabetical order, all books (and nonbook materials, if they are included in the catalog) by a particular author or on a particular subject, regardless of their locations in the library.
3. It provides several ways of finding materials, listing them by author, title, subject; by coauthor, translator, or illustrator, if there is one; and often by series, if the work belongs to a series.

Kinds of Catalogs

A library catalog may be a single alphabetical arrangement or it may be divided into author, subject, and title catalogs.

1. A *subject* catalog is made up exclusively of subject entries.
2. An *author* catalog includes only the author or main entry cards.
3. A *title* catalog is made up of only title entries.
4. A *dictionary* catalog has all entries—author, title, subject, and other entries—filed in one alphabet.

Large libraries usually have three separate catalogs: author, title, and

---

[11] The same kind of information is given about audiovisual materials. See pp. 160–161.

[12] In modern cataloging practice, the information which appears on the catalog card is referred to as cataloging information or as the bibliographic record. Since most library catalogs are made up of cards—either 3- by 5-inch cards or photographic or microphotographic reproductions of them— the term "catalog card" is still appropriate. An exception is the cataloging information in an on-line catalog, which may not look like the traditional card. All types provide the same kind of information. The term "catalog card" is used in this chapter in describing the contents of the library catalog. The word "entry" is used to refer to the way a work is entered in the catalog; by author, subject, title, or added entry.

subject. In general, small libraries have a dictionary catalog. It is important to know how the catalog in your library is arranged in order to avoid making such mistakes as looking up an author's name in the title catalog.

Kinds of Entries (Cards) in the Catalog

An entry is a single listing of a publication. Most publications have at least two entries in the catalog. (1) They are entered under author, and (2) they are entered under title or subject. Most publications other than fiction are listed under author, title, and subject. In addition, a work may be entered in the catalog under coauthor, editor, translator, and illustrator.

AUTHOR ENTRY

The author entry (Figures 5.1 and 5.9) is the basic cataloging record and is called the "main entry." In general, it gives the following information:

1. Author's full name, inverted (some cards give the dates of the author's birth and death, if applicable)
2. Title and subtitle of the work
3. Edition, if it is not the first
4. Coauthor, illustrator, translator
5. Imprint, which includes place of publication, publisher, and date of publication
6. Collation, which includes number of pages or volumes, illustrative material, and size in centimeters
7. Series to which the work belongs, if it is one of a series
8. Subjects which are treated fully
9. Full name and usually the birth and death dates of the coauthor, translator, editor, or illustrator

It may give other pertinent information, such as a note concerning the contents or the pages on which a bibliography is located. (See Figures 5.1, 5.2 and 5.6.)

The author or main entry for a publication may be:

1. An individual (Figures 5.1 and 5.9)
2. An individual who edits rather than writes the work (Figure 5.2)
3. An institution or an organization (Figure 5.3)

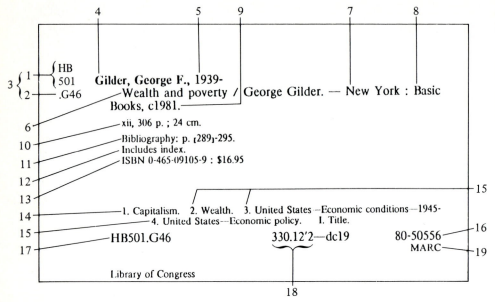

FIGURE 5.1
Author card or main entry: (1) class number; (2) author or book number; (3) call number; (4) author's name, inverted; (5) author's date of birth; (6) title of book; (7) place of publication; (8) publisher; (9) date of publication; (10) collation; (11) bibliographical note; (12) descriptive note; (13) identifying number of book (International Standard Book Number); price at time of publication; (14) subject heading (the subject treated fully); (15) other subjects treated; (16) Library of Congress catalog card number; (17) Library of Congress classification and book number; (18) Dewey Decimal class number; (19) information on this card is available in machine-readable format (MARC means "machine-readable cataloging").

    a Library of Congress
    b Modern Language Association
4. A publication or a title
    a *The American Scholar*
    b *Whales Weep Not* (Figure 5.4)

TITLE ENTRY

A title entry (Figure 5.5) is made for a publication which has a distinctive title. The title is typed at the top of the card in black, above the author's name. If the title is used as the main entry, the work will not have a title entry in the catalog.

807
S53 **Sloan, Thomas O**   *ed.*
The oral study literature ₍by₎ Robert Beloof ₍and others₎
Edited with an introd. by Thomas O. Sloan. New York,
Random House ₍1966₎

xii, 209 p. 19 cm. (Studies in speech, SSP3)

Includes bibliographical references.

1. Oral interpretation.   2. Literature—Study and teaching.
ɪ. Beloof, Robert Lawrence, 1923–   ɪɪ. Title.

PN4145.S53   807   66–11149

Library of Congress   ₍5₎

F I G U R E 5.2
Editor as main entry.

F I G U R E 5.3
Organization as author or main entry.

332.401
Am 52r **American Economic Association.**
Readings in monetary theory, selected by a committee of
the American Economic Association. Philadelphia, Blakiston, 1951.

ix, 514 p. diagrs. 22 cm. (Blakiston series of republished articles
on economics, v. 5)

"Classified bibliography of articles on monetary theory, by Harlan
M. Smith": p. 457–505.

1. Money—Addresses, essays, lectures. 2. Currency question—Addresses, essays, lectures.   ɪ. Title.

HG221.A46   332.401   51—4205

Library of Congress   ₍61n²2₎

QL
737
.C435

Whales weep not [motion picture] / producer, James R. Donaldson ; directors, Lana Jokel, James R. Donaldson. — Deerfield, IL : Coronet/MTI Film & Video, 1986.

1 film reel (26 min.) : sd., col. ; 16 mm.

Title from data sheet.
Credits: Narrator, Jason Robards.
Made in 1983.
Audience: Ages 12 through adults.
Issued also as videorecording.
Summary: Documents the little-known habits and characteristics of the endangered sperm whale.

1. Sperm whale. [1. Sperm whale. 2. Whales] I. Donaldson, James R. II. Jokel, Lana. III. Coronet/MTI Film and Video.
[QL737.C435]   599.5—dc11a   86-700160
                                                          AACR 2   MARC

ALA Booklist
for Library of Congress   F

F I G U R E 5.4
Title as main entry.

F I G U R E 5.5
Title entry.

PN
1992
.75
M36

      `Computers in video production`

McQuillin, Lon B.
    Computers in video production / by Lon McQuillin. — White Plains, NY : Knowledge Industry Publications, c1986.

x, 186 p. : ill. ; 29 cm. — (Video bookshelf)

Bibliography: p. 167-170.
Includes index.
ISBN 0-86729-182-6 : $39.95

1. Television—Production and direction—Data processing. I. Title. II. Series.
PN1992.75.M36   1986   791.43'0232—dc19   86-7314
                                                        AACR 2   MARC

Library of Congress

SUBJECT ENTRY

There is no set number of subject entries for each publication listed in the catalog; a subject card (Figure 5.6) is made for every subject which is discussed fully. A subject card differs from all other types of entries in that the subject is typed at the top of the card in red letters, or in black capital letters. No other kind of heading is typed in this manner. The remainder of the card is an exact duplicate of the main entry card.

Subject headings describe the contents of a work and therefore indicate to the reader its usefulness for a particular purpose. Subject headings in a given library catalog are uniform and are used consistently throughout the catalog. The subject headings used for one publication on a given subject will be used for *all* the publications in the library which deal fully with that same subject. A reader who is searching for material on folk music will find that all the works in the library in which this subject is discussed fully (works which are included in the catalog) are listed under the heading "folk music." They will be filed together in the catalog, alphabetically by author. A subject heading may be a word, a phrase, or a compound heading, inverted to emphasize the important words:

Poetry

Art in literature

Authors, American

FIGURE 5.6
Subject entry.

```
                    MOGUL EMPIRE--HISTORY
    DS
    461     Hansen, Waldemar.
    .H33       The Peacock Throne : the drama of
    1981     Mogul India / Waldemar Hansen. -- Delhi
             : Motilal Banarsidass, 1981.
                xi, 560 p. : ill. ; 25 cm.
                Bibliography: p. 533-545.
                First Indian reprint of the 1972 edition.
                Includes index.

                1. Mogul Empire--History.  2. India--
             History--1500-1765.  3. Taj Mahal--
             History.  4. Shahjahan, Emperor of
             India, ca. 1592-1666.  I. Title.

    FTS     02 Nov 81     7899974   FHMMsc
```

The subject heading may be determined by the form of the work (Engineering—Dictionaries), or by location (Education—U.S.), or it may be a location subdivided by subject (France—Social life and customs).

A knowledge and understanding of subject headings is essential to the efficient use of the catalog. If the student knows the author or title of a publication, finding it in the catalog is relatively simple, if the library has it. If, however, the assignment is to find material *on a subject*, the student must have an understanding of the nature of subject headings—how they are determined and how they are phrased—in order to know how to look for the topic in the catalog. For example, if the topic is contemporary American drama, the student will look in the catalog for American drama—20th century. If the topic is the history of printing, the student will look for Printing— History.

Examples of other topics and their subject headings are:

Topic	*Subject heading*
Medieval art	Art, Medieval
Early American paintings	Paintings, American
History of art	Art, History
Writing for publication	Authorship
A dictionary of English literature	English literature— Dictionaries
Finding a job	Applications for positions
The American Revolution	U.S.—History—Revolution

Careful reading of the subject headings listed on each card will result in the discovery of related subjects under which material can be found.[13]

To ensure consistency in the subject headings used in the catalog, most libraries follow the headings used by the Library of Congress and listed in the publication *Library of Congress Subject Headings* (10th ed., 1986).[14] This volume is useful also to researchers because (1) it tells them under what headings a given subject may be found in the catalog; (2) it directs them to other headings under which material can be located and to other useful aspects of a subject; and (3) it breaks a subject down into its several parts; thus aiding the researchers in limiting their subjects. In some libraries, this

---

[13] See Figures 5.1–5.9.

[14] School libraries and some public libraries follow the *Sears List of Subject Headings* 13th ed. (New York: The H. W. Wilson Company, 1986) which is also based on the Library of Congress subject headings.

volume is kept near the catalog to be used by the public. Other sources which may be useful in deciding how to phrase a subject or which give subdivisions of a subject are indexes to encyclopedias and to periodicals and thesauri (which are lists of subject headings used in on-line searches).

An understanding of subject headings (called "descriptors" in the field of computers) is essential to the successful use of any mechanized information retrieval system as well as to the use of the traditional library card catalog. Information is fed into the computer under given subject headings (descriptors) and retrieved by using the *same* subject headings. In general, a list of descriptors is referred to as a "thesaurus."

OTHER ENTRIES

If a publication has a joint author or an important editor, illustrator, or translator, an entry is made for each one. The name of such a person is typed above the author's name, in black. These cards are called "added entries" (Figure 5.7).

When a title card and an author card are made for each of the stories, plays, or essays in a collected work, they are called "analytical entries" and are referred to as "analytics" (Figure 5.8). Analytics may be made for each

---

	Shultz, George Pratt, 1920- joint author
HD	
6331	**Baldwin, George Benedict.**
.B25	Automation, a new dimension to old problems ₍by₎ George P. Shultz and George B. Baldwin. Washington, Public Affairs Press ₍1955₎
	20 p. 23 cm. (Annals of American economics)
	Cover title.
	Author's names in reverse order in previous ed.
	1. Automation. 2. Industrial relations. ɪ. Shultz, George Pratt, 1920- joint author.
	HD6331.B25 331 55–11116 rev
	Library of Congress ₍r56q6₎

FIGURE 5.7
Joint author as added entry.

```
QA          Shuman, Bruce A.
76.55
.N37            "Who's user-friendly? A comparative
1983            appraisal of Dialog, Orbit, and BRS."
                (In Proceedings of the Fourth National
                Online Meeting, New York, April 12-14,
                1983.  Medford, N.J., 1983.  pp. 491-498.)
```

FIGURE 5.8
Analytical entry.

important subject discussed in a yearbook or for each biographee in a biographical work which includes several persons.

Arrangement of Entries in the Catalog[15]

Rules for arranging entries in the catalog are adopted by each library. There are some variations, but in general these practices are followed:

1. Alphabetical arrangement is word-by-word rather than letter-by-letter.

Word-by-word	*Letter-by-letter*
New Guinea	Newcomer
New Hampshire	Newfoundland
New Mexico	New Guinea
New Orleans	New Hampshire

[15] In library catalogs in which cards are filed according to the *ALA Filing Rules* (1980), the arrangement of some of these entries will differ from the ones given here. The librarian will explain if necessary.

New products	Newman, John
New thought	New Mexico
New York	New Orleans
Newcomer ·	Newport
Newfoundland	New products
Newman, John	News agencies
Newport	Newsboys
News agencies	News broadcasts
News broadcasts	Newsome, Mary
Newsboys	Newspapers
Newsome, Mary	New thought
Newspapers	Newton, Robert
Newton, Robert	New York
Port	Port
Port Arthur	Portage
Port Elizabeth	Port Arthur
Port Jackson	Port Elizabeth
Port of Spain	Porter, Cole
Port Orange	Port Jackson
Port Royal	Portland
Port Said	Portobello
Portage	Port of Spain
Porter, Cole	Port Orange
Portland	Portrait
Portobello	Port Royal
Portrait	Port Said
Portsmouth	Portsmouth
Portugal	Portugal

2. Definite and indefinite articles at the beginning of titles and other headings are ignored.

The academic library
Addition and subtraction
Airports
The All American team
An American Primer

American speech
An annual review

3. Abbreviations are filed as if they were spelled out: "St." is filed as "Saint," "Mr." is filed as "Mister," and so on.

Mr. Mack

St. Augustine

Mrs. Miniver

St. Joan

Money and banking

Saint Nicholas

Mt. Olympus

School days

Mountie

Spelling bee

4. Names beginning with "Mc" are arranged as if they were spelled "Mac."

McHenry, William
machines
McNeill, Richard
mammals

5. Numbers are filed as if they were spelled out.

1984

20th century

Odyssey World Atlas

twins

100 Days

200 gold pieces

Origins

6. Historical subheadings are filed in chronological order.

UNITED STATES—HISTORY—COLONIAL PERIOD
UNITED STATES—HISTORY—REVOLUTION
UNITED STATES—HISTORY—1789–1801
UNITED STATES—HISTORY—WAR OF 1812
UNITED STATES—HISTORY—1821–1823
UNITED STATES—HISTORY—CIVIL WAR

7. Works *by* a person are filed before works *about* that person.

Shaw, George Bernard, 1856–1950   (as author)
SHAW, GEORGE BERNARD, 1856–1950   (as subject)

An example of the simplest form of arranging catalog cards in a dictionary catalog, following these practices, is as follows:

The a cappella chorus book	Mr. Mack
Aaron, Daniel, editor	Monetary fund
The Abbey Theater	100 days
Ability	Only a rose
Ability—Testing	St. Augustine
Accent on teaching	School days
Accents on opera	Shaw, George Bernard,
Education—History	1856–1950 (as author)
Educational psychology	SHAW, GEORGE
Literature	BERNARD,
Literature—Dictionaries	1856–1950 (as subject)
Literature—History	U.S.—History—Colonial
McHenry, William	period
Machines	U.S.—History—Revolution
McNeill, Richard	U.S.—History—Civil War

Listed below are some entries as they would be filed in an author, a title, a subject, and a dictionary catalog:

Author catalog

Wiggim, Albert Edward
Wiggin, Kate Douglas
Wigglesworth, Edward
Wightman, David
Wigman, Mary, 1886–1973
Wijk, Axel
Wild, Earl
Wilde, Oscar, 1856–1900
Wilder, Alec

Title catalog

The wigwam and the cabin
Wilberforce
The Wilcox banner

Wild Alaska
Wild animals I have known
The wild cherry tree
Wilderness

Subject catalog

WIGMAN, MARY 1886–1973
WILD FLOWER GARDENS
WILD FLOWERS
WILD FLOWERS—NORTH AMERICA
WILDE, OSCAR 1856–1900
WILDLIFE CONSERVATION

Dictionary catalog

Wiggim, Albert Edward
Wiggin, Kate Douglas
Wigglesworth, Edward
Wightman, David
Wigman, Mary 1886–1973
WIGMAN, MARY 1886–1973
The wigwam and the cabin
Wijk, Axel
Wilberforce
The Wilcox banner
Wild, Earl
Wild Alaska
Wild animals I have known
The wild cherry tree
WILD FLOWER GARDENS
WILD FLOWERS
WILD FLOWERS—NORTH AMERICA
Wilde, Oscar 1856–1900
WILDE, OSCAR 1856–1900
Wilder, Alec
Wilderness
WILDLIFE CONSERVATION

On-Line Catalogs

Some libraries have computer terminals which are on-line to a data base containing all the cataloging information of that particular library in a file of machine-readable cards. Such systems are known as on-line catalogs.

On-line catalogs are not standardized at the present time. They differ in the kinds of instructions given for accessing information, the ways the information appears on the screen, and the amount of information given.

In general, an item can be found in an on-line catalog under author, subject, and title, just as in a card catalog. But before beginning a search in an on-line catalog, the user must read a set of instructions.

Each on-line system has different steps which must be followed in calling up catalog information. These steps are carefully outlined in the instructions at each computer terminal. They must be followed exactly and in the order given. For example, if you are searching for an author and the instructions are "Press keys AU, type in the author's name, and press the Enter key," you will first press capital A, then press capital U, then type in the author's name, and then press "Enter". If the instructions are "Press keys a =, type in the author's name, and then press the Enter key," you will first press the a key, then press the = key, then type in the author's name, then press Enter. The information for the author has been fed into the computer using a specific sequence, and it can be retrieved *only* in the same way. The instructions for subject and title searches will be similar to the instructions for author searches. Most systems are easy to learn to use.

In most on-line catalogs, the subject headings have been taken from The *Library of Congress Subject Headings*,[16] a copy of which will be near the terminal, and only those headings can be used to retrieve information by subject. If another list of subject headings has been used, only those headings can be used to retrieve the subject information. The LC subject headings (or whatever list is used in the data base) must be consulted in order to find the correct headings before beginning a subject search.

Even though the instructions vary from one on-line catalog system to another, the same information is given about a book that is found on the traditional catalog card: author, title, place of publication, publisher, date of publication, call number, subjects treated in the book, pages, and other descriptive information. The order of information will be different, and there may be additional information on the computer screen that pertains to that

---

[16] U.S. Library of Congress, Subject Cataloging Division, *Library of Congress Subject Headings*, 10th ed. (Washington, D.C.: Library of Congress, 1986), 2 vols.

```
1                         2                              3   6   9

LUIS SEARCH REQUEST:   A=GILDER GEORGE F
BIBLIOGRAPHIC RECORD -- NO. 7 OF 8 ENTRIES FOUND

4┌─Gilder, George F., 1939-
5────Wealth and poverty / George Gilder. -- New York :
     Basic Books, c1981.
7────xii, 306 p.
    ┌Bibliography: p. (289)-295.
8───┤Includes index.
    └SUBJECT HEADINGS (Library of Congress; use s= ):
     ┌Capitalism.
     │Wealth.
10──┤United States--Economic conditions--1945-
     └United States--Economic policy.

11 ───────────────┐
    LOCATION: TAMPA circulating collection
12──CALL NUMBER:  HB501 .G46
13───────CHARGED to a user. Due: 11/05/87




14────────────────────FOR ANOTHER COPY AT THIS OR ANOTHER LOCATION,
                      press ENTER


    ┌TYPE m FOR NEXT RECORD. TYPE h FOR HELP.
15─┤TYPE i TO RETURN TO INDEX.  TYPE r TO REVISE SEARCH,
    │h FOR HELP, e FOR LUIS INTR
    └TYPE COMMAND AND PRESS ENTER==>
```

FIGURE 5.9
Author entry: (1) acronymn for this on-line catalog; (2) this search was made by author: a = ; (3) eight entries were found under the author; (4) author's name and birth date; (5) title of book; (6) place of publication, publisher, date; (7) number of pages; (8) book has a bibliography and an index; (9) subject headings are from Library of Congress; subject headings; to find material under them begin search s = ; (10) subjects treated in the book; (11) the name of the library that has the book; (12) the call number: class number and author number; (13) status of the book: charged out, due date; (14) how to locate another copy; (15) computer instructions for various steps. (University of South Florida LUIS record. LUIS is the NOTIS Systems, Inc., name for the on-line public access catalog supported by their NOTIS software. By permission from Florida Center for Library Automation.)

computer or to the particular library. A comparison of the information on the author card from an on-line catalog (Figure 5.9) and the information on a traditional author catalog card (Figure 5.1) illustrates these points.

Entries can be added to an on-line catalog at any time, and therefore it can be kept up to date. Terminals can be placed throughout the library and in other buildings on campus, making the catalog more accessible.

CD-ROM Catalogs

A CD-ROM is a plastic disk 4.72 inches in diameter (or larger) on which data are encoded by using a laser to burn pits into the surface. When accessed at a terminal, the pits are read by a laser and reproduced on the computer screen. A CD-ROM has a storage capacity of 600,000 catalog records. Information on the disk cannot be edited, erased, or added to. To update a CD-ROM data base, a new disk must be produced.

The CD-ROM catalog workstation is made up of a special keyboard, a TV monitor, a CD-ROM disk drive, a disk, and perhaps a printer. The catalog information is the same as that in other catalogs, but the information may be listed, as in Figure 5.9, or it may be in another format. Instructions must be followed exactly.[17]

Summary

The catalog card stands for the work it describes. The main entry gives the items which appear on the title page and the copyright date on the verso of the title page. In addition, it describes the work as to size, number of pages, and kinds and amount of illustrative material. It indicates whether the work has a bibliography, and it may list the contents. The main entry gives the subject or subjects treated in the order of emphasis, the first subject heading listed being the one which is treated most completely. It is often possible to select or to reject a book or other publication by reading and understanding the information on the catalog card.

The form of the catalog may be book, microform (COMcat), card, or on-line to a data base or CD-ROM. It may be an author catalog, a title catalog, a subject catalog, or a catalog with all entries filed in one alphabetical arrangement.

Whatever the form, all library catalogs give the same kinds of information about the items described; provide aids to the user such as guide cards, cross references, and instructions on how to access the information; and require an understanding of subject headings and the various ways they are phrased.

---

[17] For other uses of CD-ROM, see pp. 165–167.

Review Questions

CHAPTER 5. LIBRARY CATALOGS

1. Explain the difference between classification and cataloging.
2. Name the kinds of information on a catalog card or computer printout. In what ways does this information help you look for material on a subject?
3. Name the kinds of library catalogs. Give the advantages and disadvantages of each one.
4. Examine the catalog cards on pp. 69, 71, 73. Under what subjects can you find material on: American literature, the Taj Mahal, Automation, Money?
5. Look in the *Library of Congress List of Subject Headings* under any of the headings in Question 4. What additional headings are given?
6. Examine the author card on p. 68 and the author printout on p. 80. In what ways do they differ?
7. Name the different ways a book or other item can be found in the library catalog.

PART

3

General Information Sources

CHAPTER

6

Reference Sources

The word "reference" comes from the verb "refer," which means "to turn to for aid or information." Thus any person or thing referred to for these purposes is a reference. A source which is consulted for aid or information on a topic, a theme, an event, a person, a date, a place, or a word is a reference source. In this sense, the entire library is a reference collection, because it was selected, organized, and arranged for study and reference.

In any library there are some sources which are consulted more frequently than others for certain kinds of information; there are books which, because of their organization and arrangement, lend themselves to quick and easy use; and there are other publications which were planned and written to be *referred to* for pieces of information rather than to be read completely. In most libraries these kinds of materials are brought together in one room or area and constitute what is called the "reference collection," the "reference room," or the "reference department." The use of these materials is restricted to the library. Questions may be answered completely from the resources in the reference collection, or a given source may only indicate other books and materials which the information seeker must consult to secure the full answer to a question. The other sources may be in another part of the library or in another library.

The reference collection, room, or department is not a separate library within itself but is only one of the parts of the total library that students will use in their search for material.

Reference Books

The term "reference book" has come to mean a specific kind of publication which has been planned and written to be consulted for items of information, rather than read throughout. It contains facts that have been brought to-

85

gether from many sources and organized for quick and easy use, either in an alphabetical or chronological arrangement or by the use of detailed indexes and numerous cross references.

Using reference books effectively and advantageously depends upon developing a facility in using them independently. An understanding of what reference books are, the kinds that are available, the types of questions each kind will answer, and how each book is arranged will help the user acquire this facility.

There are two types of reference books: (1) those which contain the needed information, such as dictionaries, encyclopedias, handbooks, biographical dictionaries, atlases, and gazetteers; and (2) those which tell the user where the information can be found, such as indexes and bibliographies.

These two types of reference books are of two classes, general and specialized; the latter are referred to in this text as "subject" information resources.

GENERAL REFERENCE BOOKS

General reference books are those which are broad in scope, not limited to any single subject, but useful for all, or at least for many, subject areas. The kinds of general reference books, according to their form and the material which they include, are dictionaries, encyclopedias, indexes, yearbooks, handbooks, almanacs, biographical dictionaries, directories, atlases, gazetteers, and bibliographies.

Each kind of reference book is designed to do specific things. Theoretically, a given reference book does the specific things it is planned to do better than any other reference book can do them; thus it should be consulted *first* for the kind of information it covers, even though other reference books may include some of the same information. For example, a dictionary or an encyclopedia may give information about a geographical location; but a gazetteer, which is designed for the sole purpose of providing information about geographical names and places, is the first place to look for information concerning a geographical location.

The kinds of general reference books, the purposes they serve, and examples of each kind are listed below.

1. A dictionary provides information about words—meaning, derivation, spelling, pronunciation, syllabication, usage, and current status.
   a   *Webster's Third New International Dictionary of the English Language*
   b   *American Heritage Dictionary of the English Language*
2. An encyclopedia is concerned with subjects. It gives an overview of a

topic, including definition, description, background, and bibliographical references.

a   *Encyclopedia Americana*
b   *The New Encyclopaedia Britannica*

3.   An index points out where information can be found. There are indexes to articles which appear in periodicals and there are indexes to articles, essays, poems, and other writings which appear in collected works.

a   *Readers' Guide to Periodical Literature*
b   *Essay and General Literature Index*

4.   A yearbook, often called an annual, presents the events of the past year in brief, concise form.

a   *The Annual Register of World Events*
b   *Britannica Book of the Year*

5.   A handbook, literally a small book which can be held conveniently in the hand, provides miscellaneous items of information. It may also be called a miscellany, a manual, or a companion.

a   *Robert's Rules of Order*
b   *Famous First Facts*

6.   An almanac, originally a projection of the coming year—days, months, holidays, and weather forecasts—is the name now given to a collection of miscellaneous facts and statistical information.

a   *The World Almanac and Book of Facts*
b   Whitaker's *Almanack*

7.   A biographical dictionary is a collection of sketches of varying lengths about the lives of individuals, arranged alphabetically by surname.

a   *Who's Who*
b   *Dictionary of American Biography*

8.   A directory lists the names and addresses of persons, organizations, or institutions. It may provide other pertinent information, such as the purposes, the dues, and the officers of organizations.

a   *American Library Directory*
b   *The Foundation Directory*

9.   An atlas is a volume of maps, plates, or charts, with or without explanatory text.

a   *National Atlas of the United States of America*
b   *National Geographic Atlas of the World*

10.   A gazetteer is a volume which provides geographical information and data about places. It does not define geographical terms.

a   *Columbia-Lippincott Gazetteer of the World*
b   *Webster's New Geographical Dictionary*

11.   A bibliography is a list of books and other materials which have some

relationship to each other. The materials listed are described as to author, title, publisher, price, and number of pages. In some bibliographies the materials are evaluated.

a   *Cumulative Book Index*
b   *Guide to Reference Books*

OTHER GENERAL REFERENCE SOURCES

1. Periodical publications—newspapers, magazines, and journals— provide news or material of current interest in a particular field or at a particular time.
    a   *The New York Times*
    b   *National Geographic Magazine*
    c   *College English*
2. Abstract journals give digests or summaries of periodical articles and other literature.
    a   *Chemical Abstracts*
    b   *Psychological Abstracts*
3. Government publications include all the kinds of sources mentioned above. They are discussed in Chapter 15.

SUBJECT REFERENCE SOURCES

Subject reference sources are those in which the material is devoted to a specific subject area, such as literature, art, or history. In most subject fields, there are the same kinds of reference sources as there are in the general field. Subject reference materials are discussed in Chapters 16 to 24.

Nonbook Reference Sources

The many nonbook reference sources include pamphlets, clippings, audio, visual, and audiovisual materials, data bases, and microforms. They are discussed in Chapter 14.

Determining the Usefulness of a Reference Source

The usefulness of a reference source for a particular purpose may be determined by answering some basic questions.

Auth 1. Are those who produced the subject matter—the editorial staff as listed on the title page or in the preliminary pages—specialists in their fields, as indicated by the academic position or by some other position which they hold?

S 2. Is the usefulness of the subject matter of the reference source under consideration affected by time, and if so, is this source out of date?

S 3. Does it attempt to cover more than can be handled in a work of this size?

Arr 4. Is it arranged for quick and easy use, with adequate index and cross references?

S 5. Does it provide text alone, or does it include illustrative material as well? Is the illustrative material well chosen?

T. 6. Is the treatment of material, as stated in the preface,
   a Simple for the nonspecialist?
   b Technical for the expert?
   c Scholarly for the scholar?

Auth 7. Is there any indication of bias in the treatment of material?

S 8. Does the source provide bibliographies, and are they up to date?

Arr 9. Is the print clear and legible?

S 10. What kinds of questions will it answer:
   a Factual?
   b Statistical?
   c Historical?
   d Current information?

S 11. What subject areas are emphasized:
   a Science?
   b Literature?
   c Social science?

Choosing a Reference Source

In choosing a reference source to answer a given question most conveniently and effectively, it is necessary to understand the nature of the question and to know the usefulness of the various reference sources in answering given questions. First analyze the question, then decide which reference source or sources provide the kinds of information it requires.

1. What kind of information is needed to answer the question:
   a A definition of terms?
   b Statistical information?
   c An exhaustive explanation or discussion?
   d A brief summary?
2. In what subject area does the question belong:

    a History, economics, geography?
    b An area touching several subject fields?
3. What factors affect the question:
    a Date?
    b Location?
    c Economic conditions?
    d Historical events?
4. What kind of reference source is needed:
    a A general dictionary for definitions?
    b A subject dictionary for specialized terminology?
    c An encyclopedia for an overview or a summary?
    d A periodical article or a newspaper article for current information?
    e A yearbook for statistics?
    f An audiovisual source?
    g A combination of several reference sources?

Using Reference Sources

Use of any reference source is easier and more efficient if the user understands its distinguishing features. These features are explained in the preliminary pages and include:

1. Plan followed in the organization and presentation of material:
    a Alphabetical, word-by-word or letter-by-letter[1]
    b Chronological
    c Topical, with detailed indexes giving page numbers or some other kind of numerical reference, such as the number of a poem in an anthology or the number of an entry
2. Symbols and abbreviations used in the text
3. Diacritical marking or the phonetic transcription used to indicate pronunciation
4. Kinds of indexes it has

In Chapters 7 to 15, each kind of general reference source is discussed, with emphasis upon its usefulness for a particular purpose.

---

[1] See pp. 74–75.

Review Questions

CHAPTER 6. REFERENCE SOURCES

1. What is a reference?
2. What is a reference source in a library? Define each kind and give an example.
3. Name the *kinds* of reference sources that are available in your library.
4. On what bases can the authority of a reference source be judged?
5. What points should be considered in choosing a reference source for a given purpose?
6. In what ways are the contents of reference books arranged?

CHAPTER

7

Dictionaries[1]

The earliest dictionaries were those in which the meanings of the words of one language were given in the words of another. Among the clay tablets recovered from the ruins of the Sumerian civilization are dictionaries which give Sumerian words with their Semitic-Assyrian meanings. The word "dictionarius," meaning "a collection of words," was first used in the English language about 1225 as the title of a collection of Latin terms. Several Latin-English dictionaries, as well as English and other modern language dictionaries, appeared before the end of the sixteenth century. In the seventeenth century, the name "dictionary" was gradually given to works explaining English words in English.

The first general and comprehensive dictionary of the English language was the *Universal Etymological English Dictionary* by Nathan Bailey, published in 1721, which gave pronunciation and authority for pronunciation but only very brief definitions.

Samuel Johnson's *Dictionary of the English Language*, which appeared in 1755, was designed to list all "good" words in the language with their "proper" meanings. There were many quotations to illustrate the uses of words, and these illustrative quotations have been repeated by makers of dictionaries since that time. Johnson's *Dictionary* was used in England and America until 1828, when it was superseded by Noah Webster's *American Dictionary of the English Language*. *Webster's Third New International Dictionary of the English Language*, which we use today, is the successor to the 1828 work.

[1] Dictionaries are included in Part Three, General Information Sources, because they cover words in all areas. See also Chapter 20, Language (Philology).

The next important English dictionary was *A New English Dictionary on Historical Principles*. James Murray, as editor, began the task of publishing this scholarly ten-volume work in 1878. It was not completed until 1928. Reissued in 1933, with some corrections and additions, as *The Oxford English Dictionary* (often abbreviated *OED*), it is an example of the application of the historical method to words, giving the origin, meaning, and historical development of English words in general use now or at any time since 1150.

Characteristics of Dictionaries

Following the pattern established by the distinguished *American Dictionary of the English Language* and *The Oxford English Dictionary*, the dictionary today is, first of all, a collection of words in which each word is treated as to pronunciation, derivation, usage, meaning, and syllabication. In addition, the dictionary may give synonyms, antonyms, illustrative quotations, maps and plates, biographical facts, and geographical and historical information. Thus a dictionary may be a combination of wordbook, gazetteer, biographical dictionary, and encyclopedia.

Because most dictionaries are arranged alphabetically for convenience of reference, the word "dictionary" has come to mean any alphabetical arrangement of words or topics. A collection of items of information in a special subject area, arranged in alphabetical order, is often called a dictionary. There are dictionaries of psychology, education, philosophy, music, mathematics, and many other subjects, as well as dictionaries of dates, events, battles, plants, and sports. In fact, dictionaries of subjects and of things surpass in number those of words or language.

When only a few words, a small part of those belonging to a subject, are given, or when these words are only partially explained, the work is a "vocabulary." When it is a list of explanations of technical words and expressions in some particular subject or in a book, it is a "glossary."

Determining the Usefulness of a Dictionary

The primary purpose of any dictionary is to answer questions about words. The usefulness of a dictionary is determined by the way in which it answers them. In order to use a dictionary most effectively, it is necessary to understand what it has to offer and in what manner the material is presented. The user must learn the kinds of dictionaries and the distinguishing characteristics of each kind, in order to decide which one or ones will answer a given question most completely and most satisfactorily.

In judging the usefulness of a dictionary, consider these points:

1. What part of the language does the dictionary include? Slang, dialect, obsolete, and technical words, as well as standard words?
2. What period of the language does it cover?
3. Is usage indicated?
4. Are plurals, verb tenses, and participles spelled?
5. Is syllabication indicated?
6. In what way is pronunciation shown? If diacritical marks are used, are they explained?
7. Are the definitions clear?
8. Are the definitions given in order of historical or current usage?
9. Is the etymology of the word given?
10. Is illustrative material—quotations, maps, pictures, charts—used? If so, is it adequate and appropriate?
11. Does it give synonyms and antonyms, and are they explained?
12. Are abbreviations and symbols explained?
13. Is encyclopedic information—that is, geographical, biographical, and historical facts and like material—included?
14. Is the dictionary easy to use?
15. How does it compare with other dictionaries on each of these points?

Many of the questions listed above will be answered as one uses the various dictionaries; other answers will be found in the preface and introduction of each dictionary. Making a dictionary is a very complicated and technical task, and any good dictionary will have a large staff of specialists as editors. These editors will explain the steps they have followed in making the dictionary. In order to use a dictionary most efficiently, the student should examine the table of contents, the preface, and the introductory material of the dictionary when consulting it for the first time.

Kinds of Dictionaries

Dictionaries can be divided into (1) general word dictionaries, which provide overall information such as pronunciation, derivation, syllabication, and meaning, about the words of a language; (2) dictionaries which have to do with certain aspects of language, such as etymology, synonyms and antonyms, slang, colloquialisms, dialect, and usage; and (3) dictionaries which are concerned with a specific subject area.

General word dictionaries are (1) unabridged, that is, complete—covering all the words of a language; (2) abridged, that is, reduced in content but retaining the features of the unabridged work; or (3) general-purpose desk dictionaries which are not abridgments of a work but which include only a selection of the words of a language. They include both English-language and foreign-language dictionaries.

Dictionaries which are concerned with certain aspects of language are discussed in Chapter 20, Language (Philology).

Dictionaries in the subject fields are included in Chapters 17 to 24.

Representative Dictionaries[2]

GENERAL WORD DICTIONARIES—*UNABRIDGED*

Craigie, William A., and others (eds). *A Dictionary of American English on Historical Principles*. Chicago: University of Chicago Press, 1938–1944. 4 vols. Follows the plan of *The Oxford English Dictionary;* continues the story of the English language into colonial America and to the end of the nineteenth century; indicates which words originated in America; does not include slang and dialect.

Funk & Wagnalls New Standard Dictionary of the English Language. New York: Funk & Wagnalls Company, 1963 (original ed. 1913). Includes all live words of the language; gives current meaning first; provides pronunciation, spelling, etymology; includes many technical terms, illustrative quotations from newspapers and periodicals, and geographical entries; has an appendix of foreign words and phrases.

Murray, James Augustus Henry, and others (eds.). *The Oxford English Dictionary*. Being a corrected reissue, with an introduction, supplement, and bibliography, of *A New English Dictionary on Historical Principles*. London: Oxford University Press, 1933. 12 vols. and supplement. Presents the historical development of each word introduced into the English language since 1150, giving the date it was introduced and the uses which have survived; each meaning illustrated with a quotation from literature; gives pronunciation, etymology, inflectional forms, and synonyms.

The Random House Dictionary of the English Language. 2d ed.—unabridged. New York: Random House, Inc., 1987. Based on current usage, reflects changes and growth in the language in all fields; many definitions are dated; illustrative phrases are given for some definitions; encyclopedic

---

[2] See also Chapter 20, Language (Philology).

information includes biographical and geographical names, titles of literary works, a world atlas, and four foreign language dictionaries: French, Spanish, Italian, and German; has more than 2000 illustrations.

A Supplement to the Oxford English Dictionary. Edited by R. W. Burchfield, Oxford: Clarendon Press, 1972–1986. 4 vols. The four-volume *Supplement* incorporates the material in the 1933 *Supplement* and contains all words that came into common use in English during the publication of the *OED*, 1884–1928, and words which have come into use from 1928 to the present. It aims to record the vocabulary of the twentieth century, including literary, scientific, technical, legal and other professional terminology, and popular, colloquial, and modern slang expressions.

12,000 Words: A Supplement to Webster's Third New International Dictionary. Springfield, Mass.: Merriam-Webster, Inc., Publishers, 1987. Gives meanings that have become established in the language since *Webster's Third* was published in 1966.

Webster's New International Dictionary of the English Language. 2d ed. Springfield, Mass.: G. & C. Merriam Company, 1959. Gives definitions in historical sequence; features a pronouncing gazetteer and biographical information; includes slang, dialect, obsolete, and technical words; provides pronunciation, etymology, inflectional forms; indicates British pronunciation; includes foreign words and phrases in the main vocabulary. (Now out of print.)

Webster's Third New International Dictionary of the English Language. Springfield, Mass.: G. & C. Merriam Company, 1981. Covers current vocabulary of standard written and spoken English; earliest meaning given first; single-phrase definitions are based on examples of usage; provides a simplified pronunciation key, etymologies, synonyms, illustrations; quotations from contemporary sources; has more than 460,000 entries; 200,000 examples of usage.

GENERAL WORD DICTIONARIES—*DESK TYPE*

Abridged

Funk & Wagnalls Standard Desk Dictionary. New updated ed. New York: Thomas Y. Crowell Company, 1980. Has more than 100,000 entries; includes usage notes, discriminated synonyms, idioms, and encyclopedic information; appendixes include pronouncing gazetteer, biographical information, abbreviations, and a secretarial handbook.

The Random House College Dictionary. Rev. ed. New York: Random House, Inc., 1984. Based on the unabridged *Random House Dictionary of the*

English Language; contains more than 150,000 entries in one alphabet; includes many of the latest technical and slang words, general words, idioms, synonyms and antonyms, geographical and biographical information; gives usage labels; has pictures and maps.

The Shorter Oxford English Dictionary on Historical Principles. 3d ed. Completely reset, with etymology revised by G. W. S. Friedrichsen and with revised addenda. Oxford: Clarendon Press, 1973. An authorized abridgment of *The Oxford English Dictionary* with the features of that work; includes some new materials.

Webster's Ninth New Collegiate Dictionary. Springfield, Mass.: Merriam-Webster, Inc., Publishers, 1984. Based on *Webster's Third New International Dictionary*; aims to present the English language as it is spoken and written today, including general vocabulary and specialized terminology; contains more than 160,000 entries, including new words; new meanings are given; the date the word was first used in English and examples of usage are new features; has pictorial illustrations and a number of appendices.

Other desk dictionaries

American Heritage Dictionary of the English Language. 2d college ed. Edited by William Morris. Boston: Houghton Mifflin Company, 1985. Contains 200,000 entries and 3,000 illustrations; includes new words from business, science, technology; gives clear definitions; includes guides to punctuation and grammar and notes on preferred usage.

Chambers Twentieth Century Dictionary. New ed. New York: Cambridge University Press, 1986. A dictionary of international English with 170,000 entries; includes literary, scientific and technical, popular, and archaic words.

Oxford American Dictionary. Compiled by Eugene Ehrlich and others. New York: Oxford University Press, 1980. Compiled by American editors and designed to serve the everyday needs of users; has a selected vocabulary of 35,000 entries—words and phrases likely to be found in everyday life, including slang, informal words, technical words, idioms, and new words from the 1970s; gives brief concise definitions with the most current meaning first; offers guidance on correct usage; does not give etymologies; uses a simple system of pronunciation.

Webster's New World Dictionary. 2d college ed. Englewood Cliffs, N.J.: Prentice-Hall, Inc., 1986. Has 160,000 entries, including 20,000 new words and meanings; gives new meanings and etymologies of American place names; has many current words of American origin; includes scientific and technical terminology, slang, and colloquial expressions; all in one alphabet.

FOREIGN-LANGUAGE DICTIONARIES[3]—*BILINGUAL*

French

Harrap's New Standard French and English Dictionary. Edited by J. E. Mansion. Revised and edited by R. P. L. Ledésert and Margaret Ledésert. New York: Charles Scribner's Sons, 1973. Vols. 1, 2: *French-English*. Updated with new entries and new definitions; offers many new words, including scientific and technical terms; gives examples of usage. Vols. 3, 4: *English-French*, revised by R. P. L. Ledésert and Margaret Ledésert. London: Harrap, 1980. *Supplement*. 3d ed. Compiled by R. P. L. Ledésert, with the assistance of P. H. Collen. London: Harrap, 1961. *Harrap's New Collegiate French and English Dictionary*. London: Harrap, 1982.

New Cassell's French Dictionary: French-English, English-French. Completely revised by Denis Gerard and others. New York: Funk & Wagnalls Company, 1973. Includes new words in science, art, and commerce; gives pronunciation and translation of phrases and expressions; omits obsolete terms.

German

Betteridge, Harold T. (ed.). *Cassell's German Dictionary: German-English, English-German*. Rev. ed. New York: The Macmillan Company, 1978. Includes technical words and geographical and proper names; reflects current usage.

Greek

Liddell, H. G., and Scott, Robert (comps.). *Greek-English Lexicon*. 9th ed. Revised and augmented by Sir Henry Stuart Jones and others. Oxford: Oxford University Press, 1940. *Supplement*. Edited by E. A. Barber. 1968. The standard English-Greek lexicon, updated by scholars in many countries; includes scientific and technical terms.

Italian

The Cambridge Italian Dictionary. Compiled by Barbara Reynolds. Cambridge: Cambridge University Press, 1962, 1981. 2 vols. Vol. I: Italian-English; Vol. II: English-Italian. Designed for English-speaking users

---

[3] For additional foreign-language word dictionaries, see Robert Lewis Collison, *Dictionaries of Foreign Languages*, 2d ed. (New York: Hafner Publishing Company, 1971).

but also useful for Italians; presents Italian and English vocabulary, usage, and idioms; translation rather than definition of words and phrases; attention is given to specialized terms in arts, sciences, technology, industry, philosophy, etc.; illustrative phrases are used to clarify meaning.

Rebora, Piero, and others (comps.). *Cassell's Italian Dictionary: Italian-English, English-Italian*. London: Cassell & Co., Ltd., 1967. A general dictionary of the Italian language; includes colloquialisms and new words as well as obsolete words and words found in the classics.

Latin

Simpson, D. P. (ed.). *Cassell's New Latin Dictionary: Latin-English, English-Latin*. Completely revised. New York: Funk & Wagnalls Company, 1960. Useful for beginning students.

Russian

Falla, P. S. *The Oxford English-Russian Dictionary*. Oxford: Clarendon Press, 1984. For English-speaking users at the university or similar level; has some technical terms.

Müller, Vladimir Karlovich (ed.). *English-Russian Dictionary*. 7th ed. New York: E. P. Dutton & Co., 1965. A general dictionary of the Russian spoken language.

Smirnitsky, Aleksandr Ivanovich. *Russian-English Dictionary*. Rev. ed. New York: E. P. Dutton & Co., 1973. Gives general coverage.

Wheeler, Marcus. *The Oxford Russian-English Dictionary*. 2d ed. Oxford: Clarendon Press, 1984. A general-purpose dictionary of Russian as it is written and spoken; designed for English-speaking users. Companion to *The Oxford English-Russian Dictionary*.

Spanish

Cuýas, Arturo (ed.). *Appleton's New Cuýas English-Spanish and Spanish-English Dictionary*. 5th ed., revised and enlarged by Lewis E. Brett (Part I) and Helen S. Eaton (Part II). New York: Appleton-Century-Crofts, 1972. 2 vols. Includes idioms and specialized terms; gives particular emphasis to usage in the United States and Latin America and to scientific and technological terms; gives pronunciation, definitions, parts of speech.

The New Revised Velázquez Spanish and English Dictionary. New York: New Century Publishing Company, 1985. Spanish-English; English-Spanish; has thousands of new terms and idiomatic expressions of general use replacing those no longer in common usage; has many encyclopedic features, such as geographical terms, abbreviations, proper names, monetary units.

Summary

The primary purpose of all dictionaries is to give information about words. They differ in the ways this information is presented and in the amount of information given. As Collison said, "No one dictionary of a language is sufficient . . . the more dictionaries there are, the richer the people."[4]

Differences in dictionaries can be seen clearly in the following excerpts from three college dictionaries.[5]

re·search (rĭ-sûrch', rē'sûrch) *n. Abbr.* **res.** Scholarly or scientific investigation or inquiry. *—v.* **researched, -searching, -searches.** *—intr.* To engage in or perform research. *—tr.* To study thoroughly. [Old French *recerche,* from *recercher,* to seek out, to search again : *re-,* again + *cerch(i)er,* to SEARCH.] **—re·search'er** *n.*

(a) *The American Heritage Dictionary of the English Language*

re-search (rē sûrch'), *v.t., v.i.* to search again.
re·search (ri sûrch', rē'sûrch), *n.* **1.** systematic inquiry into a subject in order to discover or revise facts, theories, etc. **2.** a particular instance or piece of research. *—v.i.* **3.** to make researches. *—v.t.* **4.** to make an extensive investigation into. [< MF *recerch(er)* (v.) (to) seek, OF = *re-* RE- + *cercher* to SEARCH] **—re·search'a·ble,** *adj.* **—re-search'er, re·search'ist,** *n.* **—Syn. 1.** scrutiny, study. See **investigation. 4.** study, inquire, examine, scrutinize.

(b) *The Random House College Dictionary,* revised edition

¹re·search \ri-'sərch, 'rē-₁\ *n* [MF *recerche,* fr. *recerchier* to investigate thoroughly, fr. OF, fr. *re-* + *cerchier* to search — more at SEARCH] **1 :** careful or diligent search **2 :** studious inquiry or examination; *esp* **:** investigation or experimentation aimed at the discovery and interpretation of facts, revision of accepted theories or laws in the light of new facts, or practical application of such new or revised theories or laws
²research *vt* **1 :** to search or investigate exhaustively <~ a problem> **2 :** to do research for <~ a book> ~ *vi* **:** to engage in research — **re·search·able** \-ə-bəl\ *adj* — **re·search·er** *n*
re·search·ist \-'sər-chəst, -₁sər-\ *n* **:** one engaged in research

(c) *Webster's New Collegiate Dictionary*

---

[4] Robert Lewis Collison, *Dictionaries of Foreign Languages* (New York: Hafner Publishing Company, 1955), p. xv.

[5] (a) © 1969, 1970, 1971, 1973, 1975, 1976, 1978, Houghton Mifflin Company. Reprinted by permission from *The American Heritage Dictionary of the English Language.* (b) *The Random House College Dictionary,* rev. ed. (New York: © 1975 by Random House). (c) By permission. From *Webster's New Collegiate Dictionary.* © 1977 by G. & C. Merriam Co., publishers of the Merriam-Webster dictionaries.

They differ in (1) the number of main entries for the word; (2) the method of indicating pronunciation; (3) punctuation and use of symbols; (4) order and extent of etymology; (5) number of meanings; (6) order of meanings (oldest first or current meaning first); (7) number of illustrative examples; (8) number and form of inflectional forms; (9) number of synonyms given; (10) abbreviations given.

In the library catalog, dictionaries are listed in several ways, for example:

Under the language: English language—Dictionaries
Under a subject: Botany—Dictionaries; Mathematics—Dictionaries
Under a kind of dictionary: Dictionaries, Juvenile
Under a general heading: Encyclopedias and dictionaries

Each dictionary is listed under author or editor, title, and subject.

Review Questions

CHAPTER 7. DICTIONARIES

1. What is the basic purpose of a dictionary?
2. List the kinds of information about words a dictionary should provide.
3. Examine any of the dictionaries discussed in this chapter to see if it carries out the basic purpose. How much information does it give about the entries in it?
4. What other kinds of information do some dictionaries give? (The extra information is called "encyclopedic information.") What dictionaries include encyclopedic information?
5. Explain unabridged and abridged dictionaries. Which dictionaries are abridged, and what are their parent volumes?
6. Compare two dictionaries on the basis of the ways in which they provide the information you listed as an answer to Question 2.
7. Look up a given word in *The Oxford English Dictionary*. When did it enter the English language? How many definitions are given? How many illustrative quotations are given? (See pp. 229–230 for other dictionaries of the historical development of words.)

CHAPTER

8

Encyclopedias

Since ancient times, it has been the aim and desire of encyclopedia makers to bring together into one work *all* human knowledge.

The first encyclopedias were works of a single author, designed to summarize the knowledge and thinking of the time. Aristotle produced a large number of encyclopedic treatises. The *Historia Naturalis* of Pliny the Elder, dating from A.D. 77, has been called the first encyclopedia because of its method of compilation. It is the oldest encyclopedia in existence.[1]

In general, the encyclopedias of the Middle Ages were devoted to one or another of the sciences; but Isadore, Bishop of Seville, attempted to cover every branch of knowledge in his work *The Etymologiae*, which is sometimes called the "Encyclopedia of the Middle Ages."

In 1630 the first modern encyclopedia (the first work to be given the title "encyclopedia") was published in Switzerland by Johann Heinrich Alsted. French contributions to encyclopedia making in the seventeenth century were the *Grand Dictionnaire* of Louis Moréri and the *Dictionnaire Historique et Critique* of Pierre Bayle.

English encyclopedias began with the two-volume *Cyclopaedia* of Ephraim Chambers in 1728, which became the model for all encyclopedias that followed. Translated into French, it provided the working basis for *L'Encyclopédie du XVIIIᵉ Siècle*, which was edited by Diderot and d'Alembert from 1751 to 1772, with all the savants of France as members of the editorial staff.

---

[1] Translated into English by Philemon Holland in 1601, the *Historia Naturalis* was the standard authority for many centuries on the subjects it included: physics, geography, ethnology, physiology, zoology, botany, medical information, minerals, and art. Forty-three editions were published before 1536.

The *Encyclopaedia Britannica* was first published in Edinburgh in 1771 in three volumes as a dictionary of the arts and sciences. The next edition, in ten volumes, added history and biography. Other and larger editions followed, including the scholarly ninth and eleventh editions. In 1920 it was acquired by Sears, Roebuck and Company, which gave it to the University of Chicago in 1943. It has been published since that time by Encyclopaedia Britannica, Inc., which was organized for that purpose.[2]

Encyclopedia editing in the United States began with the publication of the *Encyclopedia Americana* in 1829. The *New International Encyclopedia*, which introduced the journalistic style into encyclopedia writing, appeared in 1884.

By derivation, "encyclopedia" means "instruction in the circle of arts and sciences"—considered by the Greeks to be essential to a liberal education. Today, as it has from the beginning, the encyclopedia purports to be a repository of information on all branches of knowledge, presenting the basic general principles and the most essential details of each of the arts and sciences. It gives an overview of each subject, with definition, description, explanation, history, current status, statistics, and bibliography. It is organized, usually in alphabetical arrangement, for rapid and easy use. Most encyclopedias have an index volume. Use of the index enables the researcher to find small items in long articles.

A work of this magnitude calls for the most careful planning and editing and the most experienced writers. Reputable publishers of encyclopedias spare no expense in making their works authoritative and accurate. Because of the amount of work involved, it is not possible to revise an encyclopedia every year. Therefore, the chief means of keeping an encyclopedia up to date is by publishing an annual supplement or yearbook. (The yearbook does not bring the articles in the encyclopedia up to date; it presents topics of interest from the past year.) In addition to publishing yearbooks, the major encyclopedia publishers have programs called "continuous revision." This means that their editorial specialists are always at work on the subjects for which they are responsible and annually a certain number of articles are brought up to date. The new material in the revised articles, and new articles and additions, call for a new copyright. Therefore, each annual issue is a new edition; and instead of appearing as numbered editions, such as the tenth or the eleventh, most encyclopedias are identified by the year, such as the 1988 edition.

There are encyclopedias written for scholars and educated adults, there are some addressed to the general public, and there are others designed for young people and children. Some encyclopedias are available in on-line

---

[2] See Herman Kogan, *The Great E B: the Story of the Encyclopaedia Britannica* (Chicago: The University of Chicago Press, 1958), pp. 257–258.

format. In each of these encyclopedias, the basic factual material may be the same; they differ in style of writing, in amount of additional material included, and in manner of presentation.[3]

Choosing an Encyclopedia

Encyclopedias are of two types:

1. The dictionary type treats subjects under many specific alphabetically arranged headings.
2. The monographic type presents its subjects under large headings with many subdivisions. The monographic encyclopedia may be arranged alphabetically or by broad topic. In either case, a detailed index and many cross references are needed to locate topics within long articles.

The usefulness of an encyclopedia depends upon the extent to which it fulfills its stated purposes. In order to decide which encyclopedia can most satisfactorily provide material on a given subject, the student should become acquainted with each encyclopedia as to:

1. Its authoritativeness
   a Is the publisher well known and reputable?
   b Is the work dependable, as evidenced by an editorial staff of specialists in each field of knowledge?
2. Its purpose
   a What is the editor attempting to do?
   b For whom is the work intended?
      (1) Scholars?
      (2) The general public?
      (3) Young people or children?
          (a) Is it planned to supplement a curriculum?
          (b) Is it written on grade or age levels?
3. Its scope
   a Is it comprehensive in coverage?
   b Is it limited to one branch of knowledge?

---

[3] The name "encyclopedia" is given also to a work designed to present information on all phases of one particular branch of knowledge. This kind of encyclopedia is usually referred to as a "subject encyclopedia" as distinguished from a "general encyclopedia," which covers all branches of knowledge. Subject encyclopedias are included in Chapters 17 to 24.

4. Its up-to-dateness
    a Is it a new work?
    b Is it based on an old edition of the same title or of another title?
    c Is the material in the articles, including statistics, maps, and charts, out of date?
    d Are the bibliographies adequate and up to date?
        (1) Are they references for further reading on the subject?
        (2) Are they the sources used in writing the articles?
        (3) Do they follow each article, or are they collected into a single volume?
5. Its strong points
    a What subject areas are emphasized?
    b What features are superior to those in other encyclopedias?
6. Its physical makeup
    a Does the physical makeup— that is, the size of the volumes, the kind of paper, the type, the headings, and the lettering on the spine—add to the ease of use?
    b Is the illustrative material adequate and suitable to the text?

Some of these questions can be answered by reading the preliminary pages in each encyclopedia; others will be answered as the student uses the several encyclopedias.

Using an Encyclopedia

In using an encyclopedia for the first time, it is important to read the preface carefully in order to determine:

1. Organization of the material
    a Are there short articles on small subjects?
    b Are there long articles on large, general subjects?
2. Arrangement
    a Is it alphabetical letter-by-letter or word-by-word?
    b Is it arranged by broad topics?
3. Kind of index provided
    a Is there a detailed index which points out small subjects within the long articles?
    b Is there an index to each volume or a single index for the entire work?
4. Kinds of aids to the reader
    a Is pronunciation indicated? If so, what system is followed?
    b Are cross references provided?
    c Are abbreviations and symbols explained?

The outstanding features of the general encyclopedias listed below are given in the annotations.

Representative Encyclopedias

GENERAL ENCYCLOPEDIAS

Academic American Encyclopedia. Danbury, Conn.: Grolier Educational Corporation, 1988. 21 vols. A completely new, up-to-date reference work; aims to provide quick access to information on a wide range of subjects for high school and college students and adults; major emphasis is on science and technology, the arts and humanities, and biography; articles are short; there are many illustrations—75 percent in color—and maps; Vol. 21 is the index. Computer-produced, the entire contents are in machine-readable form. Available on CD-ROM.

The Canadian Encyclopedia. Edmonton, Alberta: Hurtig Publishers, Ltd., 1985. 3 vols. A national encyclopedia, it covers all aspects of Canadian life; treats subjects from the Canadian viewpoint; includes topics in art, literature, science, technology, politics, religion, and popular events.

Chambers's Encyclopedia. 4th ed., revised. New York: Pergamon Press, 1967. 15 vols. The only major encyclopedia produced in England, presents the British and European viewpoints; covers entire range of human knowledge. Updated in 1973.

Collier's Encyclopedia. New York: Macmillan Educational Corporation, 1988. 24 vols. Emphasizes current subjects; aims to cover every major area of knowledge; contains new articles on the latest developments in the social sciences, in science and technology, and in the arts and humanities; makes extensive use of maps and other illustrations—many in color. Vol. 24 includes the index, bibliographies on more than 120 broad subjects, and study guides to a number of selected topics.

The New Encyclopaedia Britannica. Edited by Philip W. Goetz. 15th ed., revised. Chicago: Encyclopaedia Britannica, 1985. 32 vols. The greatly revised *Encyclopaedia Britannica* is made up of the 1-vol. *Propaedia*, the 12-vol. *Micropaedia*, the 19-vol. *Macropaedia*, and a 2-vol. *Index*. The *Propaedia* is an outline of knowledge and a guide to the set; the *Micropaedia* has 60,000 articles ranging in length from 300 words to 3000 words. The *Macropaedia* contains 641 essay articles averaging over 30,000 words each. The *Index* gives access to the *Propaedia*, the *Micropaedia*, and the *Macropaedia*. There are many illustrations (many in color) and maps.

The Encyclopedia Americana. Danbury, Conn.: Grolier Educational Corporation, 1988. 30 vols. A scholarly work which includes short articles on small subjects, as well as long articles; comprehensive in scope and depth of material; provides extensive coverage of science and technology; offers new articles in the field of medicine and health, politics, environment, population origins; includes new biographies; has many illustrations and maps; bibliographies follow articles.

The New Columbia Encyclopedia. Edited by William H. Harris and Judith S. Levey. New York: Columbia University Press, 1975. (Distributed by J. B. Lippincott Company.) The 4th ed. of the *Columbia Encyclopedia*; has about 7000 short, concise articles covering recent events, persons, problems, and scientific and technological advances; is universal in coverage; includes numerous American writers; gives pronunciation; is a ready-reference source.

The Random House Encyclopedia. New rev. ed. New York: Random House, Inc., 1983. 2 vols. Divided into two parts: the *Colorpedia* and the *Alphapedia.* The *Colorpedia* presents human knowledge in text and illustrations; 876 full-color spreads, each beginning with a lengthy essay which is keyed to the illustrations, transmits information by words and pictures as a unit. The *Alphapedia* is a traditional ready-reference volume with entries ranging in length from one sentence to one column. Cross references are made to the *Colorpedia*. Other kinds of information include a bibliography, illustrations of national flags, and an 80-page atlas by Rand McNally.

The World Book Encyclopedia. Chicago: World Book Inc., 1988. 22 vols. Provides up-to-date and easy-to-read information in all areas of knowledge; vocabulary used in a given article is geared to the grade level of the article; many long articles begin with simple concepts and reading level and build to more advanced concepts and reading levels; illustrations— more than half in color—are combined with text; new areas of interest are covered (energy, the economy, computers, music, sports, minority groups, new nations); features reading lists, reading and study guides, and guidance in conducting research; provides maps. *World Book Year Book* and the 2-vol. *World Book Dictionary* add to the usefulness of the *World Book Encyclopedia.*

FOREIGN ENCYCLOPEDIAS

Bol'shaia Sovetskaia Entsiklopediia. 3d ed. Moscow: Sovetskaia Entsiklopediia, 1970–1978. 30 vols. and index. Sponsored by the Soviet government; international in scope; English translation in progress. (See *Great Soviet Encyclopedia.*)

Brockhaus Enzyklopädie in zwanzig Bänden. 17. Vols. 1–22. Völlig Neubearb.

Aufl. des Grossen Brockhaus. Wiesbaden: Brockhaus, 1966–1975. New edition of a standard work; has many new entries; provides long articles on countries and continents.

Brockhaus' Konversations-Lexikon. Der Grosse Brockhaus. Wiesbaden: F. A. Brockhaus, 1977. 14 vols. and index. A model for encyclopedias in other languages; has frequent revisions.

Enciclopedia Italiana di Scienze, Lettere ed Arti. Rome: Instituto della Enciclopedia Italiana, 1929–1937. 35 vols. Provides long articles, many bibliographies, illustrations of all kinds, and biographies; illustrations for travel and art subjects are most notable. Vol. 36: *Indici.* 1939. Appendixes I–III cover 1938–1960. 10-year supplements.

Enciclopedia Universal Ilustrada Europeo-Americana. Barcelona: Epasa, 1905–1933. 70 vols., with a 10-vol. supplement and a 1-vol. appendix. *Suplemento Anual.* 1934– . Comprehensive in coverage; gives Spanish and Spanish-American biography and geographical names.

Encyclopaedia Universalis. Paris: Encyclopaedia Universalis, Editeur, 1968–1974. 20 vols. Divided into three parts—the encyclopedia proper (Vols. 1–16), a 1-vol. summary of human knowledge with long and short articles (Vol. 17), and a thesaurus or analytical index to the encyclopedia (Vols. 18–20)—the *Encyclopaedia* gives long, comprehensive articles with bibliographies and references to related articles, biographical sketches of important figures, and many illustrations, maps, and charts. Annual *Supplement.* 1974–

Grand Larousse Encyclopédique. Paris: Librairie Larousse, 1960–1964. 10 vols. *Supplement I,* 1960–1968. 1969; *Supplement II,* 1968–1975. 1976. A dictionary as well as an encyclopedia; covers contemporary subjects; vocabulary from contemporary and classical authors; bibliography in each volume.

La Grande Encyclopédie. Paris: Librairie Larousse, 1971–1976. 20 vols. and index volume. Emphasizes twentieth century with special attention given to recent developments in the sciences; offers both long and short articles.

Great Soviet Encyclopedia: A Translation of the Third Edition. New York: Macmillan, Inc., 1974–1982. 31 vols. and index. A volume-by-volume translation of the 3d ed. of *Bol'shaia Sovetskaia Entsiklopediia;* general in scope but concentrates on the Soviet Union; more than 100,000 articles give comprehensive treatment of Soviet life, including history, peoples, science, technology, economic life, military affairs, institutions, culture, and philosophy—past to present; includes current and past biography; a cumulative index is published after every five volumes. *Index,* 1983.

Summary

The encyclopedia gives an overview of a subject. Bibliographies which follow each article are sources for further study. The person who writes an encyclopedia article (and signs it) may have written more extensively on this subject—a book or a series of articles—and is therefore a source to consult. Signed articles are an important criterion in judging the quality of an encyclopedia.

The detailed index of the encyclopedia enables the researcher to locate all material on or related to a subject. Indexes are useful also for showing subdivisions of a topic, and they aid the researcher in limiting a topic for a research paper or they suggest headings under which to look for material in the library catalog, periodical indexes, and other sources.[4]

Encyclopedias are written for different levels of readers and in some ways supplement each other.

The authoritativeness of an encyclopedia is of the greatest importance. Librarians base their choice of encyclopedias on reputable review sources[5] as well as on their own experience in using them.

Each encyclopedia is listed in the library catalog under title and editor or compiler. Examples of general subject headings under which encyclopedias can be located if the title is not known are:

Encyclopedias and dictionaries
Encyclopedias, French
Music, Encyclopedias and Dictionaries

Review Questions

CHAPTER 8. ENCYCLOPEDIAS

1. Discuss the difference between a dictionary and an encyclopedia.
2. Name and discuss some important criteria in evaluating an encyclopedia.
3. Which encyclopedias can be used for ready reference? For in-depth research? Which encyclopedias have a yearbook? An index?
4. How are encyclopedias kept up to date? Explain.
5. Compare two encyclopedias on the basis of the points given on pp. 104–105.
6. How does an encyclopedia index subdivide the subjects in Question 4, Chapter 4?

[4] See p. 309.
[5] See pp. ix, x.

CHAPTER

9

Indexes

The word "index" comes from the Latin *indicare*, "to point out." Thus an index does not provide the information which is sought; it *indicates* where it can be found.

The index of a book points out the page or pages on which certain information can be found. The library catalog is an index to the materials in a library. Each catalog card indicates, by means of a call number, the location of a book or other kind of material. The catalog card may give the pages on which certain material can be found in a given book; for example, the card may have the notation, Bibliography: pp. 210–212.

In addition to library catalogs and the indexes of books, three other kinds of indexes[1] are needed by the student who seeks material on a particular subject: (1) indexes to literature appearing in periodicals, (2) indexes to materials appearing in newspapers, and (3) indexes to literature appearing in collections or anthologies.

Periodicals

Periodicals appeared in the sixteenth century soon after the invention of printing. They began as pamphlets, grew into a series of related pamphlets, and by the seventeenth century had taken on the characteristics of our modern periodicals. Throughout the eighteenth century, the word "periodical" was used chiefly as an adjective, e.g., "periodical literature," "peri-

---

[1] Some libraries compile indexes to special collections or special types of materials to supplement the published indexes, e.g., archival materials, pamphlets, and some nonbook materials. Libraries also have thesauri to be used with certain abstract journals and to gain access to a data base.

odical publication." By the end of that century the term was applied to all regularly issued publications except newspapers.

The word "journal" originally meant a daily newspaper or publication; it has since come to mean any publication which contains news or material of current interest in a particular field.

The historical meaning of the word "magazine," deriving from the Arabic *makhāzin*, was "storehouse." The first publication in English with the word "magazine" in the title was the *Gentlemen's Magazine*, founded in London in 1731 and planned as a kind of repository for news, essays, and other outstanding and interesting pieces of literature. The word "magazine" referred at first to content only; it now includes form also, and means a collection of miscellaneous stories, articles, essays, poems, and other material, including illustrations, appearing at regular intervals. Since magazines appear periodically—weekly, monthly, bimonthly, or quarterly—they are often referred to as periodicals.

The first magazine in America was published on February 13, 1741, when Andrew Bradford issued his *American Magazine, or a Monthly View of the Political State of the British Colonies*. Three days later, Benjamin Franklin published his *General Magazine, and Historical Chronicle, for All the British Plantations in America*. Both periodicals carried the publication date January 1741. Bradford's magazine lasted three months; Franklin's, six months. Several other magazines were published before 1775, but none survived the American Revolution. Magazine publishing began again in 1779.[2]

From these meager beginnings, magazine publishing has grown until now more than 70,000 magazines, including general-interest magazines, trade journals, vocational and recreational periodicals, and professional journals, are published in the United States and Canada.[3] A certain number of issues, usually covering six months or a year, constitute a volume. Some magazines publish an index for each volume, but many others do not provide an index of any kind.

The search for information on any subject must include the examination of material which appears in periodical publications. The importance of this material cannot be overemphasized.

1. The most recent material on a subject, especially in the fields of science, technology, statistics, politics, and economics, will be found in periodicals.

[2] Frank Luther Mott, *A History of American Magazines, 1741–1850* (Cambridge, Mass.: Harvard University Press, 1938), I, 2–8, 24.

[3] *The Standard Periodical Directory*, 1987 (New York: Oxbridge Publishing Company, 1987). See also *Ulrich's International Periodicals Directory*, 27th ed., 1988.

2. Subjects too new, or even too obscure or too temporary, to be covered by books are treated in periodicals.
3. The trend of interest or opinion at any given period is traced easily in periodical literature, the current issues giving contemporary information and the old issues giving a record of past ideas, problems, and accomplishments.
4. Books, or parts of books, often appear first in periodicals, before they are published as separate volumes.
5. Professional literature is supplemented by periodicals which keep teachers, scientists, physicians, economists, lawyers, and members of other professions up to date.

Periodical literature can be divided into two classes, general and professional. A general periodical is not limited to one area of interest but touches many interest areas. Examples are *Harper's Magazine, Reader's Digest*, and *The New Yorker*. A professional periodical—usually called a "professional journal"—consists of articles on subjects of concern to a particular branch of knowledge, which are usually written by members of the profession. Examples are *College English, Journal of Geography, American Journal of Psychology*, and *American Historical Review*.

Periodical Indexes

It would not be possible to make use of the countless pieces of information in periodicals without the aid of indexes.[4] Even the indexes to each volume, when they are provided, may not bring to light all the important topics discussed. To aid the researcher in the use of periodicals, there are indexes to periodical literature. The function of an index to periodical literature is to point out the location of the topics discussed in the periodicals covered by the index. In carrying out this function, the index lists not only the large, general subjects treated, but also the various subdivisions of each subject; it indicates where material can be found on each of the several aspects of a subject. For example, for purposes of indexing, the subject "Music" includes the following subdivisions:[5]

---

[4] Periodicals may be listed in the library catalog with a cross reference to a special file—called the serials file or the periodicals file—for complete information on the library's holdings. This file shows the volumes in the library; it is not an index to individual articles in periodicals. See Chapters 17 to 24 for indexes to periodicals in the subject fields. Not all periodicals are covered by the indexes to periodical literature.

[5] Entries from *Humanities Index*, June 1981 issue. (*Humanities Index* Copyright © 1981 by the H. W. Wilson Company. Material reproduced by permission of the publisher.)

Music	Music, American
Music—Analysis	Music, Popular (songs, etc.)
Music—Criticism	Music and literature
Music—History and criticism	Music and science
Music—Performance	Music and society
Music—Rhythm	Music as a profession
Music—Scores	

This detailed breakdown of a subject and the innumerable cross references which are provided are valuable aids to the student who is trying to choose a subject for a research paper, or who is trying to narrow and restrict a chosen subject.

Each of the indexes to periodical literature covers a group of periodicals of a certain kind—general, scientific, educational, business, and so on. The list of periodicals covered is given in the front of each issue of the index. In general, one index does not include periodicals which have been covered by another index. Note the absence of duplication in the references given for the subject "Television broadcasting" in the excerpts from *Readers' Guide to Periodical Literature* (Figure 9.1), *Social Sciences Index* (Figure 9.2), *Humanities Index* (Figure 9.3), and *Education Index* (Figure 9.4), which cover approximately the same period of time. Note also the absence of duplication in the *see* and *see also* references.

It is necessary, therefore, to consult several indexes in order to locate the several kinds of periodicals which can be of help in answering a question or in providing material for a research paper.

The location of a periodical article is given by volume, page, and date of issue. In general, each article is listed under author and subject, with complete information under the author entry. Not all periodical indexes use both forms of listing. Some indexes include a title entry; others index by subject only.

Some indexes point out only certain kinds of articles appearing in periodicals, such as book reviews (see Figure 9.5), bibliographies, or biographies.

In using a periodical index, as in using any other reference book, it is necessary to understand the system of indexing, the kinds of articles covered, the arrangement of items, and the method of abbreviating.

DETERMINING THE USEFULNESS OF A PERIODICAL INDEX

The usefulness of a periodical index depends upon several factors:

1. Number and kinds of periodicals covered by the index
2. Inclusion of books or parts of books and other materials

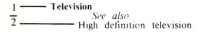

```
1 ─────── Television
            See also
2 ──────────── High definition television
```

```
          Television—See also—cont.
2 ───────        Scrambling (Television signals)
                 Video art
          Television, Cable  See  Cable television
          Television actors and actresses  See  Television performers
          Television and literature
                 See also
                 Television and reading
          Television and politics
                 See also
                 Presidential debates
                 Television broadcasting—Government use
          Television broadcasting
                 See also
                 American Broadcasting Companies, Inc.
                 CBS Inc.
                 Fox Broadcasting Company
                 Television program reviews
                 Television stations
3 ─────────────────── Arts programs ───────────── 5
4 ───────  The arts. Sunday morning, and Charles Kuralt. M.
           Rhodes. il por  Horizon  30:6 Je '87
6 ─────────────────────────────────────────────── 8
7 ──────────
```

FIGURE 9.1

Excerpt from Readers' Guide to Periodical Literature: *(1) Subject. (2) See also references from the subject "Television"—topics under which to look for additional material on the subject. (3) Subdivision of the subject "Television," that is, "Television—Arts programs." (4) Title of the article on the subject "Television—Arts programs." (5) Author of the article. (6) The article is illustrated. (7) The article has a portrait. (8) Title of the magazine in which the article is located,* Horizon: *volume 30, page 6, June 1987. (*Readers' Guide to Periodical Literature, *September 10, 1987, issue, Copyright © 1987 by The H. W. Wilson Company. Material reproduced by permission of the publisher.)*

3. Period of time covered in the index—when it began and whether or not it is still being issued

4. Completeness of the indexing of any periodical—all articles or only certain types of articles

5. Fullness of the information given—author, title, volume, page, date—as well as information about bibliographies and illustrations

6. Method of indexing—by subject as well as by author and title

7. Frequency of issue—bimonthly, monthly, quarterly, less often

8. Ease of use

Television
> *See also*
> Video recordings
> > **Apparatus and supplies**
> > *See also*
> > Videotape recorders and recording
> > > **Receivers and reception**
> > > *See also*
> > > Video games

Television advertising
All by numbers. A. Gottlieb. *Economist* 301:survey 9-10 D 20 '86
Forgettable commercials. J. C. Horn. *Psychol Today* 20:16 D '86

> **Laws and legislation**
> The fight for freedom in broadcasting. S. Brittan. *Polit Q* 58:3-23 Ja/Mr '87

> **Public opinion**
> 'Ask a silly question . . .': public attitudes to commercials on the BBC. S. Barnett. *Media Cult Soc* 9:97-109 Ja '87

Television and children
> *See also*
> Television and youth

Television broadcastng
> *See also*
> Cable television
> Television programs

> **Economic aspects**
> The failure of cultural programming on cable TV: an economic interpretation. D. Waterman. bibl *J Commun* 36:92-107 Summ '86

Television programs
The failure of cultural programming on cable TV: an economic interpretation. D. Waterman. bibl *J Commun* 36:92-107 Summ '86
The "lead-in" strategy for prime-time TV: does it increase the audience? J. T. Tiedge and K. J. Ksobiech. bibl *J Commun* 36:51-63 Summ '86
Selective television viewing: a limited possibility. N. Signorielli. bibl *J Commun* 36:64-76 Summ '86

> **Documentary programs**
> "Assignment Africa". M. Maren. *Afr Rep* 32:68-9 Mr/Ap '87

> **News programs**
> *Objectivity*

FIGURE 9.2

Excerpt from Social Sciences Index. *(Social Sciences Index, June 1987 issue, Copyright © 1987 by The H. W. Wilson Company. Material reproduced by permission of the publisher.)*

Television
> *See also*
Africa in television
Dancing and television
Television broadcasting
Theater and television
Video art
>> **Apparatus and supplies**
> *See also*
Video recorders and recording
>> **Data transmission systems**
Teletext viewing habits and preferences. L. L. Henke and T. R. Donohue. *Journal Q* 63:542-5+ Aut '86
Videotex news: a content analysis of three videotex services and their companion newspapers. N. A. Brown and T. Atwater. *Journal Q* 63:554-61 Aut '86
>> **History**
The golden age. I. Johns. *Plays Players* no401:36-7 F '87
>> **Playwriting**
> *See* Television authorship

Television broadcasting
> *See also*
Broadcasting
Cable television
Fox Broadcasting Company
Television programs
Video recorders and recording
>> **Audiences**
> *See* Television audiences
>> **Censorship**
> *See* Broadcasting censorship
>> **History**
> *See* Television—History
>> **Law**
> *See* Broadcasting laws and regulations
>> **Moral and religious aspects**
> *See also*
Broadcasting censorship
>> **Music**
> *See also*
Television broadcasting—Opera
Television program rating *See* Television programs—Rating
Television program reviews
>> **Single works**
Antony Tudor
> *Dance Mag* 61:106 Mr '87. J. Gruen
Die Fledermaus
> *Dance Mag* 61:84 Ap '87. J. Gruen
> *Opera* 38:343-4 Mr '87. A. Blyth
L'heure espagnole
> *Opera* 38:343 Mr '87. A. Blyth
Oberon
> *Opera* 38:217-18 F '87. N. Goodwin
Television programming *See* Television broadcasting—

FIGURE 9.3

Excerpt from Humanities Index. *(*Humanities Index, *June 1987 issue, Copyright © 1987 by The H. W. Wilson Company. Material reproduced by permission of the publisher.)*

Television
Data transmission systems
Media frames, media characteristics, and knowledge struc-
tures: a theoretical exploration of young adolescents'
use of a videotex encyclopedia: theoretical outline.
E. S. Fredin and K. A. Krendl. bibl *Int J Instr Media*
13 no4:273-80 '86
Industrial applications
See Television in business and industry
Transmitters and transmission
Data distribution network uses VBI or SAP [central
education network] *EITV* 18:24 D '86
Interactive television. M. Bisesi and B. D. Felder. bibl
New Dir Higher Educ no56:37-45 '86
Television, Closed circuit
See also
Teleconferencing

Television and reading
TV viewing habits, family rules, reading grades, heroes
and heroines of gifted and nongifted middle school
students. J. A. Roderick and P. Jackson. bibl il *Roeper
Rev* 9:114-19 N '86
Television audiences
Education of television audiences: nature and objectives.
M. R. Torres. bibl *Prospects* 16 no3:391-6 '86
Television broadcasting
See also
Characters in television
Television—Transmitters and transmission
Elton Rule—associate degree preferred [interview] C. C.
Andersen. pors *Community Tech Jr Coll J* 57:16-17
O/N '86
Appreciation
Television as a language art, seriously [watching Amos]
D. A. England. *Teach Engl Two-Year Coll* 13:298-303
D '86
Art programs
See also
Television in art education
Audiences
See Television audiences
Children, Effect on
See Television broadcasting and children

FIGURE 9.4
Excerpt from Education Index. *(Education Index, March 1987 issue, Copyright © 1987 by
The H. W. Wilson Company. Material reproduced by permission of the publisher.)*

CHOOSING AND USING A PERIODICAL INDEX[6]

In order to choose the right index in a search for material on a particular
subject, the researcher should try to answer the following questions:

1. What is the nature of the subject?
   a Does it concern a topic or a person too new to be discussed in books?
   b Is it a subject so limited in appeal that it does not receive treatment in
   a book?

---

[6] See Chapters 17 to 24 for examples of indexes in the subject fields.

    c Is it a subject which is treated in a book but about which more recent information is needed?

    d Is it a topic which would be clarified by the discussions in one or more periodicals?

2. In what area does the subject belong?

    a Science

    b History

    c Literature

    d Education

    e General

3. Which of the periodical indexes covers the literature of the area in question?

4. What years are involved, and which indexes cover those years?

5. Is an article from a general periodical, an article from a professional journal, or an article from each kind required?

Some useful indexes to periodical literature are listed below. The outstanding features of each index are given with the bibliographical entry.

Abridged Readers' Guide to Periodical Literature. New York: The H. W. Wilson Company, 1935– . (Monthly except June to August.) For schools and small public libraries; indexes by author and subject on sixty-three periodicals of general interest; includes book reviews in a separate section.

✓ *Biography Index.* New York: The H. W. Wilson Company, 1946– . (Quarterly; annual permanent volumes.) Gives birth and death dates and occupation or profession of each person listed; includes an index by profession; indexes biographical material in periodicals covered by The H. W. Wilson Company indexes and in current books of individual biography; international in coverage; indicates nationality of persons who are not American.

✓ *Book Review Digest.* New York: The H. W. Wilson Company, 1905– . (Monthly, except February and July; annual cumulations.) Indexes reviews of current books appearing in eighty-three selected American, British, and Canadian periodicals; books are entered by author; information includes title, publisher, date of publication, and price of the book, citations to all reviews, and excerpts from some reviews; has a subject and title index. (See Figure 9.5.)

Book Review Index. Detroit: Gale Research Company, 1965– . (Bimonthly.) Indexes reviews appearing in more than 450 periodicals in several disciplines; excerpts are not given, only the source of the review. Title index in each issue.

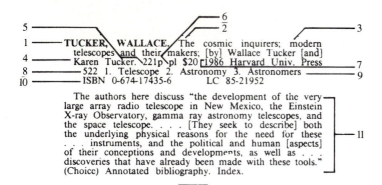

5 ──────
1 ────── **TUCKER, WALLACE.** The cosmic inquirers; modern
telescopes and their makers; [by] Wallace Tucker [and]
4 ────── Karen Tucker. 221p pl $20 1986 Harvard Univ. Press ── 7
8 ────── 522 1. Telescope 2. Astronomy 3. Astronomers ── 9
10 ────── ISBN 0-674-17435-6   LC 85-21952

The authors here discuss "the development of the very
large array radio telescope in New Mexico, the Einstein
X-ray Observatory, gamma ray astronomy telescopes, and
the space telescope. . . . [They seek to describe] both
the underlying physical reasons for the need for these
. . . instruments, and the political and human [aspects]   ── 11
of their conceptions and developments, as well as . . .
discoveries that have already been made with these tools."
(Choice) Annotated bibliography. Index.

───

"[A] splendid book. . . . The 'cosmic inquirers' are
an interesting and brilliant set of human beings. most
of them admirable. Intelligent general readers as well as
astronomy majors will find this book to be both instructive
and enjoyable."
Choice 24:156 S '86. D.L. Anderson (160w)

"[The authors] provide fascinating insight into how 'Big
Science' operates. The scientific rationale for each project
is clearly explained, and the 'people' stories give added
appeal."
Libr J 111:156 Ap 1 '86. Thomas E. Margrave (130w)

"[A] brief and readable narrative by engaged professionals
that gives the reader access to all the facets of the
astronomical enterprise today, social, personal, intellectual
and competitive. . . . [The book presents] sharp case studies
drawn from life . . . not [a] comprehensive survey. .
. . It is difficult to miss the feeling that we are reading
12 ──── about victorious generals. These are men of peace, all
right, but they share the tasks of such leaders. They all
but dwell at the conference table and in the committee
room, they persuade, they dream, they decide in the face
of ignorance and risk, they devise novel tactics against
budget cutters and against refractory Nature."
Sci Am 255:38 O '86. Philip Morrison (1000w)

FIGURE 9.5

Explanation of an excerpt from Book Review Digest: *(1) Author of the book that is reviewed.
(2) Title of the book. (3) Subtitle of the book. (4) Coauthor of the book. (5) Number of pages in
the book. (6) The book has plates. (7) Date of publication and publisher. (8) Dewey Decimal class
number. (9) Subjects treated in the book. (10) The identifying number of the book—the
International Standard Book Number. (11) Excerpt from a review that appeared in the journal*
Choice. *(12) Excerpt from a review that appeared in* Scientific American, *volume 255, page
38, October 1986, written by Philip Morrison. This review has 1000 words. (*Book Review
Digest, *June 1987 issue, Copyright © by The H. W. Wilson Company. Material reproduced
by permission of the publisher.)*

√ *Catholic Periodical and Literature Index.* New York: Catholic Library Association, 1930– . (Bimonthly.) An author, title, and subject index to a selected list of Catholic periodicals published mainly in the United States, Canada, England, and Ireland; notes articles written from the Catholic point of view elsewhere. In July 1968, incorporated the *Guide to Catholic Literature*; includes an author-title-subject bibliography of books by Catholics or of interest to Catholics; formerly the *Catholic Periodical Index.* Indexes book, theater, and film reviews.

INFOTRAC Data Base (12-inch Videodisc) Belmont, Calif.: Information Access Company, 1985– . Provides indexing by subject to articles in more than 900 business, technological, and general-interest magazines and journals for the current year; includes sixty days of *New York Times* and twelve months of *Wall Street Journal.*

The Magazine Index. Belmont, Calif.: Information Access Corporation, 1977– . (Monthly.) Indexes more than 400 popular magazines and professional journals. Each issue is on one reel of 16-mm Computer Output Microfilm; must be read with a COM reader;[7] also available on-line through the DIALOG System.

Nineteenth Century Readers' Guide to Periodical Literature, 1890–1899. New York: The H. W. Wilson Company, 1944. 2 vols. Author, subject, and illustrator index to fifty-one leading periodicals published in the 1890s; records authorship of many articles which were originally published anonymously.

Poole's Index to Periodical Literature, 1802–1907. Boston: Houghton Mifflin Company, 1891. (Reprinted in 1938 by Peter Smith, New York.) Indexes by subject only about 470 English and American periodicals chiefly of a general nature; fiction, poems, and plays are indexed by first important word of title; includes book reviews; was the first of the periodical indexes.

√ *Readers' Guide to Periodical Literature.* New York: The H. W. Wilson Company, 1900– . (18 issues per year.) Indexes more than 180 periodicals of a general nature representing all important areas of contemporary interest; follows closely the publication date of the periodicals indexed; gives author and title of article, name, volume, date of periodical, and number of pages; indicates whether illustrations, bibliography, and maps are included in the article; book reviews appearing in the magazines indexed are listed in a separate section of the index.

---

[7] See p. 64.

Newspapers

Newspapers developed from the seventeenth-century broadside, which was a single large page printed on one side only. These early newspapers were issued weekly or biweekly and were sometimes called "news-pamphlets" or "news-books."

"Corantos" was the name given to the periodical news-pamphlets issued between 1621 and 1641 to provide news of foreign countries. The "diurnalls," or news-books, gave the domestic news during the years from 1641 to 1645.

The biweekly *Oxford Gazette* was the first newspaper in the modern sense to be published in England. It appeared in November 1665. A year later it was renamed the *London Gazette*,[8] it is still issued—not as a newspaper, however, but as a record of official matters.

The first newspaper published in America appeared in Boston in 1690 and was called *Publick Occurrences, Both Foreign and Domestick*; there was only one issue. The first newspaper to be published for a continuous period was the *Boston News-Letter*, which appeared in April 1704. The first daily newspaper in America was the *Pennsylvania Packet and General Advertiser*, established in Philadelphia in 1784. *The New York Times*, founded in 1851, was, from the very beginning, one of the world's outstanding newspapers. In the twentieth century there have been such developments as chains of newspapers, tabloids, and syndicated news services.

In addition to news events, the modern newspaper provides other features, such as illustrations; book reviews; articles on education, art, music, drama, and recreation; literary contributions; and biographical features.

The function of newspapers now, as in the past, is to keep the reader up to date on events. They are valuable sources of information on questions of the day and on trends of opinion in the past. They provide a contemporary history of any given modern period.

Newspaper Indexes

There is no general index to newspapers comparable to the periodical indexes, but since all newspapers publish news items at about the same time, the date of the event will serve as the needed clue. A chronology, like that in the *Americana Annual*, or an index to one newspaper, such as *The New York*

---

[8] The word "gazette" probably came from *gazzetta*, the Italian name for a small Venetian coin which was the price charged (in the sixteenth century) for a copy of a newssheet or for permission to read it [*The Oxford English Dictionary*. IV (1933), 88–89].

Times Index, will serve as an index to all newspaper items of general interest, wherever published. This is not true, of course, in the case of strictly local-interest items.[9]

Facts on File: World News Digest with Index. New York: Facts on File, October 1940– . (Weekly; annual bound volumes.) Digests the important news of the day from the major metropolitan newspapers in the United States and the other countries of the world. Covers all subject areas.

The National Newspaper Index. Menlo Park, Calif.: Information Access Company, January 1979– . (Monthly.) Indexes completely the *Christian Science Monitor*, *The New York Times*, and *The Wall Street Journal*; one roll of 16-mm Computer Output Microfilm contains each issue; must be read with COM reader; gives date, section, page, and column for each entry. Also available on-line through Lockheed's DIALOG System.

New York Times Index. New York: New York Times, 1913– . (Semi-monthly; annual cumulation.) Gives exact reference to date, page, and column; summaries of articles may answer question without reference to the paper itself. Indexes book reviews. Available on-line from the *New York Times Information Bank*, which also offers brief abstracts from 80 other newspapers and magazines.

Newsbank. New Canaan, Conn.: Newsbank, Inc., 1970– . (Monthly; cumulated quarterly.) A reference service providing access to full-text articles from over 450 United States newspapers; microfiched articles, printed index produced monthly. Covers all subject areas. CD-ROM available for articles since 1982.

The Newspaper Index. Wooster, Ohio: Bell & Howell, 1972– . (8 monthly, 4 quarterly issues.) Indexes subjects and names in *The Chicago Tribune*, *The Los Angeles Times*, *The New Orleans Times-Picayune*, *The Denver Post*, *The Detroit News*, *The Houston Post*, and *The San Francisco Chronicle*; covers national, regional, state, and local news; separate index available for each newspaper; also available on-line. Comprehensive indexing of the significant articles with brief abstracts.

The Times Index. Reading, England: Research Publications, Ltd., 1906– . (Bimonthly.) Compiled from the final editions of *The Times*, *The Sunday Times*, *The Times Literary Supplement*, *The Times Educational Supplement—Scotland*, and *The Times Higher Education Supplement*. Gives day of month, page, and column. Includes book reviews; gives brief abstracts.

---

[9] A library may have an index to the local newspaper.

Literature in Collections

The practice of gathering extracts from the works of several writers into a collection is not a recent one. The name usually given to such a collection is "anthology," a word of Greek derivation which means "flower-gathering" and indicates that only the best pieces of literature are included.

The *Greek Anthology*, a collection of about 4500 poems, inscriptions, and other kinds of writings by more than 300 writers, dates from about 60 B.C. The earliest English anthology dates from A.D. 975.

The original use of "anthology" to mean a volume containing only the "flower" of literature has been extended to mean any collection of extracts from the writings of various authors—often on one subject or of one kind, such as a collection of poems, short stories, essays, plays, speeches, or quotations.

Volumes of collected writings, including those called "readings," constitute an important part of any well-chosen library collection. Some of these collected works are analyzed in the library catalog. Most of them contain so many selections that it is not possible to include all of them in the library catalog.

Indexes to Literature in Collections

The student will find that it is a tedious, and perhaps impossible, task to locate a particular essay, speech, or quotation, or a selection on a particular subject, by examining the index of every anthology. The reference tool designed to facilitate this kind of search is the index to literature in collections.

Indexes to literature in collections follow the general pattern of indexes to periodicals and newspapers, but they cover books only. There are indexes to general literature in collections—that is, essays, articles, and speeches covering a variety of subjects. An example of this kind of index is the *Essay and General Literature Index* (Figure 9.6). There are indexes to collections of poetry, stories, and plays. Examples are *Granger's Index to Poetry*, the *Short Story Index*, and the *Play Index*. Indexing is by author, subject, and title, and the location reference includes the name of the compiler of the anthology, the title of the anthology, and the page or pages on which the essay, poem, story, or play can be found.

Indexes to poetry, short stories, and plays are discussed in Chapter 23, Literature. Examples of indexes to collections of literature which cover several subject areas are listed below.

1——Television broadcasting ⟋——3 ⟋————4
2———— Altman. R. Television/sound. (*In* Studies
in entertainment; ed. by T. Modleski p39-54) ——5
Mellencamp, P. Situation comedy,
feminism, and Freud: discourses of Gracie
and Lucy. (*In* Studies in entertainment; ed.
by T. Modleski p80-95)

6——Television broadcasting of news
Morse, M. The television news personality
and credibility: reflections on the news in
transition. (*In* Studies in entertainment; ed.
by T. Modleski p55-79)

Television comedy programs *See* Comedy
programs

Television journalism *See* Television broadcasting of news

Television news *See* Television broadcasting
of news ⟍————7

FIGURE 9.6
Excerpt from Essay and General Literature Index: *(1) Subject. (2) Author of the essay* ⹁
"Television/sound." (3) Title of the essay. (4) Title of the collection in which the essay
"Television/sound" is located. (5) Editor of the collection Studies in Entertainment *in which*
the essay "Television/sound" is located on pages 39–54. (6) Another subject relating to television
broadcasting. (7) A cross reference from the subject "Television news," which is not used, to
*"Television broadcasting of news," which is used. (*Essay and General Literature Index,*
June 1987 issue, Copyright © 1987 by The H. W. Wilson Company. Material reproduced by
permission of the publisher.)

Biography Index. New York: The H. W. Wilson Company, 1946–   . Indexes
current books of individual and collective biography.

✓ *Essay and General Literature Index*. New York: The H. W. Wilson Company,
1934–   . Indexes English-language collections of essays, articles, and
speeches relating to all subject fields.[10]

Review Questions

CHAPTER 9. INDEXES

1. What is the purpose of an index?
2. Name the kinds of indexes and explain the importance of each kind.
3. An index can help limit a subject. Take the subjects you used in

[10] See also p. 277.

Question 4, Chapter 4, and see how they are subdivided in a periodical index, a newspaper index, and an index to collected works.

4. Examine the excerpts from indexes on pp. 114–119, 124. Compare the coverage of these indexes on the basis of:

   a The number of articles on the subject "television"
   b The number of subdivisions of the subject
   c The total number of references in each excerpt
   d The number of articles repeated in the indexes

5. Find a review of one of your textbooks or of a favorite book. In what journal is the book review located? Who wrote the review? Do you agree with the review?

6. What is the complete reference for the entry on television from *Essay and General Literature Index*, p. 124?

7. What index will give the most recent periodical articles? The most recent newspaper articles?

8. If your library does not have all the sources listed in a given index, how can the librarian help you get the article you want?

9. Which review of the book shown in the excerpt from *Book Review Digest*, p. 119, would be most helpful in deciding whether to read the book? Who wrote it? In what journal is it located?

CHAPTER

10

Biographical Dictionaries

The word "biography," from the Greek *bios*, "life," and *graphein*, "to write," is that form of history which is applied to individuals rather than to nations or civilizations. It is the purpose of biography[1] to tell accurately the history of a person from birth to death in a manner that will reveal various aspects of character, personality, and philosophy.

Since ancient times, people have been interested in the lives of others, either from a desire to eulogize them, to learn from them, or to imitate them, or just from simple curiosity.

Toward the end of the first century after Christ, Plutarch wrote his *Parallel Lives*, the life histories of forty-six Greeks and Romans. The word "biography," however, did not appear in the English language until 1683, when John Dryden described this work of Plutarch's as the "history of particular men's lives." This meaning of "biography"— the history of the life of a person—has become established as a literary form.

Other literary forms contribute to biography but must be distinguished from it. They are:

1. Autobiography, the narration of a person's life by himself or herself
2. Memoirs, the history of a person's times as seen by the individual who writes them
3. Diary, a day-by-day account of the happenings and events in a person's life, recorded by that person

---

[1] Biography is a subject area; biographical dictionaries, which cover persons in many fields and are general in that sense, are included in general reference materials.

4. Letters, written communications of a personal nature (as distinguished from belles lettres, meaning literature), which may be intimate narratives, records of events, or expressions of the writer's thoughts and philosophy

Biography may draw from these and other sources to present all the significant characteristics of the subject.

The outstanding example of individual biography in English—or in any language—is James Boswell's *Life of Samuel Johnson*, written in the eighteenth century. Since that time biography has become an increasingly important form of literature and occupies a prominent place in all library collections. The student who seeks material on a country, a civilization, or a period of history will do well to investigate the lives of outstanding persons who were a part of that country, civilization, or period of history.

Biography as a literary form differs in purpose, style, and content from simple biographical information about a person.

In the nineteenth century, there appeared in most European countries publications called "dictionaries of national biography," presenting biographical information about all important national figures. These collections of biographical articles were the forerunners of the modern biographical dictionary, a work which combines biography (factual information about the life of an individual) and dictionary (alphabetical arrangement).

The biographical dictionary, with biographical sketches arranged alphabetically by surname, does not qualify as true biography, since it does not present all aspects of an individual's life. However, the *Dictionary of National Biography* and the *Dictionary of American Biography* are outstanding for their scholarly and objective treatment of the persons included.

Biographical dictionaries are among the most frequently used books in the academic library (or in any library). Questions about notable people and about people in the news—their lives, interests, education, background, affiliations, position, and even addresses—come from faculty and students alike.

There are numerous sources of biographical information concerning individuals; these include encyclopedias, encyclopedia annuals, dictionaries, newspapers, and magazines. However, the reference sources which were written for the specific purpose of providing the kinds of biographical information mentioned above or indicating where it can be found are:

1. Biographical indexes, which point out books, periodicals, and other sources in which the information can be found
2. Biographical dictionaries, which contain the information sought

Kinds of Biographical Dictionaries²

Biographical dictionaries can be divided into three classes according to the nationality, the profession, and the dates of the persons included:

1. Universal—not limited to any state, country, or profession
    a Persons not living
    b Living persons and persons not living
    c Living persons
2. National or regional—limited in coverage to particular countries or regions but including persons from all the professions and occupations
    a Persons not living
    b Living persons and persons not living
    c Living persons
3. Professional or occupational—limited to persons in a specific profession or occupation
    a Universal
        (1) Persons not living
        (2) Living persons and persons not living
        (3) Living persons
    b National or regional
        (1) Persons not living
        (2) Living persons and persons not living
        (3) Living persons

Choosing a Biographical Dictionary

To determine which biographical dictionary will provide information on a particular person, it is helpful to know the scope and purpose of each biographical dictionary and to establish, if possible, the following facts about the person before beginning the search for information:

1. Dates of birth and (if not living) death
2. Nationality
3. Profession or occupation

² Some biographical dictionaries are called "directories," e.g., *Directory of American Scholars* (see p. 193). They provide biographical sketches of the persons included.

Sources which will aid in establishing these facts are:

1. Library catalog. If the individual has written a book, and if this book is listed in the catalog, dates of birth and death may be given following the person's name on the catalog card. The subject matter of the book or books by and about this person may indicate field or work, and the place of publication may provide a clue to nationality.
2. *Cumulative Book Index.* If the library catalog does not include any books by or about the person in question, the *Cumulative Book Index*, which is a world list of books in the English language, will list the books he or she has written in English.
3. *Biography Index.* This index to biographical articles appearing in books and magazines (excluding biographical dictionaries) gives the dates and the profession of all persons included. If the individual is not an American, nationality is given also.
4. Periodical indexes. Any periodical articles by or about the person on whom the student seeks information should be listed in one of the indexes to periodical literature. The periodicals in which the articles appear often include a brief statement about the author. The dates of publication of these articles may provide a clue to the time when the individual might have been included in a biographical dictionary or was in the current news. The subject matter of the articles will indicate field of interest, and the place of publication may suggest nationality. Indexes to periodical literature also list obituaries, which often provide full biographical information.
5. A book by the person in question. The title page may list the author's position, such as Professor of History, McGill University, or Professor of English, Duke University, immediately following his or her name. The location of the university may be a clue to the nationality of the person teaching there. The position held indicates profession.
6. A yearbook or a handbook may give the nationality and dates of an individual and this information will tell the researcher which biographical dictionary is likely to provide information on the person.

The advantage gained by establishing the dates, the nationality, and the profession of a person before consulting any biographical dictionary will more than make up for the time spent in locating this information. For example, if the subject is an important contemporary American politician, the following biographical dictionaries will be eliminated from consideration immediately:

Dictionary of American Biography
Dictionary of National Biography
Appleton's Cyclopaedia of American Biography

Among the biographical dictionaries which are possible sources of information about a living American politician are:

Who's Who in America
Current Biography
International Who's Who

Living American scientists are covered in *American Men and Women of Science*, but not in *Dictionary of Scientific Biography*. For other biographical sources in the subject fields, see Chapters 17–24.

It is necessary to point out that in some cases none of the sources mentioned above—library catalog, periodical indexes, *Cumulative Book Index*, *Biography Index*, books by the individual or yearbooks—will provide dates, nationality, or profession. In such cases, locating biographical material about the individual becomes a tedious process of trial and error. Even when dates, nationality, and profession have been established, it is not always possible to find the subject in the biographical dictionary or dictionaries designed to cover the person's profession, nationality, and time of prominence. Information in the several biographical dictionaries is provided, for the most part, at the request of the publisher by the individuals included. The fact that a person is not included may mean that he or she failed to furnish the biographical information requested and that the publisher was unable to secure it from other sources. In such cases, it may be necessary to identify individuals by piecing together bits of information from the jackets of their books, from a few titles of periodical articles by or about them, or from the fact that they edit, or contribute to, professional journals.

Using a Biographical Dictionary

Before using any biographical dictionary the first time, it is helpful to read the preliminary pages to determine (1) whether the alphabetical arrangement is letter by letter or word by word; (2) what special features are included; and (3) what abbreviations and symbols are used. The method of selecting names to be included should be noted, as a test of the objectivity of the work.

Summary

A biography of an individual provides information not only about the person but also about the events which occurred during the time he or she lived. Biographical dictionaries generally give only brief factual information, but some give a lengthy discussion of a person's life and contributions, e.g., *Dictionary of American Biography*, *Dictionary of National Biography*, and *Dictionary of Canadian Biography*.

Since achievement is a criterion for being included in a biographical dictionary, this kind of source will at least identify persons who are or were important at one time or another. There are biographical dictionaries which cover persons in a given region, and persons of a given race, profession, or religion as well as persons who lived during a certain period. It saves much time if you can establish the nationality, profession, and dates of the person before beginning to try to locate him or her in a biographical dictionary.

Representative Biographical Dictionaries[3]

UNIVERSAL BIOGRAPHY

Persons not living

New Century Cyclopedia of Names, New York: Appleton-Century-Crofts, Inc., 1954. 3 vols. Identifies proper names of importance today: persons, places, events, literary characters, plays, operas, and mythological and legendary names; provides a chronological table of world history.

Living persons and persons not living

Chambers Biographical Dictionary. Rev. ed. Edited by J. O. Thorne and T. C. Collocott. Edinburgh: W. & R. Chambers; New York: Cambridge University Press, 1986. Offers more than 15,000 biographies of persons who are "likely to be looked up," in all areas, living and deceased; international in coverage.

The McGraw-Hill Encyclopedia of World Biography. New York: McGraw-Hill Book Company, 1975. 12 vols. Includes persons not living and living persons; articles include basic biographical facts and commentary on the person's background and character, evaluation of his or her role in history, a portrait whenever possible; Vol. XII contains historical maps, index, and study guides.

---

[3] See Chapters 17 to 24 for biographical dictionaries in the subject fields.

Webster's New Biographical Dictionary. Springfield, Mass.: Merriam-Webster, Inc., Publishers, 1980. Lists names of 40,000 noteworthy persons with pronunciation and concise biographies; is not limited by period, race, religion, or occupation; includes table of heads of state and other high officials, historical and contemporary.

Living persons

Current Biography. New York: The H. W. Wilson Company, 1940– . (Monthly except December.) *Current Biography Yearbook,* 1946– . Aims to cover all important contemporary figures in all fields; includes pronunciation for unusual names, a photograph of the biographee, and a bibliography of the sources used. Yearbooks contain indexes by names and professions and a cumulated five-year index.

Dictionary of International Biography. 14th ed. Cambridge: International Biographical Centre, 1978. 2 vols. First published in 1963; aims to be a record of contemporary achievement; reports personal information, professional positions, publications, honors; covers many countries and many walks of life.

International Who's Who. London: Europa Publications, Ltd., 1935– . (Annual.) Includes sketches of important people in the world today.

The New York Times Biographical Service: A Compilation of Current Biographical Information of General Interest. New York: New York Times, 1970– . (Monthly.) Gives profiles of people in the news; contains from twenty to fifty articles each week reprinted from the *Times;* represents all sections of the country; some articles are obituaries; some are news items; others are interviews. Loose-leaf format.

NATIONAL OR REGIONAL BIOGRAPHY

Persons not living

Appleton's Cyclopaedia of American Biography. Rev. ed. New York: D. Appleton and Company, Inc., 1887–1900. 6 vols. Includes all important persons identified with American history from its earliest beginnings; has lengthy articles and many portraits.

Concise Dictionary of American Biography. 3d ed. Edited by Joseph G. E. Hopkins. New York: Charles Scribner's Sons, 1980. Provides the essential facts for each biographee in the larger work and in the supplements to January 1960; useful for quick reference.

Concise Dictionary of National Biography. Oxford: Oxford University Press, 1952, 1961. 2 vols. Pt. I: to 1900; Pt. II: 1900–1981. Provides abstracts of the articles in the original set.

Dictionary of American Biography. Published under the auspices of the American Council of Learned Societies. New York: Charles Scribner's Sons, 1927–1981. 21 vols. Provides scholarly, signed articles on persons who influenced their time; gives bibliographic references for further information on the person; covers only persons not living. Volume 21 is the first supplement; Supplements 2 to 7 bring the work to 1965. Now available in ten base volumes (A–Z) and Supplements 1 to 7. *Complete Index Guide*, 1981, indexes the entire work. *Concise Dictionary of American Biography*, 1981.

Dictionary of Canadian Biography/Dictionnaire Biographique du Canada. Toronto: University of Toronto Press, 1966–   . (In progress.) Vol. I: 1000–1700; Vol. II: 1701–1740; Vol. III: 1741–1770; Vol. IV: 1771–1800; Vol. VI: 1821–1835; Vol. IX: 1861–1870; Vol. X: 1871–1880; Vol. XI: 1881–1890. Follows the scholarly tradition of the *Dictionary of National Biography*; arranged by period, each volume covering a given range of years; includes persons born and residing in Canada and persons from other countries who have made contributions to Canadian life. Is expected to have some 20 vols.

Dictionary of National Biography. Edited by Leslie Stephen and Sidney Lee. London: Oxford University Press, 1922. 22 vols. *Supplements*, 1901–1911, 1912–1921, 1922–1930, 1931–1940, 1941–1950, 1951–1960, 1961–1970. Provides full, accurate biographies of all notable inhabitants of Great Britain and the colonies (exclusive of living persons) from the earliest historical period to the present time; includes bibliographical references.

James, Edward T. (ed.). *Notable American Women 1607–1950. A Biographical Dictionary*. Cambridge, Mass.: Belknap Press of Harvard University Press, 1971. 3 vols. Sponsored by Radcliffe College; covers 300 years of women's history in America; modeled after *Dictionary of American Biography*; includes women who have achieved distinction in their own right; includes bibliographies; articles are written by a person with "special knowledge of the subject or her field" (Preface). *Notable American Women, the Modern Period: A Biographical Dictionary*, edited by Barbara Sicherman and others (Cambridge, Mass.: The Belknap Press of Harvard University Press, 1980), supplements *Notable American Women 1607–1950* and brings it to December 31, 1975.

Who Was Who. London: A. & C. Black, Ltd., 1929–1981. 7 vols. Companion volume to *Who's Who*; contains biographies of persons in *Who's Who* who have died, with the date of the death added. These volumes cover the period 1897–1980. *Index*, 1981.

Who Was Who in America. Chicago: Marquis—Who's Who, Inc., 1942–1985.

8 vols. Gives biographies of persons in *Who's Who in America* who have died, with date of death added. *Index*, 1985.

Who Was Who in America: Historical Volume 1607–1896. Chicago: Marquis— Who's Who, Inc., 1963. Supplements *Who Was Who in America.* Treats Americans and other outstanding figures in the early development of America.

Living persons and persons not living

Clark, Judith Freeman. *Almanac of American Women in the 20th Century.* Englewood Cliffs, N.J.: Prentice-Hall Press, 1987. Covers significant issues and events marking women's achievements in recent United States history; has a chronology of events to 1987.

Encyclopedia of American Biography. Edited by John A. Garraty. New York: Harper & Row, Publishers, Incorporated, 1974. Presents about 1000 biographical accounts of persons living and not living; selection is based on their significance, achievement, and fame. Each sketch consists of a summary of the essential biographical data, followed by an interpretative essay evaluating the person's career; includes minorities and women who may have been omitted from other sources.

The National Cyclopedia of American Biography. Clifton, N.J.: James T. White & Company Publishers, 1881–1984. 63 vols. Based on original materials; provides detailed biographical articles about noteworthy Americans from the beginning of this nation to the present; includes every field of activity and every period of history; covers men and women who are distinguished locally as well as nationally; in two series: the Permanent Series covers deceased persons; the Current Series covers living Americans. Index volume includes names of all subjects in all volumes and thousands of topical entries.

Webster's American Biographies. Edited by Charles Van Doren and Robert McHenry. Springfield, Mass.: G. & C. Merriam Company, 1979. Covers some 3000 persons, living and not living, who have made a significant contribution to American life; special attention is given to groups often neglected (Indians, western pioneers, and women); geographical indexes and careers and professions indexes are provided.

Living persons

Who's Who, London: A. & C. Black, Ltd., 1849– . (Annual.) The first "who's who"; includes persons of distinction in all fields; covers Great Britain and the Commonwealth nations.

Who's Who among Black Americans. 5th ed. Lake Forest, Ill.: Educational Communications, 1988. Gives biographical sketches of more than 15,000 living notable black American men and women in many fields, selected on the basis of significant achievement; has geographical and occupation indexes.

Who's Who in America. Chicago: Marquis—Who's Who, Inc., 1899–   . (Biennial.) Includes persons of special prominence in every line of work and those who are selected arbitrarily because of their positions in government, religion, education, industry, and other fields. Since 1972–1973, in 2 vols. Supplement to 44th ed., 1987.

Who's Who in the World. 8th ed. Chicago: Marquis—Who's Who, Inc., 1987. Aims to identify important personalities of the world; contains more than 28,000 names from some 150 countries of persons who are "shaping today's world and tomorrow's future"; entries are chosen by members of the Marquis staff.

Other useful biographies of the "who's who" type, which include eminent living persons from all professions, are:

American Catholic Who's Who
Who's Who in France
Who's Who in Germany
Who's Who in Italy
Who's Who of American Women

In addition to those listed above, there are biographical dictionaries by section of a country and by profession, e.g., *Who's Who in the East, Who's Who in American Art.*

Professional and occupational biographical dictionaries are discussed in the chapters which treat each subject field.

Indexes to Biography[4]

In addition to the biographical dictionaries which provide the desired information, there are indexes which point out biographies in books and in periodical literature. Indexes to periodical literature, indexes to newspapers, and indexes to collected works include biographical articles. The following indexes cover only biographical material. They point out where biographical articles or books can be found and give the titles and pages of books or the volumes, dates, and pages of periodicals.

[4] See also Chapter 9, Indexes.

Biography and Genealogy Master Index. Detroit: Gale Research Company, 1980. (Annual.) Contains more than 3 million citations to biographical articles which have appeared in some 350 works of individual and collective biography; covers persons living and not living.

Biography Index. New York: The H. W. Wilson Company, 1947–   . (Quarterly; annual cumulations.) Locates biographical materials in some 2600 periodicals indexed in Wilson indexes; also indexed are current books of individual and collective biography, autobiographies, diaries, collections of letters, memoirs, juvenile literature, biographical material in non-biographical works, and obituaries of national interest published in *The New York Times*; bibliographies, portraits, and other illustrations are noted if they are included in the indexed material; provides an index by professions and occupations.

Hyamson, Albert M. (ed.). *A Dictionary of Universal Biography of All Ages and All Peoples.* 2d ed. New York: E. P. Dutton & Company, Inc., 1951. An index to individuals who are included in twenty-four biographical dictionaries of various countries; gives dates, nationality, and profession for each name and indicates the biographical source by a symbol.

Review Questions

CHAPTER 10. BIOGRAPHICAL DICTIONARIES

1. Discuss biography as a subject field.
2. What is a biographical dictionary? What are the three major classes of biographical dictionary?
3. What items of information about a person are given in a biographical dictionary?
4. If you are seeking biographical information on a person in the news, what facts about the person will help you decide which biographical dictionary to use?
5. Name two or more of the biographical dictionaries in this chapter that include your favorite author, musician, or historical figure.
6. Discuss indexes to biography. How can you use them in answering Question 5?

CHAPTER

 **11**

Atlases[1] and Gazetteers

Before they could write, and perhaps before they could speak, primitive people left landmarks (cairns) to show where they had been. The oldest known map is a Babylonian clay tablet dating from about 2300 B.C. There are many other clay tablets which show geographical locations.

The Greeks, using their knowledge of science, philosophy, mathematics, geography, and astronomy, succeeded in developing mapmaking (cartography) to a point not again attained until the sixteenth century. Greek geographers from the fifth century B.C. believed that the earth is a sphere. About A.D. 150, Claudius Ptolemy of Alexandria, perhaps the greatest single contributor in history to cartography and geography, compiled his eight-volume *Geographia*, the first scientific and comprehensive treatment of cartography. It contained, in addition to the text, twenty-eight maps and a list of all the principal places then known. The *Geographia* disappeared during the Middle Ages and was not found until the fifteenth century. Its rediscovery[2] helped make possible the voyages of Columbus, Magellan, Vasco da Gama, John Cabot, and others, thus hastening the era of discovery and exploration. In turn, the discoveries of these explorers greatly increased the demand for maps.

Important contributors to mapmaking during this period were Mercator, famous for his celestial and terrestrial globes and for his system of projection, and Ortelius, credited with the publication of the first modern atlas in 1570. Both were members of the Dutch school of cartography.

---

[1] Atlases and gazetteers belong in the subject field of geography. They are included here because of their general reference value.

[2] The *Geographia* had been preserved by the Arabs.

Atlases

A map is a representation, usually flat, of the earth's surface or a part of it or of the celestial sphere or a part of it.[3] An atlas is a collection of maps, usually bound together in one volume. The word "atlas" was first used in this sense by Mercator, from the figure of the mythological Atlas, which was often used as the frontispiece of early collections of maps. It has come to mean any volume containing not only maps, but also plates, engravings, charts, and tables, with or without descriptive text. It is sometimes used as the name of a volume in which subjects are presented in tabular form.

While it is generally recognized that atlases are essential in studying history,[4] geography, and other branches of the social sciences, it is becoming increasingly apparent that many atlases are valuable also as general reference sources because of the descriptive materials they contain in addition to maps. Today, maps are necessary companions to the daily newspaper and radio and television news commentary, verifying names, places, and events in the news and presenting them in proper geographical relationship to other names, places, and events.

There are many sources of maps. Most of the general encyclopedias include maps either in a separate volume or as illustrative material within the text; encyclopedia annuals include up-to-date maps; many handbooks, almanacs, newspapers, and periodicals also contain maps. However, the atlas is the reference source designed primarily to provide maps.

Atlases vary in quality, and they also vary according to the country of publication. For example, an atlas of the world which is published in America will include more or larger maps of America than one published in France. The latter will include larger maps of France.

CHOOSING AN ATLAS[5]

To be able to choose an atlas to answer a given question, it is necessary to know certain things about each atlas.

1. Scope
    a Is it worldwide in coverage, or is it limited to one or more regions?

[3] *Webster's New Collegiate Dictionary* (Springfield, Mass.: G. & C. Merriam Company, 1960), p. 513.

[4] A historical atlas is made up of maps which delineate past events or periods of history; it is not a collection of old maps.

[5] For examples of atlases in the subject fields, see Chapters 17–24.

    b Does it include all kinds of maps, political, topographical, thematic, relief, etc., or only one kind of map.

    c Does it provide descriptive material about the various geographical locations?

2. Place of publication as an indication of emphasis

3. Date of publication as an indication of up-to-dateness

4. Kind of index

    a Is there one comprehensive index for the entire volume, or are there separate indexes for each map or section of maps?

    b Is the index a separate volume, or is it part of the atlas?

    c Does it indicate pronunciation?

    d Is the reference to the location on a given map clear and definite?

5. Quality and content of the maps

    a Is the scale indicated clearly?

    b Are the symbols distinct and easily read?

    c Are the projections in keeping with the purpose of the map?

    d Is the lettering clear and legible?

    e Is the coloring varied and well differentiated?

    f Is the legend clearly explained?

    g Are the names of countries given in the language of each country or in translation?

Gazetteers

A gazetteer gives information about geographical places; it does not define them. In addition to geographic location, it gives historical, statistical, cultural, and other relevant facts about these places. It may also indicate pronunciation. Because they provide a variety of factual material about places, gazetteers are important reference sources. Recent editions describe a place as it is now; old editions give historical information about it. The economic growth or decline of a town or city, as indicated by data on population, number of industries, schools, and so on, will often be shown by the brief facts given in gazetteers over a period of years.

In using a gazetteer, it is important to note the copyright date as an indication of the recency of the material; the system of pronunciation and the abbreviations used; the arrangement of the material; and any additional material, such as maps and tables, which may be included in appendixes.

Useful Atlases and Gazetteers[6]

ATLASES

Bartholomew, John W. (ed.). *The Times Atlas of the World*. Vol. I: *The World, Australasia & East Asia*. Vol. II: *South-west Asia & Russia*. Vol. III: *Northern Europe*. Vol. IV: *Southern Europe & Africa*, Vol. V: *The Americas*, Midcentury Edition. London: The Times Publishing Company, Ltd., 1955–1959. Each volume has its own index-gazetteer; provides inset maps of many cities; is outstanding for the beauty and accuracy of maps. *The Times Index Gazetteer of the World* (1965) lists in 1 vol. the place names separately indexed in the 5 vols. of the Midcentury Edition.

Goode's World Atlas. 17th ed. Chicago: Rand McNally & Company, 1986. Includes physical and political maps, special maps relating to climate, religions, the ocean floor, etc.

Hammond Medallion World Atlas. Maplewood, N.J.: C. S. Hammond & Company, 1986. Places all the information about a continent, country, state, or province on consecutive pages; maps of various kinds plus all other relevant political, economic, and geographical data placed together. 1980 Census figures. Other atlases which are comparable in arrangement are *Hammond Ambassador World Atlas* (1986), *Hammond Citation World Atlas* (1986), and *Hammond World Atlas International Edition* (1981).

The National Atlas of the United States of America. Washington, D.C.: U.S. Department of the Interior, Geological Survey, 1970. The official national atlas of the United States; has 765 maps and an index which identifies more than 41,000 place names; includes many thematic maps which present the physical, economic, social, and historical features of the country; includes six plastic overlays correlated with the thematic and special maps; divided between "General Reference Maps" and "Special Reference Maps."

National Geographic Atlas of the World. 5th ed. Washington, D.C.: National Geographic Society, 1981. Provides 172 pages of political maps, an 18-page section on science, and a 30-page section of physical maps of the world both above and beneath the sea; includes profiles of countries; has insets of world, metropolitan, and regional areas; also gives world resources maps and an index to 155,000 place names. 1980 Census figures.

[6] See also Chapter 24 for additional materials in the field of geography.

The New International Atlas. Chicago: Rand McNally & Company, 1982. Offers political, physical, urban area, strategic, and geographic area maps of the countries of the world; gives population tables for all countries and principal cities; presents the world in broad view and also in detail; includes maps and charts on such topics as population distribution, energy production and consumption, and climate; has a glossary and abbreviations of geographical terms which appear on the maps; does not define terms; place names are in the language of the country. 1980 Census figures have been added.

The New Oxford Atlas, 3d ed. Prepared by the Cartographic Department of the Oxford University Press. London: Oxford University Press, 1978. Includes general reference, thematic, and relief maps; covers oceans, temperature, climate, rainfall, land use, vegetation, and population data (1974 Census).

Oxford World Atlas. Saul B. Cohen, Geographic Editor. Prepared by the Cartographic Department of the Clarendon Press. London: Oxford University Press, 1973. Presents political, geophysical, demographic, and economic data in maps; many factors are shown in the same map; includes climate, ocean features, population distribution, mineral resources; has gazetteer.

The Prentice-Hall Great International Atlas. Englewood Cliffs, N.J.: Prentice-Hall, Inc., 1981. Gives full map coverage to the countries of the world; contains historical, cultural, scientific, and geographical information on every part of the world; extensive use of colored illustrations and color in maps.

Rand McNally Cosmopolitan World Atlas. New census ed. Chicago: Rand McNally & Company, 1981. Describes in maps the environments in various regions of the world; includes maps of the world and special regions (polar regions, oceans, etc.), regional maps, United States city maps, and travel maps of the United States; a 32-page table gives census figures for more than 19,000 cities and towns in the United States.

Rand McNally Premier World Atlas. New census ed. Chicago: Rand McNally & Company, 1981. Covers space, the planets, special regions, mountains, lakes, rivers, all countries of the world, and population; includes United States highway maps; gives explanation of map projection.

The Times Atlas of the World. Comprehensive 6th ed. New York: Times Book Company, 1980. Gives physical-political maps for regions, nations, and localities of the earth; has thematic maps for world physiography, oceanography, climatology, vegetation, population; includes air routes and city maps; has geographical glossaries and a 210,000-item gazetteer. Maps are by John Bartholomew & Sons, Ltd.

GAZETTEERS

Columbia-Lippincott Gazetteer of the World. Edited by Leon E. Seltzer with the Geographical Research Staff of Columbia University Press and with the cooperation of the American Geographical Society. With 1961 *Supplement.* New York: Columbia University Press, 1962. Gives information about history, population, trade, industry, cultural institutions, and agricultural and natural resources.

Webster's New Geographical Dictionary. Springfield, Mass.: G. & C. Merriam Company, 1980. Provides geographical, economic, and historical information about countries, cities, regions, and natural features of the world; gives pronunciations; includes maps.

Summary

Atlases are generally recognized as being essential in the study of geography and history; they are becoming increasingly important in other areas of study and are necessary companions to the daily newspaper, radio, and television commentary.

Scope, place and date of publication, kind of index, and quality and content of maps are important features to consider in judging the usefulness of an atlas for a given purpose.

Gazetteers do not define geographical places: they locate them and give geographical and other important information about them. Each atlas is entered in the library catalog under title, editor or compiler, and subject. Some general subject headings for atlases are:

Atlases
Atlases, American
Atlases, British
Geography, Atlases

Gazetteers can be found in the catalog under title and editor or compiler and subject. They can be located under a general subject heading such as:

Names, Geographic—Dictionaries

Review Questions

CHAPTER 11. ATLASES AND GAZETTEERS

1. Discuss the difference between an atlas and a gazetteer.

2. What features should an authoritative atlas have? How do atlases differ?

3. Which of the atlases described on pp. 140–142 have inset maps of cities? Thematic maps? Population data?

4. Discuss the difference between a gazetteer which is found in an atlas and a gazetteer like those described on p. 142.

5. What information about your hometown is given in a gazetteer?

CHAPTER

 12

Yearbooks and Handbooks[1]

Every library has a number of books for quick reference which provide brief information on a multitude of subjects. Among these "ready-reference" works are yearbooks and handbooks.

A yearbook is a publication which is issued annually for the purpose of giving current information in narrative, statistical, or directory form. There are several types of yearbooks:

1. Encyclopedia annuals, issued by the major encyclopedia publishers as a means of keeping the encyclopedia up to date, are comprehensive in coverage and give a summary of all the major events of the preceding year.
2. Yearbooks, which treat several subject areas, include social, political, educational, cultural, and other information.
3. Almanacs, which were originally calendars of months and days with special dates and anniversaries, forecasts of the weather, and astronomical calculations, are now collections of miscellaneous facts and statistics.
4. Directories, which list persons or organizations in alphabetical or classified arrangement, include addresses and affiliations for individuals and officers and other data for organizations. Not all directories are issued annually.

A handbook (literally, a small book which can be held in the hand) is a volume which treats broad subjects in brief fashion. It may include odd bits

---

[1] See also yearbooks and handbooks in each of the subject fields.

of information about a variety of topics. Among the most useful types of handbooks are:

1. Manuals, which give instruction on, or serve as guides to, occupations, hobbies, art forms, trades, etc. Example: *Robert's Rules of Order*.
2. Miscellanies, which include bits of unusual and hard-to-find information on many subjects. Example: *Famous First Facts*.
3. Companions, which explain and interpret various aspects of a subject. Example: *The Oxford Companion to Ships & the Sea*.
4. Digests, which present in condensed form information that is classified and arranged under proper headings or titles; examples are digests of laws, digests of articles from periodicals, or digests of the plots of novels, short stories, dramas, or poems.[2] Example: *Masterplots*.

Selection and Use of a Yearbook or Handbook

Each yearbook or handbook is designed to provide certain kinds of information for the purpose of answering specific kinds of questions. Therefore, before attempting to choose a yearbook or a handbook, the student should examine the question to be answered:

1. Does it require statistical information?
2. Is it a directory-type question?
3. Is it a "trend" question?
4. Does it come under the heading of miscellany?

In order to use a yearbook or a handbook quickly and satisfactorily, it is necessary to understand:

1. Organization and arrangement of material
   a   Is it organized into chapters or into broad general subjects, and does it have a detailed table of contents, a comprehensive index, or both?
   b   Is it broken down into small topics, arranged alphabetically?
   c   Does it have tables only, or does it give both text and tables?
2. Kinds of material included
   a   Is it statistical? If it is, does it give the source for the statistics presented?
   b   Does it give instructions and directions?
   c   Is it a collection of miscellaneous information?

[2] See also pp. 283–284.

3. Scope
    a Does it cover all countries and all subjects?
    b Is it limited to one country and to a selected number of subjects?
4. Period covered
    a Is it one year? Two years?
    b If it is a handbook, is it revised often?
5. Special aids to the reader
    a Does it provide bibliographical references for further reading?
    b Does it provide cross references?
    c Is the illustrative material—charts, tables, maps, pictures—appropriate and adequate?
6. Kinds of questions it will answer
    a Will it answer factual and statistical questions?
    b Will it provide "trend" and background information?

Representative Yearbooks and Handbooks

YEARBOOKS

Encyclopedia annuals

Americana Annual. New York: Grolier, Incorporated, 1923– . Covers events of the previous year; features a brief chronological listing of events.

Britannica Book of the Year. Chicago: Encyclopaedia Britannica, Inc., 1938– Gives a calendar of events, many short articles under specific titles, statistics, and bibliography.

Collier's Year Book. New York: P. F. Collier & Son Corporation, 1938– . Surveys the events of the year; is especially strong in sports and chronology.

Other yearbooks and annuals

Europa Yearbook 1987: A World Survey. 28th ed. London: Europa Publications Limited, 1987. 2 vols. Covers some 1500 international organizations and all countries; provides information about the press, political parties, trade, industry, television, statistics, education, and religion.

The Statesman's Yearbook. London: Macmillan & Company, Ltd., 1864– . Covers government, area, population, education, religion, social welfare, money, industry, defense, international relations, energy, economic conditions, trade, communications, and other information about the countries of the world; arranged alphabetically by country.

U.S. Bureau of the Census. *Statistical Abstract of the United States.* Washington, D.C.: Government Printing Office, 1878– . (Annual.) Summarizes statistics of political, industrial, economic, and social institutions and organizations in the United States; provides bibliography.

ALMANACS

Canadian Almanac and Directory. Toronto: Copp Clark Company, 1848– . (Annual.) Gives statistical and other information for Canada on miscellaneous subjects, including geography, history, education, law, sports, and religion.

Information Please Almanac, Atlas & Yearbook. New York: Information Please Publishing Company, Inc., 1947– . (Annual.) Has a topical arrangement and subject index; covers "people & places, facts & figures, news & views, past & present" (subtitle); emphasizes sports.

Whitaker, Joseph. *Almanack.* London: J. Whitaker & Sons, 1868– . (Annual.) Gives complete statistical information regarding government finances, population, and commerce for the various nations in the world, with emphasis on Great Britain and the United States; contains material relating to astronomical and other phenomena; includes maps.

The World Almanac and Book of Facts. New York: Newspaper Enterprise Association, Inc., 1868– . (Annual.) Gives comprehensive coverage of factual material of all kinds; index is in the front of the book.

DIRECTORIES

American Library Directory. 39th ed. Compiled and edited by Jaques Cattell Press. New York: R. R. Bowker Company, 1986. Provides information on more than 35,000 libraries: public, academic, special, government, and armed forces libraries in the United States and Canada; includes name and type of library, address, telephone number, names of key staff members, income and expenditures, size of collections, special collections, and library systems to which the library belongs; lists library schools and libraries for the blind and handicapped. On-line from DIALOG.

Encyclopedia of Associations. 21st ed. Detroit: Gale Research Company, 1987. 3 vols. Covers national organizations of the United States (Vol. I), with a geographic and executive index (Vol. II), a list of new associations and projects (Vol. III), and a listing of international organizations in 1987.

The Foundation Directory. 10th ed. New York: Foundation Center, 1985. Arranged by state; lists foundations by types, geographical distribution, and economic factors; gives grant application information. *Supplement,* 1986.

Thomas' Register of American Manufacturers. New York: Thomas Publishing Company, 1905– . (Annual.) Lists major manufacturers geographically; arranged by product; has an index to manufacturers, trade names, and specific products.

U.S. Congress. *Official Congressional Directory for the Use of the United States Congress, 1809–* . Washington, D.C.: U.S. Government Printing Office, 1809– . Includes a variety of information concerning members of Congress, committees, other bodies of the government, independent agencies, diplomatic representatives, and members of the press.

HANDBOOKS

Dreyfuss, Henry. *Symbol Sourcebook: An Authoritative Guide to International Graphic Symbols.* New York: McGraw-Hill Book Company, 1972. Covers more than 6000 symbols used internationally in business, industry, the sciences, and all fields; arranged by broad subject.

Hatch, Jane (comp. and ed.). *American Book of Days.* 3d ed. New York: The H. W. Wilson Company, 1978. Arranged day by day, January 1–December 31; presents the holidays, anniversaries, birthdays, and celebrations important in the nation's history; describes the history of each occasion and ways Americans observe it.

Kane, Joseph Nathan. *Famous First Facts.* 4th ed. New York: The H. W. Wilson Company, 1981. Covers first happenings, events, discoveries, and inventions in the United States; has index by year, day, subject, personal name, and geographical location. *Supplement to the 4th ed.*, 1985, brings it up to date through the Reagan administration.

The Oxford Companion to Ships & the Sea. Edited by Peter Kemp. London: Oxford University Press, 1976. Covers a wide range of topics (terms related to the sea, names and kinds of ships, seafaring history, authors and artists of the sea, pirates, and fictional and mythological characters); has photographs, line drawings, and diagrams.

Payton, Geoffrey (comp.). *Webster's Dictionary of Proper Names.* Springfield, Mass.: G. & C. Merriam Company, 1970. Identifies over 10,000 contemporary and historical place names, nicknames, and names from the arts, science, movies, sports, and other areas; includes names unique to America; grouped in sixty-seven categories.

Post, Emily. *Emily Post's Etiquette.* 14th ed. Revised by Elizabeth L. Post. New York: Harper & Row, 1984. Treats social usage; especially useful for formal occasions.

Robert's Rules of Order. New rev. ed. A new and enlarged edition by Sarah

Corbin Robert. Glenview, Ill.: Scott Foresman Company, 1981. A guide for parliamentary procedure; provides new material.

Smith, Whitney. *Flags and Arms Across the World*. New York: McGraw-Hill Book Company, 1980. Provides information on the flags of 174 countries, including a color illustration of the official flag, the presidential flag, coat of arms or seal, and date of official adoption.

United States Government Organization Manual. Washington, D.C.: Government Printing Office, 1935– . (Annual.) The "official organization handbook of the federal government"; gives essential information regarding the executive, legislative, and judicial branches and the authority, organization, and functions of the agencies in these branches.

Webster's New World Secretarial Handbook. New rev. ed. New York: Simon & Schuster, Inc., 1981. Gives guidelines for typing, word processing, taking dictation, form and structure of business letters, grammar and usage, abbreviations, and office equipment; has a glossary of business terms.

Summary

Yearbooks and handbooks, which are quick reference sources covering many subjects, may give enough information to answer a question or may only give enough information to enable the searcher to know what other kinds of sources to consult. For example, a yearbook or handbook may give the nationality and dates of an individual, and this much information will tell the searcher what biographical dictionary to consult for additional facts about the person.

The purpose of a yearbook is to give current information on a variety of subjects, as an encyclopedia yearbook, or on topics of interest in one field, as the *Yearbook of Agriculture*.

There are several kinds of handbooks: some give how-to-do-it instructions (manuals); others present a collection of miscellaneous information covering many topics (almanacs); another type aids the user in understanding a subject (companions); and still another type offers condensations or summaries of articles, novels, short stories, plays, etc. (digests).

A handbook or a yearbook is listed in the library catalog under the author or editor, title, and subject. Handbooks and yearbooks can be found in the catalog under a given subject:

Chemistry—Handbooks, manuals, etc.
Education—Yearbooks

Review Questions

CHAPTER 12. YEARBOOKS AND HANDBOOKS

1. Why are yearbooks and handbooks called "ready reference" works? Why are they particularly useful to library users?
2. Name the kinds of information that can be found in these ready reference sources.
3. Discuss encyclopedia annuals, their content, and their usefulness.
4. Which of the ready reference sources on pp. 146–149 give information about people? Sports? Libraries? Places? Trade names? Which ready reference sources give how-to-do-it information?

CHAPTER

13

Bibliographies

The word "bibliography," deriving from two Greek words, *biblion*, "book," and *graphein*, "to write," was used in postclassical Greece in the sense of "the writing of books." The scribes who copied books were the first bibliographers. This meaning was in use as late as 1761, as is indicated by the definition of the word "bibliographer" in Fenning's *English Dictionary* of that date as "one who copies books."

The transition from the meaning of writing *of* books to that of writing *about* books dates from the eighteenth century; the latter meaning is in use today.

In the sense of "writing about books," the term "bibliography" has several uses:

1. It is the systematic description of groups of books, manuscripts, and other publications as to authorship, title, edition, and imprint, and their enumeration and arrangement into lists for purposes of information.[1]
2. It is the name given to a list of books, manuscripts, and other publications, systematically described and arranged, which have some relationship to each other. Thus, there are several kinds of bibliographies.
   a General—not limited to one author, subject, country, or period of time
   b Author—listing the works by and about one author
   c Subject—restricted to one subject or to one subject field
   d National or regional—including material relating to one country or to one region

[1] See pp. 316–324.

    e Trade—directed to the book trade and supplying information needed in buying and selling books

3. It is the science of books, that branch of learning concerned with the historical and technical examination of written works, in which books and manuscripts are examined to discover or verify their origin, dates, number and order of pages, authorship, and textual material.

A bibliography may be complete, including *all* works of a particular kind, or it may be selective, containing only a part of the works. It may be descriptive, having only a brief descriptive note (annotation); it may be evaluative, that is, with critical comment; or it may be both descriptive and evaluative. There are bibliographies of forms other than books, such as periodicals, newspapers, and nonbook materials, and bibliographies of types of material, such as book reviews, biographical materials, and bibliographies.

Bibliographies may be found in individual books, in periodical articles, and in encyclopedias and other reference books, or they may be separate books. There are bibliographies both of a general nature and in the subject fields to aid the researcher in the quest for material.

The printed catalogs of individual and of national libraries such as the Library of Congress are forms of bibliographies. They are photographic reproductions of the cards in the card catalog of the libraries they represent. Some printed catalogs are union catalogs, that is, lists of the combined holdings of several or many libraries. Union catalogs and lists indicate by means of symbols on the cards the libraries which hold a given title and enable researchers to know where they can borrow a copy if their library does not have it or secure a photocopy of a desired piece of material. There are union catalogs (lists) of books, periodical publications, nonbook materials, and combinations of these.

Bibliographies are useful sources in any search for material on a subject.

1. They locate material on the subject in question.
2. They provide a means of verifying such items as author's name, complete title of work, place of publication, publisher, date of publication, edition, number of pages, and price.
3. If they are annotated, they indicate the scope of the work and the manner in which the subject is treated; if the annotation is critical and evaluative, it comments upon the usefulness of the publication.
4. They point out material, including parts of books, which cannot be analyzed in the card catalog.
5. They group works according to form, location, and period.

Bibliographies in the subject fields are discussed in Chapters 17 to 24.

Summary

Bibliographies are essential aids in any search for material on a subject. They vary in extent from multivolume printed catalogs to brief listings following a periodical article. Whatever the length, their usefulness depends upon the completeness and accuracy of the information they provide. A bibliography is listed in the library catalog under author or compiler, title, and subject. General subject headings for bibliographies include:

> Bibliography, National
> Bibliography, Universal
> Bibliography—Collections

Bibliographies in a subject field are listed under the subject:

> American literature—Bibliography
> History—Bibliography

Representative Bibliographies

GENERAL BIBLIOGRAPHIES

Besterman, Theodore. *A World Bibliography of Bibliographies.* 4th ed., revised and greatly enlarged. Lausanne, Switzerland: Societas Bibliographica, 1965. 4 vols. International in scope; includes bibliographical catalogs, calendars, abstracts, and digests. *A World Bibliography of Bibliographies,* compiled by Alice F. Toomey (Totowa, N.J.: Rowman and Littlefield, 1977), is a decennial supplement to Besterman, 4th ed; it covers separately published bibliographies.

The Bibliographic Index. New York: The H. W. Wilson Company, 1938– . (Three times a year; annual cumulation.) A subject list of bibliographies; includes those published as books and pamphlets and those which appear in the more than 2600 periodicals indexed in the Wilson indexes, both in English and in foreign languages. Lists bibliographies that name fifty or more citations.

UNION CATALOGS

Library of Congress Catalogs: National Union Catalog. Washington, D.C.: Library of Congress, 1956– . (Nine monthly issues; quarterly and five-year cumulations.) An author list of materials held by some 1100 North

American libraries; contains reproductions of cards for books, pamphlets, maps, atlases, and periodicals in many languages; locations for some titles are given.

Library of Congress Catalogs: Subject Catalog 1950– . Washington, D.C.: Library of Congress, 1955– . (Three quarterly issues with annual and quinquennial cumulations.) A subject catalog of 1945 and later works represented by Library of Congress printed cards; includes books cataloged by members of the National Union Catalog arrangement; after 1956 a location in at least one library is given. Formerly *Library of Congress Catalog. Books: Subjects.* Available on microfiche.

The National Union Catalog, Pre-1956 Imprints. London: Mansell Publishing, Ltd., 1968–1981. 754 vols. A comprehensive author list which includes the following works: *A Catalog of Books Represented by Library of Congress Printed Cards Issued to July 31, 1942; Supplement,* August 1, 1942–December 31, 1947; *The Library of Congress Author Catalog,* 1948–1952; *The National Union Catalog, 1952–1955 Imprints;* and *The National Union Catalog, A Cumulative Author List, 1953–1957.* Has more than 12 million entries (reproductions of catalog cards), including books, pamphlets, atlases, maps, music, periodicals, and other publications cataloged by the Library of Congress and several hundred cooperating libraries in the United States and Canada over the past century; arranged by main entry. At least one location is given for each entry.

BIBLIOGRAPHIES OF PERIODICAL PUBLICATIONS

Gale Directory of Publications. Detroit, Mich.: Gale Research Company, 1869– . (Annual.) Provides information about newspapers and periodicals printed in the United States and its possessions, Canada, Bermuda, Panama, and the Philippines.

Katz, Bill, and Katz, Linda Sternberger. *Magazines for Libraries.* 5th ed. New York: R. R. Bowker Company, 1986. Arranged by subject; lists more than 6500 titles with descriptive and critical annotations of the important features of the magazine including editorial point of view; an aid in selecting magazines for public, college, and school libraries; useful for the student and nonspecialist; includes some popular titles; gives publication details.

The Standard Periodical Directory. 10th ed. New York: Oxbridge Communications, Inc., 1987. Lists 67,000 periodical publications in the United States and Canada in 230 subject classifications, including consumer and special-interest magazines, newsletters, house organs, directories, government publications, and bulletins.

Ulrich's International Periodicals Directory. 27th ed. New York: R. R. Bowker Company, 1988. Arranged by subject; lists world periodicals in each field, giving detailed information regarding contents, sponsorship, frequency, and language of text; includes some 69,000 periodicals; provides an index of abstracting and indexing services; supplemented by *Ulrich's* Quarterly. On-line access to *Ulrich's* data base available 1981– . Also available on CD-ROM.

Union List of Serials in Libraries of the United States and Canada. 3d ed. Edited by Edna Brown Titus. New York: The H. W. Wilson Company, 1965. 5 vols. Lists more than 150,000 serial titles in 956 libraries—periodicals, proceedings, annual reports—which began publication before December 31, 1949; arranged by title; indicates by symbols the libraries which have copies of each title; supplemented by *New Serial Titles, A Union List of Serials Commencing Publication after December 31, 1949* (Washington, D.C.: Library of Congress, 1953–). (Monthly with annual cumulations; beginning 1969, has eight monthly issues, four quarterly issues, and annual and five- or ten-year cumulations.)

SELECTIVE AND EVALUATIVE BIBLIOGRAPHIES

Booklist. Chicago: American Library Association, 1905– . (Semimonthly; monthly in August.) Provides reviews of a selected list of currently published books, filmstrips, and 16-mm films and other nonprint media; each issue has special sections such as adult fiction, adult nonfiction, books for children and young people, government publications, and books for special groups; "Reference Books Bulletin" includes reviews prepared by the ALA's Reference and Subscription Books Committee; it appears in a separate section. The lengthy reviews of encyclopedias and other reference books include a statement of whether or not the books are recommended by the committee.

Reader's Adviser: A Layman's Guide to Literature. 13th ed. New York: R. R. Bowker Company, 1986–1988. 6 vols. Lists and annotates the best books in nearly every field of human knowledge from antiquity to the present. Vol. I: *The Best in American and British Fiction, Poetry, Essays, Literary Biography, Bibliography, and Reference.* Edited by Fred Kaplan, 1986. Vol. II: *The Best in American and British Drama and World Literature in English Translation.* Edited by Maurice Charney, 1986. Vol. III. *The Best in General Reference Literature of the World, the Social Sciences, History, and the Arts.* Edited by Paula Kaufman, 1986. Vol. IV. *The Best in the Literature of Philosophy and World Religions.* Edited by William L. Reese, 1988. Vol. V: *The Best in the Literature of Science, Technology and Medicine.* Edited by Paul T. Durbin, 1988. Vol. VI: *Index to Volumes 1–5.* 1988.

Sheehy, Eugene P. (comp.). *Guide to Reference Books*. 10th ed. Chicago: American Library Association, 1986. Lists and annotates some 14,000 titles; reference materials are divided into five major areas with subdivisions by subject, specific kind of work, country, or all three; annotations are evaluative; emphasis is on sources for scholarly research, but some popular titles are included.

"The Standard Catalog Series." New York: The H. W. Wilson Company. Includes *Children's Catalog*, 15th ed., 1986; *The Junior High School Library Catalog*, 5th ed., 1985; *The Senior High School Library Catalog*, 13th ed., 1987; *The Public Library Catalog*, 8th ed., 1984; and *Fiction Catalog*, 11th ed., 1986. Each catalog provides annotated lists of books for the type of library or material covered; each is kept up to date by annual supplements.

Walford, A. J. (ed.). *Guide to Reference Material*. London: Library Association, 1977–1982. 3 vols. Vol. I: *Science and Technology*, 4th ed., 1980. Vol. II: *Social and Historical Sciences, Philosophy and Religion*, 4th ed., 1982. Vol. III: *Generalities, Languages, the Arts and Literature*, 4th ed., 1987. Each title lists significant reference sources published in recent years in the subject areas included; international in scope with some emphasis on British publications.

Wynar, Bohdan A. (ed.). *American Reference Books Annual*. Littleton, Colo.: Libraries Unlimited, 1970– . (Annual.) Provides a record of the reference books published and distributed in the United States during the preceding year; gives signed, critical, and comparative reviews; ARBA covers every subject area of general and specific interest; gives citations to additional reviews in major journals.

TRADE BIBLIOGRAPHIES

American Book Publishing Record. New York: R. R. Bowker Company, 1960– . (Monthly; annual cumulation.) Presents a complete record of American book publication in the four (sometimes five) calendar weeks preceding its date of issue; lists by subject the titles in the *Weekly Record*; arranged by subject according to the Dewey Decimal Classification; gives Dewey number, Library of Congress subject headings, LC card number, LC number, and annotation.

Books in Print. New York: R. R. Bowker Company, 1948– . (Annual.) 4 vols. Lists available books by author and title; gives publisher, series, edition, date of publication, price, and number of volumes; lists a total of some 585,000 books of all kinds in print in the United States from some 8100 publishers. *Authors Index*, 2 vols.; *Titles Index*, 2 vols. *Books in Print Supplement*, 2 vols., published annually in the spring, updates the basic volume. On-line access to *Books in Print* data bases available from DI-ALOG and BRS; updated monthly, the data bases include entries from *Forthcoming Books* and *Subject Guide to Books in Print*; searches can be made by author, title, publisher, and subject; also on CD-ROM.

Cumulative Book Index. New York: The H. W. Wilson Company, 1898–   . (Monthly, except August; bound annual cumulations.) An author-title-subject international list of books published in the English language; gives author's full name, complete title, edition, series, number of pages, publisher, date of publication, price, Library of Congress card number and ISBN number; continues the *U.S. Catalog*, 4th ed. (1928), which lists books in print on January 1, 1928.

Forthcoming Books. New York: R. R. Bowker Company, 1966–   . (Bi-monthly.) Lists by author and title all books scheduled for publication in the coming five-month period. Beginning 1987, included in *Subject Guide to Forthcoming Books* (1967–1987) is *Forthcoming Books*, listing the coming books under subject.

Paperbound Books in Print. New York: R. R. Bowker Company, 1955–   . 2 vols. (Semiannually in April and October.) More than 275,000 paper-backs in print are listed by author, title, and subject with information for locating and ordering.

Publishers' Trade List Annual. New York: R. R. Bowker Company, 1873–   . 4 vols. An annual compilation of catalogs and lists from about 1500 Ameri-can and Canadian publishers; provides information on most of the books currently in print in the United States and Canada.

Subject Guide to Books in Print. New York: R. R. Bowker Company, 1957–   . 4 vols. (Annual.) Lists, according to the subject headings established by the Library of Congress, more than 500,000 nonfiction titles under some 63,000 subject headings; gives author, title, publisher, current price, and year of publication. Kept up to date by *Books in Print Supplement*. Avail-able on CD-ROM.

Weekly Record. New York: R. R. Bowker Company, 1974–   . (Weekly.) Lists by author or main entry new books published in the United States the previous week; every four weeks the titles are cumulated, arranged by subject, and published as the *American Book Publishing Record*; gives Dewey Decimal and Library of Congress classifications, author, title, edition, imprint, LC card number, price, and other information.

Review Questions

CHAPTER 13. BIBLIOGRAPHIES

1. Discuss bibliography: the purpose, kinds, and usefulness.
2. What is a union catalog? What kinds of information does it give?
3. How do the bibliographies of periodical publications on pp. 154–155 differ?
4. Of the bibliographies listed on pp. 153–157, which would be useful to a student who is trying to locate:
   a A copy of a book not in the college library that the student needs for a term paper
   b Information about a town where he or she has a new job
   c Information about journals and magazines in a subject field
   d The best books on a given subject
   e A list of recommended books for a given type of library
   f The date a book will be published
   g The publisher and price of a book
5. Using the *Subject Guide to Books in Print*, find out how many books are in print on any one of the subjects you are studying.

CHAPTER
❧ 14 ❧

Nonbook Information Sources

In addition to books, magazines, and newspapers, which have been discussed in the preceding chapters, the library provides other kinds of information sources for the student who is seeking the answer to a question, aid in solving or clarifying a problem, or illustrative material in any of the several subject fields. Since these materials are not always listed in the main catalog, it is important that users of the library know what they are, how they are organized and arranged, and the rules which govern their use. (Figure 14.1 shows some catalog cards for nonbook materials.)

Among these sources are (1) pamphlets and clippings; (2) audio, visual, and audiovisual materials; (3) microfilm, microcards, microfiche, and other microforms; (4) and automated information sources.

Pamphlets and Clippings

A pamphlet is a publication which deals with only one subject and consists of a few pages stitched together and enclosed in paper covers. Pamphlets cover topics of current importance in any subject field and appear more frequently in subject areas which are constantly changing.

When they are first published, pamphlets are excellent sources of recent information or opinion on a subject. Parts of books may appear first as pamphlets, and writings which have never been published in book form are often found in pamphlet form.

When pamphlets become out of date as current information, they serve as valuable historical sources because they indicate the trend of interest and opinion at a particular time.

Pamphlets are organized for use in several ways:

1. Some are classified, cataloged, and shelved in the general collection.
2. Some are listed in the library catalog but are arranged in a filing cabinet.
3. Others may be filed in a cabinet designated as the "pamphlet file," arranged alphabetically by subject or numerically if part of a series. In this case, there is usually a separate catalog or listing of the available pamphlets on or near the filing cabinet.

Clippings which have been taken from newspapers, magazines, brochures, and other sources are useful for current events and for providing information on subjects too brief to be treated in pamphlets or books.

Clippings may be mounted on cardboard or placed in folders. In general they are kept in a filing cabinet called the "vertical file" and are arranged alphabetically by subject. As a rule, they are not listed in the library catalog.

Audiovisual Materials

Included in the broad field of audiovisual materials are pictures (clipped from newspapers and magazines), postcards, reproductions of art masterpieces, slides, filmstrips, motion picture films, charts, graphs, maps, models, phonograph records, tape and wire recordings, sheet music, transparencies, programmed books, kits, cassettes, videorecordings, and the equipment needed for their use.

There are audiovisual materials in all subject fields. They are essential in art and music appreciation courses and in language courses; they will enhance the study of drama, literature, and history; they are useful in all the social sciences and in the pure and applied sciences.

Originally, audiovisual materials were used for recreational purposes and to supplement textbook teaching, and they are still used for these purposes. But in some courses, and for some purposes, the audiovisual medium is the course, as in a course on films or television.

Audiovisual materials are no longer considered extra or additional; they are now a significant part of all areas of learning. The student seeking information on a subject or the answer to a question may find that a film, filmstrip, slide, videotape, transparency, or other nonbook form will provide the information needed more satisfactorily than a printed source. In any search for material on a subject, nonbook forms should be included.

Many academic libraries, especially community college libraries, have production facilities, including darkrooms, where teachers and students can make their own audiovisual materials. Students can use these facilities to make slides, films, prints, tapes, transparencies, or other audiovisual materials to illustrate, clarify, and support oral and written reports.

Audiovisual materials may be listed in the library catalog, or they may be kept in separate files in special rooms or areas, with a catalog or listing for each kind of material. In general, these types of materials are kept together according to kind (films, filmstrips, tapes, and so on) and are arranged on shelves or in files according to subject classification.[1] A library may have a map file, a picture file, a room where films, slides, filmstrips and other audiovisual materials are kept and projected, and booths for listening to phonograph and tape recordings.

Audiovisual materials are entered in the catalog, as other materials are, under author, title, subject, and under other appropriate headings, such as illustrator, producer, and so on. They are described on the catalog card by author, title, imprint, and subject matter, and by their peculiar features, such as form, running time, whether sound or silent, color or black and white, and size (see Figure 14.1).

Regulations governing the use of audiovisual materials and equipment vary greatly. In some libraries, certain kinds of materials are circulated while others must be used in specified areas or rooms of the library. Other regulations govern the use of production facilities.

Microforms

Printed materials are increasing at such a rapid rate that libraries as well as business, industry, and government have to find ways of housing them and making them conveniently accessible to those who need them. One of the means they use is microforms.

"Microform" is the name given to any microphotographically produced printed matter. A number of forms and production methods have been developed. Kinds of microforms include microfilm, microprint, microcards, and microfiche.

Microfilm may be 16-mm or 35-mm roll or cartridge film. It is one of the principal forms for reproducing information. Developed as a means of saving space by microcopying back issues of newspapers and magazines, it is used also to reproduce books, reports, government publications, dissertations, and other kinds of printed material.

A microfilm is a film which carries a photographic record, on a reduced scale, of printed material. The rate of reduction determines the number of pages of printed material which it can contain. Depending on the rate of

---

[1] The Dewey Decimal Classification System or the Library of Congress Classification System may be used, or new classification systems may be devised for each kind of material. In some cases, materials may be numbered in the order they were received and shelved by that number.

Video
629.45
E39   The Eagle has landed : the flight of Apollo 11. ₁Videorecording₁ /
       United States National Aeronautics and Space Administration.
       — Washington : NASA : distributed by National Audiovisual
       Center, 1979.
          1 cassette. 29 min. : sd., col. : 3/4 in.

Transparency
611.2
H85   Human respiratory system. ₍Transparency₎ .—
       Burlington, N.C. : Carolina Biological
       Supply Co., c1970.
       2 transparencies : 1 b&w. 1 col. : 26x30 cm.

Film
574.50979
L544   Life in the desert—the American Southwest. ₁Motion picture₁ /
        Encyclopaedia Britannica Educational Corporation ; made by
        Allied Films Artist. — ₁2d ed.₁ — Chicago : The Corp. 1978.
           1 reel. 11 min. : sd., col. : 16 mm. & guide.

Microfilm
330.1   Cropsey, Joseph.
C94p   Polity and economy; an interpretation
         of the principles of Adam Smith. Ann
         Arbor, University Microfilms, 1952.

Multi-media
307.094436   The People of Paris ₍kit₎ / Charles L.
P39   Mitsakos, general editor; Edith West,
           consultant. — Newton, Mass. ; Selective
           Educational Equipment, c1976.
              7 books and booklets, 3 maps, toy

Phonodisc
M22
C516   Chopin, Fryderyk Franciszek, 1810–1849.
           ₁Preludes, piano₁ ₁Sound recording₁
           Preludes. Vox STPL 512.650. ₁196–?₁
           1 disc. 33⅓ rpm. stereo. 12 in.

           Walter Klien, piano.
           Program notes by C. Stanley on container.
           Title from container.
           CONTENTS : 24 preludes, op. 28.—Prelude in C♯ minor, op. 45.—
           Prelude in A♭ major.

              1. Piano music.   I. Klien, Walter.

           [M22]   76–761709

           Library of Congress   76   R

FIGURE 14.1
Sample catalog cards for nonbook materials.

reduction, a microfilm may have 207 frames (reduced 42 times), 269 frames (48 times), or more. Each frame can carry up to 100 lines of print. (See p. 64 for a discussion of the Computer Output Microfilm catalog.)

A microfiche is a 4- by 6-inch film card which contains rows of micro-images of pages, cards, or other printed material. The reduction ratio—low, medium, or high—determines the number of pages, cards, or other material on a fiche. A conventional fiche contains up to 98 pages of text.

In a microbook fiche, which is a photographic reproduction of printed material on a small transparent film card at very great reductions, each page is reduced photographically from 55 to 90 times, depending on the page size. Up to 1000 page images can be reproduced on a single fiche.

Microprint is a microphotograph of printed material reproduced in printed form on 6- by 9-inch cards or sheets, containing up to 100 pages of text. Images are placed on the sheet in rows.

A microcard is a microscopic photographic reproduction of printed material on standard-size 3- by 5-inch library catalog cards. A microcard contains up to eighty pages of printed material, and images are placed on the card in rows. Microfilm might be compared to the negative of a picture taken by a camera, microcard and microprint to the final snapshot. Increasingly, the microcard is giving way to microfiche.

Originally conceived of as a means of reducing in size and storing great quantities of printed material in a very compact and inexpensive form, microforms are now used for numerous purposes; e.g.: (1) to preserve information which has been printed on poor-quality, perishable paper;[2] (2) to duplicate material quickly and inexpensively; (3) to protect valuable information against loss; (4) to restore out-of-print books to in-print status; (5) to enable libraries in the United States to secure materials from foreign libraries; (6) to store very small images for production of full-size copy on demand; and (7) to store and retrieve bits of data from large data bases.

Among the kinds of materials which are available in microfilm, microcard, microprint, or microfiche are: periodicals, newspapers, reports of research, out-of-print books, rare books, new books, government publications, theses, dissertations, manuscripts, library card catalogs, records and reports of business and industry, archival materials, and telephone books.

---

[2] Preservation of print on paper is a continuing and growing concern. It is estimated that most books published in the first half of this century will not be usable by the end of the century and that materials totaling some 3 billion pages will require preservative measures. *Ninth Annual Report for the Year Ending June 30, 1965* (Washington, D.C.: Council on Library Resources, Inc., 1965), pp. 23, 30.

All microforms must be read with the aid of a device which will enlarge the microphotographic image. Microcards, microprint, and microfiche are read left to right, beginning with the top line. Many devices have been designed ranging from hand viewers to large tabletop models. They are not always easy to use, and many devices do not produce an easily read image on the screen.

A reader-printer is available in many libraries. The reader-printer prints the image which is produced on the reading machine screen on a sheet of paper in print that is easily read without the aid of any device. In a sense, the reader-printer returns the microform to its original state.

Microforms are useful to any person who is looking for information on a subject. Because of the many kinds of material—on almost every subject—which are issued in one or another of the microforms, the student must learn about them and how and when to use them.

In some libraries, catalog cards for microforms are filed with other cards in the library catalog with a form or location included in the call number (see Figure 14.1). Microforms are shelved in a separate area, usually in card catalog drawers or in other file drawers.

Some libraries have a special room, called "Microforms," "Microtext Reading Room," or the like, in which microforms are housed and reading machines are located. Light is controlled to provide good contrast for images on the reading-machine screens. A catalog or list of microforms is placed in or near this room.

Automated Information Sources[3]

Some academic libraries have terminals (cathode-ray tubes, or CRTs; see Figure 14.2) which are on-line[4] to one or more data bases and which are used in computer searches. Computer-assisted reference or automated reference service means that the computer searches a standard subject index or abstracting service, but the index or abstracting service is on magnetic tape or disks rather than in printed form. For example, *Psychological Abstracts, Chemical Abstracts*, and *Index Medicus* are printed volumes, but they are also data bases. They may be searched in the printed form manually, or the data bases can be searched by computer if the library has computer access to them. The information is the same; the format is different. The search by computer is much quicker.

[3] See Chapter 5, Library Catalogs, for a discussion of on-line and CD-ROM catalogs.

[4] "On-line" means "in direct access to a data base"; when a CRT is "off-line," requests for searches are submitted to a processing center which makes the search.

The result of a computer search is generally a list of citations which appears on the screen of the CRT. From the list of references, the searcher selects the ones which appear to be useful. In some cases, the full text can be printed at the terminal in use. They may be ordered on-line to be mailed to the user.

Since few data bases provide all the documents cited in the computer search, the user must find the book, journal, or report and read the item cited. Some data base distributors and some commercial firms offer documents on microfiche or reprints of articles. If the library does not have the item cited in the computer search, it may be possible to borrow it from another library on interlibrary loan.

The charge for a computer search will vary depending on the data base searched, the number of terms used, the number of citations obtained, and the time required to make the search.

Three large distributors of data base services are: Lockheed Information Service, which offers an information retrieval service called DIALOG; System Development Corporation, which has a group of data bases referred to as ORBIT; and Bibliographic Retrieval System (BRS). Each data base has a thesaurus, that is, a detailed list of subject headings, which must be used in making a search of that data base. Each also has its own special instructions, which must be followed. A reference librarian may conduct the computer searches, but in some libraries students carry out their own searches.

CD-ROM Data Bases

Many libraries provide information sources on CD-ROM (compact disk–read only memory). A CD-ROM is a plastic disk 4.72 inches in diameter on which can be stored up to 250,000 pages of text.[5] A CD-ROM is a self-contained system that consists of a computer, a special keyboard, a CD-ROM drive, a floppy disk, and a printer. Information, which has been encoded on the disk by using a laser to burn pits in the disk's surface, can be read by a laser and, when accessed, reproduced on the computer screen. The information on a CD-ROM cannot be edited, erased, or added to; new disks are issued to update the master disk.

Examples of information that may be available on CD-ROM are bibliographical citations to journal articles, full-text articles, directory-type material, and specialized business or legal information. The number and uses of

[5] The disk may be larger than 4.72 inches; the larger the disk, the more information can be stored. See INFOTRAC, p. 120.

FIGURE 14.2
Computer terminal (cathrode-ray tube). (Photograph reproduced by permission of System Development Corporation.)

CD-ROM are increasing rapidly, and libraries are acquiring them for various purposes. Information sources which are available on CD-ROM (as well as in print form) are: *Academic American Encyclopedia, McGraw-Hill Concise Encyclopedia of Science and Technology, Books in Print, Ulrich's International Periodicals Directory, Readers' Guide to Periodical Literature*, and other H. W. Wilson Company indexes. Other sources are being made available.

One example of a CD-ROM system (which is not available in print) is INFOTRAC,[6] a comprehensive data base containing indexes of articles from more than 900 business, technological, and general-interest magazines and journals. Information is arranged alphabetically by subject and name. No special knowledge is necessary; color-coded keys give needed instructions to the user. The system is updated monthly.

Automated information sources are being made available in many ways

[6] *INFOTRAC Data Base* (Belmont, Calif.: Information Access Company).

and in many forms. The person who seeks information on any subject must keep up with the rapidly changing and expanding field of automation in order to know what kinds of sources are available and what specific types and formats libraries have to offer.

Determining the Usefulness of Nonbook Information Sources

These questions can be asked in evaluating any nonbook source:

1. Are those who produced the material specialists in their fields?
2. Is the usefulness of the subject matter presented affected by time, and, if so, is this source out of date?
3. Does it attempt to cover more than it is possible to cover in a source of this length?
4. Is the quality of reproduction acceptable, or does it detract from the content?
5. Is the material presented clearly?
6. Is the material presented without bias?
7. What purposes will it serve:
   a Will it answer a question completely?
   b Will it supplement another source?
   c Will it illustrate and clarify a topic?
   d Will it give current information if it is needed?
8. What subject areas are emphasized?
9. Does its usefulness justify the cost, if any?

Reference Sources on Nonbook Materials

GENERAL

Audiovisual Market Place: AVMP. New York: R. R. Bowker Company, 1984. Provides information on materials, equipment, sources, persons, organizations, manufacturers, and services in the audiovisual (AV) field.

Educational Media Year Book 1982. Edited by James W. Brown. Littleton, Colo.: Libraries Unlimited, Inc., 1973– . (Annual.) Gives an annual review of important developments in educational media, including libraries, training, reference sources, and organizations.

Educators Guide to Free Audio and Video Materials. Randolph, Wis.: Educators Progress Service, 1977–   . Lists, describes, and gives information about sources for these materials.

FILMS

Educators Guide to Free Films. Randolph, Wis.: Educators Progress Service, 1941–   . (Annual.) Lists and gives pertinent information on the nature, purposes, sources, and uses of films.

National Audiovisual Center. *1986 Media Resource Catalog.* Capitol Heights, Md.: National Audiovisual Center, 1986. Lists more than 2700 titles selected from the center's collection of federally produced videotapes, films, multimedia kits, and other audiovisual materials for sale or rent; arranged by subject and title.

National Information Center for Educational Media. *Film and Video Finder.* Albuquerque, N.M.: National Information Center for Education Media, 1987. (Annual.) Gives description of content, film or video format, audience level, date, running time, and source.

U.S. Library of Congress. *Library of Congress Catalogs: Audiovisual Materials.* Washington, D.C.: Library of Congress, 1979–   . (Quarterly.) Gives a reproduction of the catalog cards for motion pictures, filmstrips, slides, videorecordings, kits, and other materials for projection released in the United States and Canada which have educational or instructional value. Continues *Film and Other Materials for Projection.* Published on microfiche. 1983–   .

FILMSTRIPS

Educators Guide to Free Filmstrips. Randolph, Wis.: Educators Progress Service, 1949–   . (Annual.) Lists, describes filmstrips and gives sources. Since 1975 in 2 vols.

National Information Center for Educational Media.[7] *Index to 35mm Educational Filmstrips.* 8th ed. Albuquerque, N.M.: National Information Center for Educational Media, 1986. 4 vols. Gives bibliographical and other data on 35-mm filmstrips in all subject areas.

---

[7] National Information Center for Educational Media (NICEM) catalogs and stores in computerized form current and comprehensive data on all types of nonbook educational media. Data bases are available through Lockheed's DIALOG System.

MICROFORMS

Guide to Microforms in Print: Author-Title. Westport, Conn.: Microform Review, 1978– . (Annual.) Lists microforms available from United States publishers; does not include dissertations and theses. *Guide to Microforms in Print: Subject.* Weston, Conn.: Microform Review, 1978. (Annual.) A companion to *Guide to Microforms in Print: Author-Title*; covers all forms of microreproductions; gives bibliographical and ordering information.

MUSIC

Roach, Helen. *Spoken Records.* 3d ed. Metuchen, N.J.: Scarecrow Press, 1970. Gives a critical evaluation of commercially produced recordings selected for their literary or historical merit, interest, or entertainment value; includes all types of recordings.

U.S. Library of Congress. *Library of Congress Catalogs: National Union Catalog: Music.* Washington, D.C.: Government Printing Office, 1973– . (Semiannual.) A reproduction of cards in the catalogs of the Library of Congress for music scores, sheet music, libretti, and books about music and musicians; arranged alphabetically; has a subject index. Continues *Music and Phonorecords* and *Music, Books on Music, and Sound Recordings*; includes sound recordings of all kinds.

TAPES

Educators Guide to Free Audio and Video Materials. Randolph, Wis.: Educators Progress Service, 1977– . (Annual.) Describes and gives pertinent information about the sources and uses of these materials.

National Information Center for Educational Media. *Index to Educational Audio Tapes.* 5th ed. Albuquerque, N.M.: National Information Center for Educational Media, 1980. Gives a brief summary of contents of each tape, audience level, availability, and description; has subject index.

————. *Audiocassette Finder.* Albuquerque, N.M.: National Information Center for Educational Media, 1986. A subject guide to literature on audiocassettes, covers more than 30,000 audiocassettes in all areas.

TRANSPARENCIES

National Information Center for Educational Media. *Index to Educational Overhead Transparencies.* 6th ed. Los Angeles: National Information Center for Educational Media, 1980. 2 vols. Gives summary, description, availability, and audience; has subject index.

EXAMPLES OF PROFESSIONAL JOURNALS[8]

American Record Guide. New York: American Record Guide, 1934– . (Monthly.) Incorporates the *American Tape Guide* (formerly *The American Music Lover*); reviews recordings and tapes; covers classical records and jazz recordings; gives reviews of music and drama.

AV Communication Review, Washington, D.C.: Association for Educational Communications and Technology, National Education Association, 1953– . (Quarterly.) Emphasizes the theoretical aspects of AV; has technical articles on the use of materials in learning; gives book reviews and abstracts of research.

Tech Trends. Washington, D.C.: Association for Educational Communications and Technology, National Education Association, 1956– . (Monthly, September–May.) Official journal of the association; each issue is devoted to one theme; has practical information about equipment and techniques; includes news items; carries an index to reviews of audiovisual materials in other publications. Formerly *Audiovisual Instruction, Instructional Innovator*.

Review Questions

CHAPTER 14. NONBOOK INFORMATION SOURCES

1. Name and discuss the various types of nonbook materials. How are these materials organized and arranged in your library?

2. Discuss CD-ROM. What CD-ROMs are available in your library? What are the advantages of the CD-ROM format?

3. Which of the nonbook materials named in Question 1 require equipment? Which ones can students produce? Which ones are useful

[8] In addition to the journals in the audiovisual fields, there are journals which carry reviews of nonbook materials as regular features, for example, *Booklist* and *Library Journal*. Professional journals in specific subject fields, such as art, music, social sciences, and so on, frequently include evaluations of nonbook materials. Additional aids in locating information about audiovisual materials are the periodical indexes; see listings under such subject headings as "Audiovisual Aids," "Audiovisual Equipment," and "Audiovisual Instruction."

in preparing a class assignment? Which ones can be used in a multimedia presentation?

4. What are the rules and regulations governing the use of nonbook sources? Do nonbook sources circulate?

5. Which of the sources listed on pp. 167–170 would help you locate free materials, an audiocassette, sheet music, a film?

CHAPTER

15

Government Publications

A government publication is a publication issued (or purchased) at public expense by authority of Congress or any other government office or institution—national, state, or local—for distribution to government officials or to the public. Documents which contain the records of government in their original form are placed in government archives. With some exceptions (for example, classified materials) they are made available to libraries, organizations, and individuals in published form.

Some kinds of government publications are issued at all levels of government—national, state, and municipal—but the chief source of government publications is the federal government. It is said that the United States government is the largest single publisher in the world. Each year the departments, offices, and agencies of the federal government prepare and issue tens of thousands of publications. The Government Printing Office operates twenty-four bookstores around the country, which carry a selection of titles. Any title currently on sale by the GPO can be ordered at these bookstores.

During the early years of our nation's history, printing was done by printers selected by Congress under a contract system. The publications of these contract printers were often poorly made and inadequately indexed, and sometimes they were not even identifiable as government publications. In 1846, Congress created a Joint Committee on Printing, composed of three members from each house, to bring about reforms in printing practices. In 1852, a Superintendent of Public Printing was appointed to supervise the work of the printers who were selected under the contract system. The establishment of a national printing plant was authorized by Congress in 1860, and the United States government began doing its own printing in 1861.

The United States Government Printing Office is an independent body in the legislative branch of the government. The Public Printer, who is appointed by the President with the approval of the Senate, is responsible for its management. The Congressional Joint Committee on Printing has jurisdiction over the Government Printing Office in matters pertaining to the materials used in printing, wages of employees, and the efficient operation of the Office; it controls the arrangement and style of the *Congressional Record* and the *Congressional Directory*. The Superintendent of Documents (an office created in the Government Printing Office in 1895) is responsible for centralized distribution of government publications.

The Superintendent of Documents sells government publications to individuals, organizations, and institutions; distributes them to depository[1] libraries; compiles and distributes catalogs and lists; and provides information, upon request, about government publications.

Individuals may obtain certain government publications free, when available, from members of Congress or from the issuing agency, or they may purchase them from the Superintendent of Documents. Free price lists are issued by certain agencies and lists of selected publications are available, free of charge, from the Superintendent of Documents.

Purpose and Kinds of Government Publications

Government publications grow out of the peculiar function of the governmental agencies which issue them and are a public record of the operation and activities of the government. They provide a means of keeping the public informed, so that each citizen can understand and make use of the services the government provides and can carry out more intelligently the duties of citizenship.

---

[1] The distribution free of charge of federal government publications to designated libraries was authorized by act of Congress, February 5, 1859. The law provided for one depository library for each congressional district in the United States and for two depositories at large for each state. All state libraries and the libraries of land-grant colleges and universities were named federal depositories. Government publications in depository libraries are permanent and are available to the public, at least for reference use. The Depository Library Act of 1962 (Public Law 87-579) increased the total number of depository libraries to 792 and made available to them practically all government publications, including those not printed at the United States Government Printing Office. There are now more than 1370 Federal Depository Libraries in the United States and its territories and possessions: Guam, the Canal Zone, Puerto Rico, and the Virgin Islands.

The contents of government publications are as varied as the departments, agencies, and bureaus which issue them, and they cover every subject area. They include annual reports, transcripts of congressional hearings, statistical analyses, manuals of instruction, recordings of proceedings, bibliographies, directories, speeches, rules and regulations, results of research, maps, atlases, nonbook materials, journals, and travel information.

They are printed or processed (that is, duplicated by some means—photocopy or other process), and they appear in almost every form: loose-leaf, unbound and bound books, pamphlets, leaflets, newspapers, periodicals, maps, charts, multivolume reports, abstracts, motion pictures, filmstrips, posters, and catalogs of art reproductions; some are examples of fine printing.

Usefulness of Government Publications

Government publications provide primary source material in many areas, especially in statistics, in government operations, and in certain areas of the sciences, such as the results of scientific and medical research or patent and copyright applications. They provide information of many kinds which is not available from any other source. They are useful in most areas of study but are particularly useful in the study of history, the social sciences, education, personnel management, and the physical and biological sciences. Prepared by specialists who are in reality writing about their particular activities, they can be considered authoritative in the subjects they cover. They are up to date in that they present the latest information available to the agency which issues them. Many government publications provide bibliographies which are useful for further study and research. In general, the publications are concise and readable.

Organization and Arrangement of Government Publications in Libraries

Library users are often confused by the great number of government publications and do not know how to select or locate them. There are several ways in which libraries organize and arrange them.

1. They may be classified, cataloged, and shelved like other library materials. This is usually the case if the library receives only a few titles. If

government publications are treated like other library materials, they will be assigned a number from the classification system in use in the library and will be arranged on the shelves according to the call number. In this case, the reader will locate them by using the library catalog, just as any other kind of library material is located.

2. They may be classified and cataloged like other library materials but kept in a special file or section of shelves. If this is the case, the words "Gov. Doc." may be added to the call number.

3. They may be classified as "Government Documents" (or "Government Publications") and arranged alphabetically or numerically on shelves or in filing cabinets. Where this system is used, a listing, index, or catalog is kept nearby.

4. Some government publications in a given library may be classified and cataloged like other library materials, and others in the same library may be treated as government publications and kept in a separate place. The physical location will be included in the call number.

5. They may be treated as a separate collection, as they are in depository libraries, and arranged by the classification number of the issuing agency.

In general, the printed bibliographies or lists published by the Superintendent of Documents serve as an index to government publications when they are treated as a separate collection, as in a depository library. Instead of looking in the library catalog for a government publication, the students will consult a printed bibliography, such as the *Monthly Catalog* (Figure 15.1), in much the same manner as they would a periodical index. The printed bibliography will give the information needed to locate the item on the shelf. The location symbol is a combination of letters of the alphabet, which designate the governmental agency which issued the publication, plus Arabic numerals, which designate the individual office and the kind of publication (leaflet, bulletin, report, etc.), and letters and Arabic numerals which make up the number for that specific publication.

For example, the Defense Department is designated D, from the first distinctive letter in the title; the Secretary of Defense is designated D 1, and all annual reports are given the symbol .1. Thus the symbol for the annual report of the Secretary of Defense is D 1.1.

Every item in the printed symbol is important in locating a given publication in a library which uses this kind of organization. Every reference to the publication is important when ordering a publication from the Superintendent of Documents.

Examples of Superintendent of Documents classification numbers and the order in which they would appear on the shelf are:

D 1.2:	D 1.6/2:	D 1.16/3:	D 1.42:	D 7.2:
B 85/977-81	C 49	8	10	P 44/976

The printed bibliographies may provide descriptive and evaluative annotations for the publications listed and are useful in determining the kind of government publication to select for a particular problem.

Reference Sources

In addition to the printed bibliographies and lists, there are reference works to aid the researcher in choosing government publications for particular purposes. Listed below are (1) printed bibliographies and lists of government publications and (2) reference sources which are helpful in finding and using them.

BIBLIOGRAPHIES AND LISTS

U.S. Library of Congress. Exchange and Gifts Division. *Monthly Checklist of State Publications*. Washington, D.C.: Government Printing Office, 1910– . Arranged alphabetically by state; lists publications received by the Library of Congress; gives full bibliographic information and, in some cases, contents.

U.S. Superintendent of Documents. *Monthly Catalog of United States Government Publications*. Washington, D.C.: Government Printing Office, 1895– . Provides complete bibliographical information about each document (author, title, issuing agency, date, etc.—see Figure 15.1.) Includes sales information. Also available on-line from DIALOG.

USEFUL REFERENCE SOURCES

American Statistics Index. Washington, D.C.: Congressional Information Service, 1973– . (Annual, monthly, and quarterly supplements.) "A comprehensive guide and index to the statistical publications of the U.S. government" (subtitle); aims to provide access to all statistics produced by Federal agencies. In two parts: *Index* section and *Abstract* section. Indexed by subject, names, and categories; a microfiche service provides most of the documents indexed; searchable on-line through DIALOG and ORBIT.

1 ——————NATIONAL INSTITUTE OF EDUCATION
Education Dept.
Washington, DC 20208

ERIC documents may be ordered in microfiche or paper copy
from the ERIC Document Reproduction Service (EDRS), 3900
Wheeler Avenue, Alexandria, VA 22304. (800) 227-3742. To
obtain an order form, contact EDRS or consult any issue of
Resources in Education (RIE) .

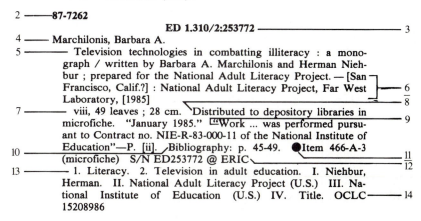

2 ————87-7262

ED 1.310/2:253772 ——————————————— 3

4 —— Marchilonis, Barbara A.
5 ———————— Television technologies in combatting illiteracy : a monograph / written by Barbara A. Marchilonis and Herman Niehbur ; prepared for the National Adult Literacy Project. — [San
Francisco, Calif.?] : National Adult Literacy Project, Far West ——— 6
Laboratory, [1985] ——— 8
7 ———————— viii, 49 leaves ; 28 cm. Distributed to depository libraries in
microfiche. "January 1985." Work ... was performed pursu- ——— 9
ant to Contract no. NIE-R-83-000-11 of the National Institute of
10 Education"—P. [ii]. Bibliography: p. 45-49. ●Item 466-A-3
(microfiche) S/N ED253772 @ ERIC ——— 11
——— 12
13 ———————— 1. Literacy. 2. Television in adult education. I. Niehbur,
Herman. II. National Adult Literacy Project (U.S.) III. National Institute of Education (U.S.) IV. Title. OCLC———— 14
15208986

Subject Index

January — June 1987

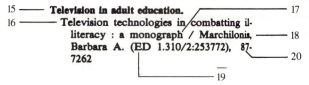

15 —— **Television in adult education.** ——— 17
16 ———————— Television technologies in combatting illiteracy : a monograph / Marchilonis, ——— 18
Barbara A. (ED 1.310/2:253772), 87- ——— 20
7262 ——— 19

F I G U R E 15.1

Excerpt from Monthly Catalog of United States Government Publications, *May 1977,
p. 54, and the* Subject Index, *pp. 1–1150. (1) Government agency which issued the
publication. (2) Location in the* Monthly Catalog: *items are listed sequentially. (3) Education
Department classification number. (4) Author. (5) Title. (6) Place, publisher, date of publication. (7) Collation. (8) Depository information. (9) Explanatory note. (10) Publication has a
bibliography. (11) Item is available to depository libraries on microfiche. (12) It is an ERIC
publication; ED number. (13) Subject headings and added entry headings. (14) The number
assigned by OCLC to identify this record in the data base. (15) Heading in the subject index.
(16) Title. (17) The publication is a monograph (government publications are issued in many
formats). (18) Author. (19) Education Department classification number: call number. (20)
Location number—not the page number—in the* Monthly Catalog.

Congressional Information Service. *Index to Publications of the United States Congress.* Washington, D.C.: Congressional Information Service, 1970– . (Monthly, with quarterly cumulation; annual cumulation in three volumes in the *CIS/Annual.*) Aims to provide access to all publications of the U.S. Congress except the *Congressional Record*; includes hearings, committee prints, reports, and other Congressional publications. In two parts: the *Index* section gives access by subject, author, and title; the *Abstract* section gives full title of the document and an abstract of most items indexed. Indexed items are available on microfiche; can be searched on-line through System Development Corporation.

Government Reference Books: A Biennial Guide to U.S. Government Publications. Littleton, Colo.: Libraries Unlimited. (Biennial.) Provides an annotated list of directories, bibliographies, indexes, dictionaries, catalogs, biographical dictionaries, handbooks, statistical works, and almanacs arranged by subject.

Morehead, Joe. *Introduction to United States Public Documents.* 3d ed. (Library Science Text Series.) Littleton, Colo.: Libraries Unlimited, 1983. Gives an overview of the function, nature, and use of United States public documents; includes a discussion of the Government Printing Office, the Superintendent of Documents, micropublishing, computer-based bibliographical services, federal audiovisual information, and the depository library system; includes only publications of the federal government.

Palic, Vladimir M. *Government Publications: A Guide to Bibliographic Tools.* 4th ed. Washington, D.C.: Library of Congress, 1976. Lists bibliographic aids in the field of government publications issued by the federal government, the states, foreign countries, and international governmental organizations; gives information about each United States agency.

U.S. Library of Congress. Serial and Government Publications Division. *Popular Names of U.S. Government Reports.* 4th ed. Compiled by Bernard A. Bernier, Jr. and Karen A. Wood. Washington, D.C.: Library of Congress, 1984.

Schwarzkopf, Le Roy C. (comp.). *Guide to Popular U.S. Government Publications.* Littleton, Colo.: Libraries Unlimited, 1986. Lists and annotates some 2900 publications in eighty-three subject areas of interest to the general reader such as energy conservation, careers, and health.

Review Questions

CHAPTER 15. GOVERNMENT PUBLICATIONS

1. Discuss the purpose, availability, sources, and usefulness of government publications.
2. How are government publications organized and arranged in a library?
3. What is a government documents depository library?
4. See p. 177. What information is given in this excerpt from the *Monthly Catalog of Government Publications?* How much of this information do you need to order this publication?
5. In what ways are government publications useful to a student doing research on a subject?

PART

4

Information Sources in the Subject Fields

CHAPTER

 16

Subject Information Sources

A general reference source, which has many subject specialists on its editorial staff, provides much information on the different subject fields; however, since the aim of the general reference source is to give wide and unrestricted coverage, specialized treatment on any one subject is necessarily limited.

For those persons who require more than general treatment of a specific subject, there are specialized reference sources in every subject area.

A subject reference source[1] can be defined as a publication in which items of information about one particular subject—literature, history, music, sports, education—are brought together from many sources and arranged so that individual items can be found quickly and easily.

Subject reference materials introduce the student (or nonspecialist) to the subject matter of the different branches of knowledge.

1. They supplement general reference by giving more specific information and by including specialized information omitted from the general reference sources.
2. They provide specialized definitions and explanations for the words and phrases in a given field which are not found in general word dictionaries.
3. They trace the growth of important ideas in a subject area.
4. They provide an introduction to the development of the literature of the subject.
5. They give authoritative information on major questions and issues in a specialized area.

---

[1] Nonbook sources are discussed in Chapter 14.

6. They explain and clarify concepts.

7. They locate, describe, and evaluate the literature of the field.

8. They provide facts which indicate trends, and they summarize the events of a given year in a given subject field.

Subject information sources are adapted to the peculiar characteristics of the subject under consideration. For example, in music there are dictionaries of musical themes and musical scores; in art, catalogs of reproductions and auctions; and in science, handbooks of tables and formulas.

Kinds and Purposes of Subject Information Sources

The kinds of information sources in each subject field are the same as those in the general area, and they serve similar purposes for a given subject. Not all the reference materials listed below provide all types of information indicated.

1. Bibliographies and guides
   a Point out the literature of the field in question
   b Indicate works which may not be in the library and therefore serve as aids to further search
   c Provide descriptive and evaluative information which the catalog card cannot include and point out materials in the library which are not listed in the catalog, such as periodical articles, parts of books, and so on
   d Arrange works according to form: dictionaries, histories, encyclopedias, handbooks, indexes, and books of criticism (if the subject field is literature), and give instructions regarding their use

   Examples:
   Bibliography of American Literature
   A Reader's Guide to the Great Religions

2. Indexes
   a Indicate where periodical articles on a subject can be found
   b Indicate collections in which plays, short stories, essays, and poems can be found
   c Analyze books and parts of books

Examples:
Short Story Index
Applied Science and Technology Index

3. Dictionaries
   a Provide specialized definitions and explanations of terminology and concepts
   b Help to establish terminology
   c Serve as a guide to current as well as historical usage of words and phrases
   d Give short, concise answers to questions
   e May give chronology
   f May give biographical information
   g May give pronunciation

Examples:
Harper's Dictionary of Music
Electronics Dictionary

4. Encyclopedias
   a Give a "summary treatment" of the different phases and aspects of a subject
   b Explain historical backgrounds, trends, and the influence of events outside the subject area, such as the influence of social conditions on the literature of a period
   c Trace the development of ideas in a subject field

Examples:
Encyclopedia of World Art
The Encyclopedia of Philosophy

5. Handbooks and manuals
   a Identify references, allusions, dates, quotations, and characters in literature
   b Summarize literary plots
   c Provide statistics and useful bits of information
   d Give instructions in specialized areas

Examples:
The Oxford Companion to American Literature
Halliwell's Film Guide

6. Yearbooks and annuals
    a Summarize events of the past year, including research projects undertaken and completed
    b Provide a source for hard-to-locate items of information

    Examples:
    Yearbook of Agriculture
    Municipal Yearbook

7. Collections (anthologies)
    a Bring together in one place selections or quotations from essays, poetry, drama, short stories, periodicals, and other forms of literature
    b Serve as source materials for courses in literature, history, education, psychology, and other subject fields

    Examples:
    The Oxford Dictionary of Quotations
    Documents of American History

8. Atlases and gazetteers
    a Provide geographical information in any subject area in maps, text, or both
    b Give overall picture emphasizing location of industries, products, literature

    Examples:
    Atlas of American History
    Oxford Economic Atlas of the World

9. Biographical dictionaries
    a Provide concise information about important persons in a subject field: authors, scholars, scientists, educators
    b May include bibliographies and evaluations of an author's work

    Examples:
    World Authors, 1970–1975
    American Men and Women of Science

10. Reference histories give factual information, trends, and main facts of development, covering
    a Chronology
    b Interpretation of events
    c Biographical data
    d Bibliographical information

    Examples:
    The Oxford History of English Literature
    The Cambridge History of American Literature

11. Professional journals provide up-to-date articles, essays, book reviews, and other material relating specifically to the subject matter of a given branch of knowledge

    Examples:
    American Journal of Philosophy
    Scientific American

12. Abstract journals contain abstracts of periodical and other literature. An abstract is a brief digest or summary which gives the essential points of an article, pamphlet, book, monograph, or report. An abstract journal is a collection of such abstracts (in a particular field) with subject and author indexes. Usually an abstract of a work gives the researcher enough information to decide whether or not the entire work should be read. Abstract journals give bibliographical information regarding the works abstracted. Abstracts may be in the original language in which the work appeared, or they may be in translation.

    Examples:
    Psychological Abstracts
    Science Abstracts

13. Nonbook information sources are available in all subject fields. They include audiovisual materials, disk and tape recordings, transparencies, multimedia kits, videorecordings, musical scores, microforms, and data bases. (See also Chapter 14 and Figure 14.1.)

14. Government publications cover every subject area. These materials are discussed in Chapter 15.

The choice of an information source in a subject field, as in a general area, depends upon the nature of the question to be answered: (1) the kind of information required, (2) the subject area of which it is a part, and (3) the factors affecting the question, such as time and location.

Using Subject Information Sources[2]

Reference materials in the subject fields are located in the library catalog under author or editor, title, and subject. Subject headings consist of the subject, subdivided by kind of material: for example, American literature— Bibliographies; Education—Yearbooks, English language— Dictionaries; Literature—Dictionaries.

Efficient use of subject sources is dependent upon an understanding of (1) the purposes of each kind of subject reference source, (2) the organization and the arrangement of the material, and (3) the distinguishing features. Before using a subject information source, one should examine the table of contents and the preliminary pages which explain the purpose, the plan and arrangement, and any special features.

Chapters 17 to 24 introduce the several subject areas and present representative sources in each area. The subject fields discussed are the major classes of knowledge as they are organized in the Dewey Decimal Classification System. They are presented in the order in which they appear in the classification schedule. Not all the materials discussed in the preceding paragraphs are found in each subject field.

Since new sources and new editions of old ones are being published continually, it is necessary to consult the library catalog frequently in order to keep up to date on the subject materials in the library. The titles listed here are only suggestions, they represent but a small portion of the thousands that are available. Each reader will supplement them and, in time, replace them with new publications.

Review Questions

CHAPTER 16. SUBJECT INFORMATION SOURCES

1. Discuss the difference between general and subject reference (information) sources.

---

[2] See also pp. 89–90.

2. What kinds of subject information sources are available? Give an example of each kind.

3. Look in the *Library of Congress Subject Headings* and see how subject information sources are listed, for example, a dictionary of music, an encyclopedia of science, and so on.

4. In what subject field is each of the titles referred to on pp. 184–187?

CHAPTER

 17

Philosophy and Psychology

Philosophy

The first subject class in the Dewey Decimal Classification System (100), as well as in the Library of Congress Classification System (B), is philosophy. When there was infinitely less to learn than there is today, philosophy comprised all learning except technical rules and the practical arts. In the medieval universities, it was the omnibus subject which covered the whole body of sciences and the liberal arts. Remnants of this comprehensive meaning are carried forward in the present in the highest academic degree, doctor of philosophy (Ph.D.), although increased specialization in the social sciences and humanities, as well as in the pure and applied sciences, has greatly narrowed the range of interest and inquiry of most "doctor of philosophy" students.

Derived from two Greek words, *philein*, "to love," and *sophia*, "wisdom," "philosophy" has historically been thought of as both the seeking of wisdom and the wisdom sought. In this day of rapidly advancing science and technology, of wide-sweeping change, and of increasingly complex domestic and world problems which overlap and intertwine and thus require the most mature thought and judgment of generalists as well as specialists, philosophy is more often thought of as the quest for wisdom than as the wisdom for which search is made. Consequently, philosophy is seen as a mode and method of thought, as a continual invitation to those of serious concern to ask reasoned questions of life and to examine and criticize rationally the ends and purposes which men and women establish and the methods they pursue in their efforts to achieve those purposes. Today, no area of investigation is denied to scientific research; correspondingly, no presupposition, premise, prejudice, assumption, belief, or disbelief—in short, no area of action and

190

thought—is "protected" from the disciplined, probing, analytical approach of philosophy.

In this concept of philosophy as the quest for wisdom, the central emphasis is on *values* (morals and ethics) and on the rational ways (logic) by which value judgments can and should be developed and criticized. Philosophy tries to locate, to understand, and to clarify the nature and importance of the issues and values at stake in situations of uncertainty, confusion, dispute, competition, and conflict. Philosophers who are true to the principles and procedures inherent in the philosophical method of inquiry are concerned about mature, serious, constructive, and hard-won matters. On the basis of facts and knowledge which they draw from wide-ranging fields of recorded and observable experience, philosophers offer for critical examination their own concepts, ideas, and propositions, and they seek to analyze rationally the concepts, ideas, and propositions set forth by others.

Consequently, since there is no such thing in a free society as an "established" philosophy—an accepted, authoritative credo of belief and action—but only philosophers and their philosophies, the basic literature of philosophy is the writings of past and present philosophers and critical commentaries upon these writings.

REFERENCE SOURCES IN PHILOSOPHY

Bibliographies and indexes[1]

Bynagle, Hans E. *Philosophy: A Guide to the Reference Literature*. Littleton, Colo.: Libraries Unlimited, 1986. Includes materials for many types of users: professionals, teachers, and graduate and undergraduate students. Illustrated.

DeGeorge, Richard T. *The Philosopher's Guide: To Sources, Research Tools, Professional Life, and Related Fields*. Lawrence, Kan.: Regents Press of Kansas, 1980. Lists materials in philosophy and reference works in related disciplines; covers histories of philosophy, individual philosophers, movements, and professional activities; useful for philosophy students and researchers.

The Philosopher's Index: An International Index to Philosophical Periodicals and Books. Bowling Green, Ohio: Bowling Green University, 1967– . Indexes major American and British philosophical journals and books in philosophy; provides some abstracts.

Tice, Terence, and Slavens, Thomas P. *Research Guide to Philosophy*. (Sources of Information in the Humanities, No. 3.) Chicago: American Library

---

[1] See also Chapter 9, Indexes, and Chapter 13, Bibliographies.

Association, 1983. Provides material on the history of philosophy, various philosophies, such as logic, and reference sources with annotations.

Walford, A. J. (ed.). *Guide to Reference Material.* Vol. II: *Social and Historical Sciences, Philosophy and Religion.* 4th ed. London: Library Association, 1982. Lists recently published sources in philosophy; international in scope.

Dictionaries and encyclopedias

Baldwin, James Mark (ed.). *Dictionary of Philosophy and Psychology.* New ed. New York: The Macmillan Company, 1925. 3 vols. (Reprinted by Peter Smith, 1946.) Out of date for modern developments, but still useful; covers the entire field.

Brugger, Walter (ed.). *Philosophical Dictionary.* (Walter Brugger, editor of the original German edition. Kenneth Baker, translator and editor of the American edition.) Spokane, Wash.: Gonzaga University Press, 1972. Translated from the German *Philosophisches Wörterbuch*: explains philosophical terms; gives the history of philosophy from ancient times to the present; includes coverage of contemporary Anglo-American concerns.

Bullock, Alan, and Stallybrass, Oliver (eds.). *The Harper Dictionary of Modern Thought.* New York: Harper & Row, Publishers, Incorporated, 1977. Covers twentieth-century words and phrases; defines words in their intellectual, historical, and cultural context.

Edwards, Paul (ed.). *The Encyclopedia of Philosophy.* New York: The Macmillan Company and The Free Press, 1967. 8 vols. For specialists and nonspecialists; covers all of philosophy and related disciplines; treats topics at length and emphasizes individual thinkers; provides bibliographies and many cross references; contributors are from all parts of the world; Vol. 8 is the index. (Also available in four vols.)

Flew, Anthony. *A Dictionary of Philosophy.* 2d ed. New York: St. Martin's Press, 1979. Covers terminology, personalities, and vocabulary of philosophers from classical to modern times.

Lacey, A. R. *A Dictionary of Philosophy.* Boston: Routledge & Kegan Paul, Ltd., 1976. Published in paperback by Charles Scribner's Sons, 1976. Intended for students and nonspecialists; covers only western philosophy; defines terms; explains concepts; gives some biographies; entries are brief; some have bibliographies.

Reese, William L. *Dictionary of Philosophy and Religion: Eastern and Western Thought.* Atlantic Highlands, N.J.: Humanities Press, 1980. Delineates the ideas of a particular thinker or school of thought; explains various meanings of a term; lists principal writings of individual philosophers.

Wiener, Philip P. (ed.). *Dictionary of the History of Ideas: Studies of Selected Pivotal Ideas*. New York: Charles Scribner's Sons, 1973. 4 vols. *Index*, 1974. A collection of long, scholarly articles by an international group of experts; provides interdisciplinary coverage of many topics in the history of ideas, including philosophy, history, religion, science, mathematics, literature, the arts, and the social sciences; bibliographies are provided.

Handbooks and digests

Burr, John R. (ed.). *Handbook of World Philosophy: Contemporary Developments since 1945*. Westport, Conn.: Greenwood Press, 1980. Surveys recent philosophical trends throughout the world. Provides a selected bibliography and a directory of associations.

Magill, Frank N. *World Philosophy: Essay-reviews of 225 Major Works*. Englewood Cliffs, N.J.: Salem Press, 1982. 5 vols. Reviews important philosophical works from the sixth century B.C. to the present with commentary and bibliographical references. Major philosophers are represented by one work; chronologically arranged; has a glossary of terms.

Reed, Jeffrey G., and Baxter, Pam M. *Library Use: A Handbook for Psychology*. Washington, D.C.: American Psychological Association, 1983. Written especially for the undergraduate; emphasizes selection and use of library resources and research methods; includes computerized sources.

Biographical dictionaries[2]

Directory of American Philosophers. Bowling Green, Ohio: Philosophy Documentation Center, Bowling Green University, 1962– . (Biennial.) Companion volume to *International Directory of Philosophy and Philosophers*; gives a list of colleges and universities in the United States and Canada, with information about the philosophy department, if any; includes a list of societies, journals, and publishers of materials in this field.

Directory of American Scholars. 8th ed. Vol. IV: *Philosophy, Religion and Law*. Edited by the Jaques Cattell Press. New York: R. R. Bowker Company, 1982. Devoted to United States and Canadian scholars; gives brief biographical information; provides a geographical index by state or province.

International Directory of Philosophy and Philosophers. 1st ed. Bowling Green, Ohio: Philosophy Documentation Center, 1966– . Published under the auspices of the International Institute of Philosophy with the aid of UNESCO; serves as a worldwide guide to philosophy; provides survey essays on the history and character of philosophy in the various parts of

---

[2] See also Chapter 10, Biographical Dictionaries.

the world; lists organizations, institutes, research centers, members of college and university philosophy faculties, and associations and societies.

Examples of professional journals in philosophy[3]

The Journal of Philosophy. New York: Journal of Philosophy, Inc., Columbia University, 1904–   . (Fortnightly.) Provides historical articles on philosophers or systems; includes notes and news.

Journal of the History of Ideas. Philadelphia: Temple University, 1940–   . (Quarterly.) "Devoted to cultural and intellectual history" (subtitle); offers articles on the history of philosophy, literature, the arts, natural and social sciences, religion, and political and social movements; emphasizes the influence of one figure or school on another; has lengthy book reviews.

Journal of the History of Philosophy. St. Louis, Mo.: Washington University, Department of Philosophy. 1963–   . (Quarterly.) Includes articles on the history of western philosophy; some are in foreign languages; has book reviews.

The Modern Schoolman. St. Louis, Mo.: St. Louis University, 1925–   . (Quarterly.) Aims to promote original and scholarly contributions in all fields of philosophy; includes book reviews.

Philosophical Review. Ithaca, N.Y.: Cornell University, 1892–   . (Quarterly.) Publishes papers on problems of interest to contemporary philosophers; discusses philosophers and their ideas; gives book reviews.

Psychology

Psychology, from the Greek words *psyche*, meaning "mind" or "soul," and *logos*, meaning "law," has historically been the science which treats of the mind in any of its aspects—function, organization and structure, and effect on behavior. Once a part of philosophy and still a close companion, psychology developed and became a separate branch of learning within the past century. Class B of the Library of Congress Classification and 100 of the Dewey Decimal Classification include both philosophy and psychology.

In recent times, psychology has been thought of as the serious study of the organism as an individual whole, as the study of the organism and its

---

[3] See also *Ulrich's International Periodicals Directory*, 27th ed., and *Magazines for Libraries*, 5th ed., edited by Bill Katz and Linda S. Katz.

activities rather than of physiological functions. For example, the study of the functions of the brain is thought of more as a physiological than a psychological theme. Thus the general theme of psychology is the study of the activities of the total organism (humans and lower animals) in its interrelations with its physical environment and with its social setting and influences.

Psychology is often referred to and identified in terms of a school or system; for example, behaviorist psychology or Gestalt psychology.

Perhaps the best and most comprehensive way in which to see modern psychology is through an acquaintance with some of its many subdivisions, which are determined by, and are named to describe, the kinds of problems studied. These kinds and fields of psychological study are so connected that one should not try to arrange them either chronologically or in order of their current importance. Some of the more important subdivisions of psychology are abnormal, analytic, animal, applied, experimental, genetic, motor, and physiological. Other subdivisions of psychology are child, adolescent, adult, educational, social, and industrial. Related fields include psychiatry, psychoanalysis, psychotherapy, and psychopathology.

REPRESENTATIVE REFERENCE SOURCES IN PSYCHOLOGY

Bibliographies[4]

Harvard University. *The Harvard List of Books in Psychology*. 4th ed. Compiled and annotated by psychologists at Harvard University. Cambridge, Mass.: Harvard University Press, 1971. A guide to important titles in psychology; arranged by types of psychology; gives some evaluations.

Indexes[5]

Council on Research in Bibliography. *Mental Health Book Review Index*. New York: Research Center for Mental Health, New York University, 1956–1972. Gives references to book reviews which appeared in some 200 journals, many of which are not listed elsewhere; worldwide in coverage; useful especially for large and specialized libraries.

Index Medicus. (See p. 238.)

Dictionaries, encyclopedias, and handbooks

Corsini, Reymond J. *Encyclopedia of Psychology*. New York: John Wiley & Sons, Inc., 1984. Treats concepts, theories, and terminology; includes biographies and bibliographical references; provides brief as well as indepth coverage.

---

[4] See also Chapter 13, Bibliographies.
[5] See also Chapter 9, Indexes.

English, Horace Bidwell, and English, Ava C. (eds.). *A Comprehensive Dictionary of Psychological and Psychoanalytical Terms*. New York: Longmans, Green & Co., Inc., 1958. Gives definitions of all terms that are used frequently in a specialized or technical sense; is not encyclopedic.

Eysenck, H. J. (ed.). *Encyclopedia of Psychology*. New York: Herder and Herder, 1972. 3 vols. International in coverage; treats all facets of psychology today; gives definitions of terms, historical overview, discussion of research and scientific controversies, and descriptions of various schools of psychology and related disciplines; gives background and summary of leading international opinion on current issues; includes bibliographies.

Goldenson, Robert M. (ed.). *The Encyclopedia of Human Behavior: Psychology, Psychiatry, and Mental Health*. Garden City, N.Y.: Doubleday & Company, 1970. 2 vols. Aims to cover all major phases of these areas: presents essential information for students and nonprofessionals; gives definitions, illustrative cases, and illustrations.

Harré, Rom, and Lamb, Roger. *The Encyclopedic Dictionary of Psychology*. Cambridge, Mass.: MIT Press, 1983. Gives an overview of psychology, definitions, and theories; treats many areas of contemporary psychology.

Biographical dictionaries and directories[6]

American Men and Women of Science: Social and Behavioral Sciences. 16th ed. Edited by Jaques Cattell Press. New York: R. R. Bowker Company, 1986. 8 vols. Provides a biographical profile of persons engaged in teaching or research in psychology.

American Psychological Association. *Biographical Directory*. Washington, D.C.: American Psychological Association, 1970– . (Triennial.) Lists affiliated organizations; gives brief biographical information on members and background information on the association.

Yearbooks

Annual Review of Psychology. Palo Alto, Calif.: Annual Reviews, 1950– . Gives interpretative and evaluative reviews by psychologists of many topics in contemporary psychology.

Examples of professional and abstract journals in psychology[7]

American Journal of Psychology. Urbana: University of Illinois Press, 1887– . (Quarterly.) Publishes reports of original research; emphasis on experimental psychology; includes short notes, discussions, book reviews.

---

[6] See also Chapter 10, Biographical Dictionaries.

Journal of General Psychology. Provincetown, Mass.: The Journal Press, 1928– . (Quarterly.) Covers experimental, physiological, and comparative psychology.

Psychological Abstracts. Arlington, Va.: American Psychological Association, Inc., 1927– . (Monthly.) Contains nonevaluative summaries of the world's literature in psychology and related disciplines; includes abstracts from journals, books, technical reports, and other scientific publications, abstracts are arranged under sixteen major subject categories; has author and subject indexes. Available on-line since 1967 as Psychological Abstracts Information Services.

The Psychological Review. Lancaster, Pa.: American Psychological Association, Inc., 1894– . (Bimonthly.) Presents articles of theoretical significance to any area of scientific endeavor in psychology.

Psychology Today. New York: Ziff-Davis Publishing Company, 1967– . (Monthly.) Presents current developments in American psychology for professionals and nonprofessionals; broad coverage.

Review Questions

CHAPTER 17. PHILOSOPHY AND PSYCHOLOGY

1. Define philosophy. Compare the definition of philosophy in a general word dictionary with the definition in a subject dictionary. In what ways do they differ?

2. Look in the library catalog or in the *Library of Congress Subject Headings* for the subdivisions of the subject "philosophy." What aspects are covered?

3. Name the kinds of literature in the field of philosophy. Give an example of the types of reference sources. What are the primary sources in philosophy?

4. What is the derivation of the word "psychology"?

5. Which of the titles listed on pp. 195–197 would cover: definitions of terminology, schools of psychology, persons in the field?

6. What kinds of sources would be helpful to a beginning student in psychology? Why?

---

[7] See also *Ulrich's International Periodicals Directory*, 27th ed., and *Magazines for Libraries*, 5th ed., edited by Bill Katz and Linda S. Katz.

CHAPTER

 18

Religion and Mythology

Religion

The story of books and libraries (Chapter 1) revealed that the earliest records of every civilization contain religious or moral works. Since the time of Cicero, who defined religion as "the worship of the gods," attempts have been made to define religion. Some definitions are:

Action or conduct indicating a belief in, reverence for, and desire to please, a divine ruling power; the exercise or practice of rites or observance implying this.[1]

Religion is a feeling of dependence upon the unseen powers which control our destiny, accompanied by a desire to come into friendly relations with them.[2]

A specific and institutionalized set of beliefs and practices generally agreed upon by a number of persons or sects.[3]

A cause, principle, or system of beliefs held to with ardor and faith.[4]

---

[1] *The Oxford English Dictionary*, VII, 1933, 310.

[2] George Thomas White Patrick, *Introduction to Philosophy*, rev. ed. (Boston: Houghton Mifflin Company, 1935), p. 37.

[3] *The Random House College Dictionary*, rev. ed. (New York: Random House, Inc., 1975). Copyright © 1982 by Random House, Inc.

[4] *Webster's New Collegiate Dictionary* (Springfield, Mass.: G. & C. Merriam Company, 1981), p. 969. By permission. From *Webster's New Collegiate Dictionary* © 1981 by G. & C. Merriam Co., Publishers of the Merriam-Webster ® Dictionary.

In Hebrew and Christian thought, religion is man's recognition of his relation to God and his expression of that relation in faith, worship, and conduct.[5]

There are many religions, and while there is no generally accepted definition of religion, religions have common characteristics, such as form or forms of worship; rites, rituals, and practices; a set of beliefs, rules or laws, or guiding principles; and sacred writings.

Religious literature is perhaps the largest subject class in extent and variety. There are the basic scriptures or writings of each religion or sect and commentaries on them, historical studies, devotional and inspirational works, rituals, informational literature, church doctrines, works of interpretation, ecclesiastical law, religious music, lives of the saints, lives of important persons in each religious group, statistical information, periodical literature, and many nonbook forms—audio, visual, and audiovisual materials.

Reference works in the field of religion, like all other reference sources, are compilations of factual information and are planned to answer specific questions about religions and the literature of the various religions and to aid in further study of a given area. These reference sources include bibliographies, guides, indexes, concordances, dictionaries, encyclopedias, books of quotations, collections of hymns, digests of religious literature, historical and Bible atlases, yearbooks, biographical dictionaries, and professional journals. (See Chapter 14 for types of nonbook sources.)

REPRESENTATIVE REFERENCE SOURCES IN RELIGION

Bibliographies, guides, and indexes[6]

Adams, Charles J. (ed.). *A Reader's Guide to the Great Religions.* 2d ed. New York: The Free Press, 1977. A collection of bibliographic essays by authorities on the literature, history, and beliefs of the world's great religions; includes religions of the ancient world, Mexico, and South America; provides guidance on what to read.

Cornish, Graham (ed.). *Religious Periodicals Directory.* Santa Barbara, Calif.: ABC-Clio, Inc., 1986. Offers a wide range of periodicals in religion and related fields such as history, anthropology, linguistics, art, and archaeology; worldwide in coverage.

---

[5] Madeleine S. Miller and J. Lane Miller, *Harper's Bible Dictionary*, 8th ed. (New York: Harper & Row, Publishers, 1973), p. 608.

[6] See also Chapter 9, Indexes, and Chapter 13, Bibliographies.

Religion Index One: Periodicals, July–December 1977– . Chicago: American Theological Association, 1978– . (Semiannual.) Formerly entitled *Religious Periodical Literature* (1949–1977); indexes periodicals published in the United States and in foreign countries; has a subject index, an author index with abstracts, and a book review index.

Sandeen, Ernest R., and Hale, Frederick. *American Religion and Philosophy: A Guide to Information Sources*. Detroit: Gale Research Company, 1978. Provides a general introduction to recent secondary literature and key primary documents in religion and philosophy, including general reference works and sources in specific subject areas; gives attention to contributions of other disciplines to religion and philosophy; has brief annotations.

Walford, A. J. (ed.). *Guide to Reference Material*. Vol. II: *Social and Historical Sciences, Philosophy and Religion*. 4th ed. London: Library Association, 1982. Includes materials in the field of religion published in recent years; international in scope.

Concordances

Cruden, Alexander (comp.). *A Complete Concordance to the Holy Scriptures of the Old and New Testaments*. New ed. Westwood, N.J.: Fleming H. Revell Company, n.d. Includes a concordance to the Apocrypha.

Morrison, Clinton. *An Analytical Concordance to the Revised Standard Version of the New Testament*. Philadelphia: The Westminster Press, 1979. Lists and analyzes both the English and the original Greek words of the New Testament; English words and phrases of the *Revised Standard Version* are arranged alphabetically, each entry followed by a definition of the Greek original and the word in Greek in transliteration; uses of the word are listed in context, with identification of the book, chapter, and verse.

Nelson's Complete Concordance of the Revised Standard Version of the Bible. Compiled under the supervision of John W. Ellison. New York: Thomas Nelson & Sons, 1957. Gives context and location of each key word.

The New American Standard Exhaustive Concordance of the Bible. Nashville, Tenn.: A. J. Holman Co., 1981. Lists each key word in the *New American Standard Bible* and every verse where it is found; has more than 400,000 entries.

Strong's Exhaustive Concordance of the Bible with Key-Word Comparison of Selected Words and Phrases in the King James Version with Five Leading Translations. Nashville, Tenn.: Abingdon Press, 1980. Largely a reprint of the original *Strong's* (1894); adds a 225-page "key-word comparison" of selected words and phrases in the *King James Version* with the *Revised Standard*

Version, the *New English Bible*, the *Jerusalem Bible*, the *New International Version*, and the *New American Standard Bible*.

Thompson, Newton Wayland, and Stock, Raymond (comps.). *Complete Concordance to the Bible (Douay Version)*. St. Louis, Mo.: B. Herder Book Company, 1945. Indexes the actual words of the Douay Roman Catholic version of the Bible.

Dictionaries

Abingdon Dictionary of Living Religions. Nashville, Tenn.: Abingdon Press, 1981. Presents the beliefs, practices, historical development, and current status of the religions of the world today; covers sects, doctrines, movements, and sacred writings; major religions are given extensive coverage; includes illustrations, maps, and drawings, and some bibliographies. Useful for students and scholars.

Achteimer, Paul (ed.). *Harper's Bible Dictionary*. New York: Harper & Row, Publishers, 1985. Revision of 8th ed.; covers archaeology, geography, persons, places, developments in theology, and religion; gives some pronunciation; illustrated.

Brandon, S. G. F. (ed.). *A Dictionary of Comparative Religion*. New York: Charles Scribner's Sons, 1970. Articles cover a wide variety of topics relating to the world's religions from prehistoric times to the present; aims to "treat the religions in proportion to their significance in the history of human culture" (Preface).

Childress, James F., and McQuarrie, John. *The Westminster Dictionary of Christian Ethics*. Philadelphia: The Westminster Press, 1986. Represents many points of view; includes contemporary issues; treats basic ethical concepts, biblical and theological; does not have biographical material.

Cross, F. L., and Livingstone, E. A. (eds.). *The Oxford Dictionary of the Christian Church*. 2d ed. London: Oxford University Press, 1974. Covers historical developments, doctrine, and definitions of terms; includes biographies and provides bibliographies; gives attention to recent developments in the churches, movements, and personalities.

Gentz, William. *The Dictionary of Bible and Religion*. Nashville, Tenn.: Abingdon Press, 1986. Gives definitions and explanations of people, places, and events in the Bible and beliefs, practices, and organizations of religion. Jewish and Christian traditions receive more attention than other major religions. Illustrated.

The Interpreter's Dictionary of the Bible. Nashville, Tenn.: Abingdon Press, 1962. 4 vols. "An illustrated encyclopedia identifying and explaining all proper names and significant terms and subjects in the Holy Scriptures, including the Apocrypha, with attention to archaeological discoveries and researches into the life and faith of ancient times" (subtitle). Serves the needs of students, scholars, teachers, preachers, and general readers. Supplementary volume, 1976.

Parrinder, Geoffrey. *A Dictionary of Non-Christian Religions.* Philadelphia; The Westminster Press, 1971. Explains terminology, concepts, gods, and religious systems of all non-Christian religions; covers primitive and classical as well as contemporary religions; emphasis is on Hinduism, Buddhism, and Islam; provides drawings and photographs.

Stoeckle, Bernard (ed.). *Concise Dictionary of Christian Ethics.* New York: Seabury Press, 1979. Intended for undergraduates and educated laypersons; gives articles on major ethical issues from a Roman Catholic perspective; brief definitions as well as longer articles.

Encyclopedias

Bodensieck, Julius H. (ed.). *The Encyclopedia of the Lutheran Church.* Minneapolis: Augsburg Publishing House, 1965. 3 vols. Prepared for the general public as well as for theologians, the clergy, teachers, and students, with contributors from all parts of the world; this standard reference work on the Lutheran Church gives the scope, history, and influence of the church; does not include biographies of living persons.

Eliade, Mircea. *The Encyclopedia of Religion.* New York: Macmillan Publishing Company, 1987. 16 vols. Discusses in detail worldwide religions of Judaism, Christianity, Islam, and Buddhism—growth, development, beliefs, texts, doctrines, practices, leading figures, and current issues; other religions are treated, including ancient religions.

Encyclopaedia Judaica. New York: The Macmillan Company, 1972. 16 vols. Presents all aspects of Jewish life and knowledge up to the present time; gives bibliographies for further reading; includes biographical articles. *Yearbook,* 1973–   .

Hastings, James (ed.). *Encyclopaedia of Religion and Ethics.* New York: Charles Scribner's Sons, 1908–1927. 12 vols. and index. Contains articles on all religions, all the great ethical systems and movements, religious beliefs and customs, philosophical ideas, moral practices, and important persons and places.

The International Standard Bible Encyclopedia. Rev. ed. Grand Rapids, Mich.: Wm. B. Eerdmans Publishing Company, 1979–   . (In progress.) 4 vols. "Aims to include every word in the Bible and the Apocrypha which has a spiritual meaning" (Preface). Defines, identifies, and explains terms and topics in the Bible; includes personal and geographical names; most articles are signed and have bibliographies. For teachers, students, pastors, and laypeople. Vol. II, 1981.

Melton, J. Gordon. *Encyclopedia of American Religions.* 2d ed. Detroit: Gale Research Company, 1986. Gives detailed information on about 1500 religions found in North America: origin, development, and practices; provides name, address, membership, publications, and other directory-type information about the religious groups. *Supplement*, 1987.

The New Catholic Encyclopedia. Prepared by an editorial staff at the Catholic University of America. New York: McGraw-Hill Book Company, 1967. 15 vols. "An international work of reference on the teachings, history, organization, and activities of the Catholic Church and on all institutions, religions, philosophies, and scientific and cultural developments affecting the Catholic Church from the beginning to the present" (subtitle). Vol. XVI: *Supplement 1967–1974.* Edited by David Eggenberger, 1974.

The New Schaff-Herzog Encyclopedia of Religious Knowledge. Based on 3d ed. Grand Rapids, Mich.: Baker Book House, 1951. 13 vols. Covers biblical, historical, doctrinal, and practical theology from the earliest times to the present; includes biography.

Roth, Cecil (ed.). *The Concise Jewish Encyclopedia.* New York: New American Library, 1980. Gives concise information on all aspects of Judaism: history, literature, communities around the world, and outstanding personalities both historical and contemporary. Entries are brief; useful for quick reference.

Books of quotations

Mead, Frank Spencer (ed. and comp.). *The Encyclopedia of Religious Quotations.* Westwood, N.J.: Fleming H. Revell Company, 1965. Contains quotations about religion and related topics from both religious and secular sources.

Stevenson, Burton Egbert. *The Home Book of Bible Quotations.* New York: Harper & Row, Publishers, 1949. Based on the *King James Version* of the Bible; has a key-word concordance index arranged by subject.

Woods, Ralph L. (comp. and ed.). *The World's Treasury of Religious Quotations.* New York: Hawthorn Books, 1966. Offers a great variety of quotations of religious thought from religious and secular sources, modern and ancient; nondenominational; does not include poetry and has only two verses from the Bible.

Digests

Magill, Frank N. (ed.). *Masterpieces of Catholic Literature in Summary Form.* New York: Harper & Row, Publishers, 1965. Presents, in the form of essay-reviews, a selection of Roman Catholic literature from earliest times to the present; includes books in the fields of philosophy, theology, and history.

————. *Masterpieces of Christian Literature in Summary Form*. New York: Harper & Row, Publishers, 1963. 2 vols. A selection of literature in essay-review form from the Protestant viewpoint.

Hymns

Christ-Janer, Albert, and others (eds.). *American Hymns Old and New*. New York: Columbia University Press, 1980. Offers more than 600 American hymns from the British psalters of the seventeenth century to hymns of this century; traces influences on hymns; groups hymns by denomination or type; includes forty new hymns written for this edition.

Julian, John (ed.). *A Dictionary of Hymnology*. Rev. ed. with new supplement. London: John Murray, 1915. Sets forth the origin and history of Christian hymns of all ages and nations.

Atlases

AlFaruqi, Isma'il R., and Sopher, David E. (eds.). *Historical Atlas of the Religions of the World*. New York: The Macmillan Company, 1974. Historical and geographical approach to the world's religions; covers major religions or groups of religions—past and present—including American Indian religions, African religions, and such universal religions as Buddhism, Christianity, and Islam. Maps, bibliographies, and chronologies are provided; covers origin and distribution; locates shrines and temples.

The Macmillan Bible Atlas. Rev. ed. Edited by Yohanan Aharoni and Michael Avi-Yonan. New York: The Macmillan Company, 1977. Uses maps and text to cover all aspects of Bible history.

May, Herbert Gordon, and others (eds.). *Oxford Bible Atlas*. 3d ed. revised by John Day. London: Oxford University Press, 1984. Covers physical geography, historical changes, and geographical name changes; maps are accompanied by explanatory text; includes articles on historical background of the region; gives archaeological data: has a gazetteer.

Yearbooks

Each denomination has its own yearbook which provides information regarding its organization, membership, officers, local officials, development, publications, and annual achievements; it may include articles on doctrine and questions regarding theology. Examples are *American Jewish Yearbook*, *Official Catholic Directory*, and *The Episcopal Church Annual*. The titles listed below cover all denominations.

Mead, Frank Spencer. *Handbook of Denominations in the United States*. 8th ed. revised by Samuel S. Hill. Nashville: Abingdon Press, 1985. Provides factual information on the history, organization, doctrines, and status of more than 250 religious bodies; includes statistical material, a glossary of terms, and bibliographies.

Yearbook of American and Canadian Churches. Prepared and edited in the Office of Research, Evaluation, and Planning of the National Council of the Churches of Christ in the U.S.A. Nashville, Tenn.: Abingdon Press, 1973– . (Annual.) Supersedes *Yearbook of American Churches*; attempts to provide information on most of the established religious groups in the United States and Canada; gives brief historical description of the religious body, names and addresses of officers, organizations, periodicals, and statistics.

Biographical dictionaries[7]

Bowden, Henry Warner (ed.). *Dictionary of American Religious Biography*. Westport, Conn.: Greenwood Press, 1977. Presents 425 biographies of men and women (no longer living) who influenced American religious life; covers more than three centuries and includes religious leaders, reformers, philosophers, and members of minority groups; emphasis is on ordained clergy, but laypersons are represented; gives essential biographical information and an evaluation of the person's contribution to religious history, a brief list of works by the biographee, and bibliographical references.

Directory of American Scholars. 8th ed. Vol. IV: *Philosophy, Religion and Law*, 1982. Covers persons active in the field of religion.

Who's Who in Religion. Chicago: Marquis—Who's Who, 1985. Covers current religious leaders; includes religious educators, church officials, and writers; emphasis is on large denominations, but small groups are included.

Professional journals in religion

Each denomination has its own journals. See *Ulrich's International Periodicals Directory*, 27th ed., and *Magazines for Libraries*, 5th ed., edited by Bill Katz and Linda S. Katz, for a comprehensive listing. The following titles are examples of general-coverage journals in the field of religion.

Church History. Oreland, Pa.: American Society of Church History, 1932– . (Quarterly.) Nondenominational; considers all aspects of church history; gives information on religion in America and abroad; includes book reviews.

---

[7] See also Chap. 10, Biographical Dictionaries.

Harvard Theological Review. Cambridge, Mass.: Harvard University Press, 1908– . (Quarterly.) Nondenominational; covers Bible studies, history and philosophy of religion, and theology.

History of Religions: An International Journal for Comparative Historical Studies. Chicago: University of Chicago Press, 1961– . (Quarterly.) Devoted to the study of historical religious phenomena; one primary aim is the integration of results of the several disciplines of the science of religion.

Mythology

"Mythology" is a collective word, usually thought of by social anthropologists as including the stories and tales (myths) which describe the origin, nature, and adventures of the gods and goddesses of a people. In other words, myths are concerned with the supernatural and are especially associated with religious feasts, festivals, rites, and beliefs. For this reason, mythology is often classified by social scientists as a part of primitive religion. Both mythology and religion have their beginnings in prehistory.

REPRESENTATIVE REFERENCE BOOKS IN MYTHOLOGY

Indexes[8]

Art Index. (See p. 253.)

Encyclopedias and handbooks

Cavendish, Richard (ed.). *Mythology: An Illustrated Encyclopedia.* New York: Rizzoli International Publications, 1980. A survey of world mythology divided into six large geographical areas: Asia, the middle east, the west, Africa, the Americas, the Pacific; brief text; more than 400 illustrations, many in color.

Cotterell, Arthur. *A Dictionary of World Mythology.* New York: G. P. Putnam's Sons, 1980. Gives short articles on the chief mythologies of the world, divided by geographical area, with historical background of the mythologies represented; arranged according to the "seven great traditions of world mythology: West Asia, South and Central Asia, East Asia, Europe, America, Africa, and Oceania." Includes illustrations and bibliographies.

Funk and Wagnalls Standard Dictionary of Folklore, Mythology and Legend. New York: Funk & Wagnalls, 1973. Presents survey articles on the folklore,

---

[8] See also Chapter 9, Indexes.

mythology, and legends of the cultures of the world; includes bibliographical references.

Frazer, Sir James (ed.). *The Golden Bough: A Study in Magic and Religion.* 3d ed., revised. New York: St. Martin's Press, Inc., 1955. 12 vols. A comprehensive collection of information about primitive religions; traces many myths and rites to their prehistoric beginnings.

Gray, Louis Herbert (ed.). *The Mythology of All Races, Greek and Roman.* 26th ed. Boston: Marshall Jones Company, 1958. 13 vols. Includes text and illustrations.

Grimal, Pierre (ed.). *Larousse World Mythology.* New York: G. P. Putnam's Sons, 1965. Translated from two French works, *Mythologies de la Méditerranée au Gange* and *Mythologies des Steppes, des Iles et des Forêts.* Includes mythology of every region in the world; has outstanding illustrations, many in color; a reference work for students of art, literature, history, theology, etc.

Larousse Encyclopedia of Mythology. Rev. ed. New York: G. P. Putnam's Sons, 1968. Covers world mythology; divided by nationalities.

Shapiro, Max. S. *Mythologies of the World: A Concise Encyclopedia.* Garden City, N.Y.: Doubleday & Company, Inc., 1979. Gives short definitions or explanations of gods, heroes, and others in about twenty mythologies from all parts of the world, including Africa and North America. Useful for quick reference.

Tripp, Edward (ed.). *Crowell's Handbook of Classical Mythology.* New York: Thomas Y. Crowell Company, 1970. Designed as a companion to reading, tells major myths of Greece and Rome in readable story form; includes personal and place names.

Review Questions

CHAPTER 18. RELIGION AND MYTHOLOGY

1. What areas of religion are included in the 200 class of the Dewey Decimal System (see p. 47)? What is the LC classification number for religion?

2. List the kinds of religious literature. What kinds are available in your library?

3. Which titles described in this chapter will give information about your religious faith or denomination?

4. Which titles will give information about:
   a All the major religions

   b The non-Christian religions
   c Specific religions or faiths
   d Hymns
   e Number of members in the various denominations
   f The geographical location of religions

5. What is mythology?

6. In what subjects would a knowledge of mythology be useful?

CHAPTER

 19

The Social Sciences and Education

Social Sciences

The social sciences[1] comprise those branches of knowledge which have to do with the activities of the individual as a member of society. Included in the social sciences class of the Dewey Decimal Classification System (300) are sociology, statistics, political science, economics, law, government, social welfare, education,[2] commerce, and customs and folklore.[3] These areas are part of Library of Congress classes H, J, K, and L.

There are numerous reference sources devoted to the subject matter of the several social sciences. They include bibliographies, guides, indexes, dictionaries, encyclopedias, handbooks, yearbooks, biographical dictionaries, atlases, and professional journals.

BIBLIOGRAPHIES AND GUIDES[4]

American Behavioral Scientist. *The ABS Guide to Recent Publications in the Social and Behavioral Sciences.* New York: American Behavioral Scientist, 1965. Lists and annotates a selection of books, pamphlets, and articles

---

[1] The social sciences are not to be confused with "social studies," which are portions of the subject matter of the social sciences suitable for study in elementary and secondary schools and are developed into courses of study which place emphasis on social aims.

[2] Education as a subject field is discussed on p. 220.

[3] For a full discussion of the social sciences, see Edwin R. A. Seligman, "What Are the Social Sciences?" *Encyclopaedia of the Social Sciences*, I (1930), 3–7.

[4] See also Chapter 13, Bibliographies.

from material cited in the "New Studies Section" of the *American Behavioral Scientist* from 1957 to 1964. Supplemented by *Recent Publications in the Social and Behavioral Sciences.* 1966–   . (Annual.)

Ballou, Patricia. *Women: A Bibliography.* 2d ed. Boston: G. K. Hall, 1986. Annotates books, pamphlets, essays, and journal articles about women.

Daniells, Lorna M. *Business Information Sources.* Rev. ed. Berkeley: University of California Press, 1985. Annotates a selected list of basic reference works in business; covers sources on investments, statistics, management, real estate, insurance, and other topics. Gives examples of textbooks and books for people in business; includes collections of readings.

Fisher, Mary L. *The Negro in America: A Bibliography.* 2d ed., revised and enlarged. Cambridge, Mass.: Harvard University Press, 1970. Lists titles on numerous subjects such as black theater, dance and the arts, music, blacks in literature and the arts; includes books, journals, pamphlets, and government documents; gives references to language and idiom, black studies, etc.

Goodman, Leonard K. *Current Career and Occupational Literature:* 1984. New York: The H. W. Wilson Company, 1984. Lists and annotates books and pamphlets under specific subject headings or specific subject, such as jobs, career planning, and financial aid; many references are to material issued by professional organizations, publishers, and government agencies.

Handbook of Latin American Studies. Gainesville: University of Florida Press, 1936–   . (Annual.) Various publishers. A critical bibliography of Latin American research, provides an annual record of important publications in the various disciplines; beginning with Vol. 26 (1964), the handbook is divided into two parts, Vol. 26 (*Humanities*) and Vol. 27 (*Social Sciences*), published in alternate years.

O'Brien, Jacqueline Wasserman, and Wasserman, Steven R. *Statistics Sources.* 10th ed. Detroit: Gale Research Company, 1986. Identifies primary sources of statistical data on some 20,000 subjects; includes information about statistical sources for each country in the world.

Porter, Dorothy B. (comp.). *The Negro in the United States: A Selected Bibliography.* Washington, D.C.: Library of Congress, 1970. A selected bibliography of materials by or about blacks in the United States; arranged alphabetically by author under twenty-three broad subject headings; designed to meet current needs of students, teachers, researchers, and others for introductory guidance to the study of the black person in the United States.

Public Affairs Information Service. *Bulletin.* New York: Public Affairs Information Service, 1915–   . (Semimonthly.) A subject index to current books, pamphlets, government publications, reports of public and private agencies, and periodicals relating to economic and social conditions, public administration, and international relations. Materials published in English throughout the world are included.

Walford, A. J. (ed.). *Guide to Reference Materials:* Vol. II: *Social and Historical Sciences, Philosophy & Religion.* 4th ed. London: Library Association, 1982.

Webb, William H. *Sources of Information in the Social Sciences.* Chicago: American Library Association, 1986. Updates and adds to Carl White's *Sources of Information in the Social Sciences;* describes monographs, periodicals, and reference sources in history, psychology, social science, and education.

INDEXES[5]

Business Periodicals Index. New York: The H. W. Wilson Company, 1958–   . (Monthly except August.) Indexes by subject periodicals in business and related fields in 298 English-language periodicals. Book reviews are arranged by author in a separate section of the index.

Index to Legal Periodicals. New York: The H. W. Wilson Company, 1908–   . (Monthly except September.) Indexes articles in more than 500 legal journals, yearbooks, bar association organs, university publications, law reviews, and government publications originating in the United States, Canada, Puerto Rico, Great Britain, Ireland, Australia, and New Zealand. Other features are a "Table of Cases," a "Table of Statutes," and book reviews of current books.

Social Sciences and Humanities Index. New York: The H. W. Wilson Company, 1965–1974. (Quarterly.) Succeeded the *International Index;* an author and subject index to 202 periodicals in the social sciences and the humanities; includes periodicals of general scholarly interest, English and foreign. Succeeded by *Social Sciences Index* and *Humanities Index* in 1974.

Social Sciences Index. New York: The H. W. Wilson Company, 1974–   . (Quarterly, annual cumulations.) Indexes by author and subject 300 periodicals in the social sciences; book reviews are in a separate section.

---

[5] See also Chapter 9, Indexes.

DICTIONARIES

Ammer, Christine, and Ammer, Dean. *Dictionary of Business and Economics*. Rev. and expanded ed. New York: The Free Press, 1984. Covers terminology, people, associations, theory, and practical applications of economic theory in business.

Black's Law Dictionary. 5th ed. St. Paul, Minn.: West Publishing Company, 1979. Defines terms and concepts; includes a guide to pronunciation, rules for admission to the bar, code of professional ethics, abbreviations.

Gould, Julius, and Kolb, William L. (eds.) *A Dictionary of the Social Sciences*. Compiled under the auspices of UNESCO. New York: Free Press of Glencoe, 1964. Defines and describes in essay form the key concepts most widely employed in the various social science disciplines with illustrative quotations from the literature; definitions are signed. Gives all major definitions of a term, including common usages as well as "accepted scientific usages." Omits highly technical terms.

Greenwald, Douglas, and others (eds.). *McGraw-Hill Dictionary of Modern Economics*. 3d ed. New York: McGraw-Hill Book Company, 1983. Written for the nonspecialist; defines 1300 selected contemporary terms in economics; has some charts and tables; lists references to additional sources; identifies some 200 organizations and agencies connected with economics.

Johnston, R. J., and others (eds.). *Dictionary of Human Geography*. New York: The Free Press, 1981. Defines terms and concepts and provides lengthy articles on theories and topics relating to the relationship of human societies and their environments.

Pearce, Donald W. *The MIT Dictionary of Modern Economics*. 3d ed. Cambridge, Mass.: The MIT Press, 1986. Gives brief definitions of terminology in economics: for beginning students.

Plano, Jack C., and Greenberg, Milton. *The American Political Dictionary*. 7th ed. New York: Holt, Rinehart and Winston, Inc., 1985. Provides an overview of important concepts, terms, court cases, statutes, and agencies; includes state and local governments.

Rosenberg, Jerry M. *Dictionary of Business and Management*. New York: John Wiley & Sons, Inc., 1978. Defines some 8000 terms from forty major areas of business activities; useful for the layperson as well as the student.

ENCYCLOPEDIAS

Collier, Simon, and others (eds.). *The Cambridge Encyclopedia of Latin America and the Caribbean*. Cambridge: Cambridge University Press, 1987. Covers all aspects, including history, people, economic problems, political events, culture, and physical environment; has many maps and photographs.

Greenwald, Douglas (ed.). *Encyclopedia of Economics*. New York: McGraw-Hill Book Company, 1982. Covers the entire field of economics: terminology, economic thought, influences such as the industrial revolution, the great depression, the Federal Reserve, collective bargaining, political philosophies, etc.; does not include biographies; has lengthy bibliographies.

Harvard Encyclopedia of American Ethnic Groups. Edited by Stephan Thernstrom. Cambridge, Mass.: The Belknap Press of Harvard University Press, 1980. Each ethnic group is described in detail (social organization, origin, migration, settlement, culture, education, religion, and politics); includes native-born American ethnic groups, e.g., Indians, Eskimos; has a detailed table of contents but no index.

International Encyclopedia of the Social Sciences. New York: Macmillan and The Free Press, 1967. 17 vols. Complements, does not supplant, the *Encyclopaedia of the Social Sciences*; aims to "reflect and encourage the rapid development of the social sciences throughout the world" (Preface); represents the social sciences of the 1960s; emphasis is on the analytical and comparative aspects of each topic; contains some biographical articles, including living persons; selected bibliographies follow articles; Vol. 17 is the index. Vol. 18: *Biographical Supplement*, 1980.

Kaplan, Frederic M., and others (eds.). *Encyclopedia of China Today*. Updated ed. New York: Harper & Row, Publishers, 1980. "A practical guide to the trade, industry, geography, politics, and culture of the People's Republic of China" (subtitle); arranged by chapters; has maps and illustrations; includes some biographies.

Kodansha Encyclopedia of Japan. Tokyo: Kodansha, 1983. 9 vols. Surveys Japanese life and culture; gives information on history, philosophy, literature, fine arts, business, politics, economics, technology, etc.

Kurian, George Thomas (ed.). *Encyclopedia of the Third World*. 3d ed. New York: Facts on File, 1987. 3 vols. Treats most of the nations of the world; gives a chronology of events for each country dating from the year of independence; covers political, cultural, economic, military, legal, and geographic aspects of each country. *Atlas of the Third World*, edited by George Thomas Kurian, 1982, is a companion volume.

Laszlo, Ervin, and others (eds.). *World Encyclopedia of Peace*. New York: Pergamon Press, 1986. 4 vols. Covers theories and philosophies of peace, contemporary peace issues, outstanding peace theorists from ancient times to the present; provides information on worldwide peace organizations and peace treaties; includes a chronology of war since the Napoleonic period. Vol. IV is a bibliography of more than 1500 citations for further study.

Levy, Leonard W., and others (eds.). *Encyclopedia of the American Constitution*. New York: Macmillan Publishing Company, 1986. 4 vols. Designed as a general introduction to the Constitution, this scholarly work also celebrates the bicentennial of the United States Constitution; covers all aspects of the Constitution: history, development, concepts, individuals associated with it, and specific cases.

Low, W. A., and Clift, Vergil A. *Encyclopedia of Black America*. New York: McGraw-Hill Book Company, 1981. Aims to present the "totality of the past and present life and culture of Afro-Americans—their education, politics, history, family life, literature, art"; articles define, describe, and elaborate; includes some 1400 brief biographical articles; alphabetically arranged; illustrated.

Porter, Glenn (ed.). *Encyclopedia of American Economic History: Studies of the Principal Movements and Ideas*. New York: Charles Scribner's Sons, 1980. Aims to present American economic history as it was understood in the late 1970s; contains articles by historians and economists; covers such topics as technology, taxation, business cycles, institutions, social history, slavery, automobiles, prices, wages, women, immigration, and economic growth and thought.

Worldmark Encyclopedia of the Nations. 7th ed., revised. New York: Worldmark Press, 1988. 5 vols. Gives factual information in uniform format relating to topography, language, religion, and certain socioeconomic categories on countries which belong to the United Nations; Vol. I is devoted to the United Nations; remaining volumes are devoted to Africa, the Americas, Asia and Australasia, and Europe.

Worldmark Encyclopedia of the States. New York: John Wiley & Sons, Inc., 1986. Gives detailed information about each state, the nation's capital, and the United States as a whole and its dependencies; covers government, population, education, agriculture, finance, social conditions, economic conditions, services provided, housing, the arts, sports, famous persons, industries, political parties, the press, and many other items in the same format for each state; has maps and tables.

HANDBOOKS[6]

Africa Contemporary Record, 1968–69– . Edited by Colin Legum. London: Rex Collings, 1969– . (Annual.) An annual survey and documents;

---

[6] See also Chapter 12, Yearbooks and Handbooks.

divided into three parts—Part One: Essays on Current Issues; Part Two: A Country-by-Country Review (Legal, Political, Social, Military, Economic); Part Three: Documents.

Banks, Arthur S., and others (eds.). *Economic Handbook of the World: 1982*. Published for the Center for Social Analysis of the State University of New York at Binghamton. New York: McGraw-Hill Book Company, 1982. Gives essential information about the economic conditions of every country in the world, including economic statistics, domestic trends, and trade; has a section on international organizations; arranged alphabetically by country.

Barone, Michael. *The Almanac of American Politics 1982*. Washington, D.C.: Barone & Company, 1981. Covers the presidents, the senators, the representatives and the governors: their records and election results, states and districts, economics, politics, social conditions, etc.

Colombo, John Robert. *Colombo's Canadian References*. London: Oxford University Press, 1976. Presents Canada in some 6000 articles on every aspect of Canadian life, past and current; includes culture, communication, education, geography, history, resources, business, politics, and technology.

Davidson, Sidney, and Weil, R. (eds.). *Handbook of Modern Accounting*. 2d ed. New York: McGraw-Hill Book Company, 1977. Covers accounting as a whole— traditional problems and procedures and new techniques arising from computer applications.

Inge, Thomas M. (ed.). *Handbook of American Popular Culture*. Westport, Conn.: Greenwood Press, 1979–1981. 3 vols. Covers such popular culture areas as the automobile, American pulp fiction, film, circus, television, the western movie, games and toys, and literature; for each area, includes a brief history, a critical guide to the most useful sources, and a description of research centers and collections of primary and secondary materials.

Klein, Barry (ed.). *Reference Encyclopedia of the American Indian*. 4th ed. Santa Barbara: ABC-Clio, 1986. 2 vols. Gives information about associations, organizations, government agencies, schools, museums, college and university courses, and other related topics. Vol. II has "who's who" type of information about 1500 prominent native Americans.

Ploski, Harry A., and Williams, James (eds.). *The Negro Almanac*. 4th ed. New York: John Wiley & Sons, Inc., 1983. Covers history and biography; gives statistical information in charts and graphs; includes photographs, reproductions of art, chronologies, tables, and bibliographies.

Political Handbook of the World. Published for the Center for Comparative Political Research of the State University of New York and the Center on Foreign Relations. New York: McGraw-Hill Book Company, 1975– . (Biennial.) Published annually since 1927 by various publishers; gives current information on the independent nations of the world regarding government, social, education, and political conditions; covers religions, geography, and borders. Has a section on the United Nations.

Smythe, Mabel M. (ed.). *The Black American Reference Book*. Englewood Cliffs, N.J.: Prentice-Hall, Inc., 1976. In thirty-four lengthy essays by prominent authors, treats virtually every aspect of the black experience, historical, social, educational, religious, artistic, and literary; points out black influence on American culture.

Sturtevant, William C. (ed.). *Handbook of North American Indians*. Washington, D.C.: Smithsonian Institution, 1978– . (In progress.) The aim of the projected 20 volumes is "to give an encyclopedic summary of what is known about the prehistory, history, and cultures of the aboriginal peoples of North America"; gives linguistic, ethnographic, historical, and archaeological information on each tribe.

YEARBOOKS[7]

The Annual Register 1987: A Record of World Events. London: Longmans, Green & Company, 1958– . (Annual.) Discusses events of the year concerning every country, the UN, other international organizations; social and economic trends, major developments in all fields; has maps, statistical charts, and reprints of important documents.

The Book of the States. Lexington, Ky.: Council of State Governments, 1935– . (Biennial.) Provides an authoritative source of information on the structure, working methods, financial and functional activities of state governments; gives a comprehensive listing of elected state officials and members of the legislatures; tables give information for each state; kept up to date by supplements.

Britain: An Official Handbook. London: Her Majesty's Stationery Office 1948– . (Annual.) Revised each year, gives a factual account of the administration and the national economy of the United Kingdom; describes activities of many of the national institutions both official and unofficial.

Canada Yearbook 1980–1981. Ottawa: Minister of Supply and Services,

---

[7] See also Chapter 12, Yearbooks and Handbooks.

1981–   . (Annual.) Gives a review of economic, social, and political developments in Canada.

China Official Yearbook. Hong Kong: Salem International Publications, 1985–   . Gives an overall view of Chinese life during the preceding year; has a chronology of events, important political and legal documents; covers politics, law, science, etc. Gives statistical information.

Demographic Yearbook. New York: United Nations, 1949–   . (Annual.) Surveys statistics of more than 250 countries and territories on population trends, marriages, births, deaths, and life expectancy. English-French.

Facts on File: World News Digest with Index. New York: Facts on File, October 30, 1940–   . (Weekly; annual bound volumes.) Digests from a number of metropolitan newspapers the important news of the day relating to national and foreign affairs, science, arts, religion, economy, and other topics.

The Far East and Australasia. London: Europa Publications, Ltd., 1969–   . (Annual.) Covers the region as a whole, then subdivisions, giving social, physical, and economic surveys of each area, including government, political parties, education, religion, finance, trade, etc. Includes a "who's who" in the Far East and Australasia.

Keesing's Contemporary Archives: Record of World Events. London: Longmans, Green, 1983–   . (Monthly.) A continuation of *Keesing's Contemporary Archives: Weekly Digest of World Events . . .* , covers important events in all countries; includes texts of speeches, documents, statistics, and obituaries; arranged in chronological, topical, and geographical sections.

Municipal Year Book. Chicago: International City Managers' Association, 1934–   . (Annual.) Gives information concerning governmental units, personnel, finance, and activities of United States and Canadian cities; has a directory of chief officers of Canadian cities over 10,000 population and of mayors and clerks of United States cities over 2500.

South American Handbook. London: Trade and Travel Publications, 1924–   . (Annual.) Covers South and Central America, Mexico, and the West Indies; presents information about government, transportation, communication, natural resources.

United Nations. Statistical Office. *Statistical Yearbook/Annuaire Statistique*. New York: United Nations, 1949–   . (Annual.) Gives political, scientific, educational, and cultural data on the countries of the world.

Yearbook of the United Nations. New York: United Nations, Department of Public Information, 1947–   . (Annual.) Provides a comprehensive account of the activities of the United Nations and its related intergovernmental agencies.

ATLASES

Allen, James Paul, and Turner, Eugene James (eds.). *We the People: An Atlas of American Ethnic Diversity*. New York: Macmillan Publishing Company, 1987. Provides information on the ethnic character of the population of the United States, e.g., people of Southern European origin, of African origin, Western European origin, Asian and Pacific origin; intended for all persons interested in their ethnic background; points out differences in ethnic composition of the population of a given area; data based on 1980 census. Text, maps, charts, diagrams, and tables are used.

Oxford Economic Atlas of the World. Prepared by the Cartographic Department of the Clarendon Press. 4th ed. London: Oxford University Press, 1972. Provides maps which show world distribution patterns for all the important industries, resources, and commodities; includes topographic maps, urban land-use maps of selected cities throughout the world, and thematic maps of a wide range of political, economic, physical, and geographical subjects; includes a gazetteer of some 8000 names and a section of statistical information. Detailed information about specific areas is provided in companion volumes, e.g., *Oxford Regional Economic Atlas of the United States and Canada* (2d ed., 1975).

Shortridge, Barbara G. *Atlas of American Women*. New York: Macmillan Publishing Company, 1986. Provides information about the current status of women: where and how they live, age groups, employment, education, occupations, health, and other topics.

BIOGRAPHICAL DICTIONARIES[8]

American Men and Women of Science: Social and Behavioral Sciences. 15th ed. Edited by Jaques Cattell Press. New York: R. R. Bowker Company, 1985. Gives brief biographical sketches of some 130,000 scientists actively engaged in teaching or research in economics, political science, psychology, and sociology.

Who's Who in American Politics, 1981–1982. 8th ed. Compiled and edited by Jaques Cattell Press. New York: R. R. Bowker Company, 1981. Covers important political figures and public servants in the United States on the national, state, and local levels from the President of the United States to local political figures about whom information is not easily

---

[8] See also Chapter 10, Biographical Dictionaries.

available; entries are arranged geographically, with a separate name index.

EXAMPLES OF PROFESSIONAL JOURNALS
IN THE SOCIAL SCIENCES[9]

American Academy of Political and Social Science. *Annals*. Philadelphia: American Academy of Political and Social Science, 1890– . (Bimonthly.) Each issue is devoted to a selected topic of current social or political interest; articles present different aspects of the subject.

American Behavioral Scientist. Beverly Hills, Calif.: Sage Publications, Inc., 1957– . (Bimonthly.) Devoted to the methods and techniques of social research, each issue has articles by specialists; the "New Studies" section is an annotated listing of new publications including books, pamphlets, and articles on sociology, psychology, and other behavioral sciences.

American Economic Review. Nashville, Tenn.: American Economic Association, 1911– . (Quarterly.) Reviews new books; has articles on such topics as wages, employment, marketing, inflation, and unemployment; provides bibliographical references.

American Journal of Economics and Sociology. New York: American Journal of Economics and Sociology, Inc., 1941– . (Quarterly.) Reports original research; covers social aspects of economic institutions and economic aspects of social and political institutions.

American Political Science Review. Washington, D.C.: American Political Science Association, 1906– . (Quarterly.) Stresses theoretical rather than practical aspects of political science; has book reviews.

Journal of Economic History. New York: Economic History Association, New York University, 1941– . (Quarterly.) The journal of the Economic History Association; presents articles on economic history and related aspects of history or economics, taxation, investments, business, and industry.

Political Science Quarterly. New York: Academy of Political Science, Columbia University, 1886– . (Quarterly.) Covers the broad field of political science; has long articles and many book reviews.

Sociological Quarterly. Columbia, Mo.: The Midwest Sociological Society, 1960– . (Quarterly.) Emphasizes trends in social thought, ideas, and

[9] See also *Ulrich's International Periodicals Directory*, 27th ed., and *Magazines for Libraries*, 5th ed., edited by Bill Katz and Linda S. Katz.

contributions of individual sociologists; is the journal of the Midwest Sociological Society.

Education

The word "education" has several meanings, and it is necessary to make clear its meaning as a *subject field* before beginning a study of reference materials in this area. A brief statement of two of the several meanings of "education" will help to clarify its meaning as a branch of knowledge.

In the broad sense, education is the sum total of all the ways, both formal and informal, by which a person develops attitudes, abilities, and behavior patterns and acquires knowledge.

In another and less broad sense, education is the social process by which people are placed under the influence of an organized and controlled environment, such as a school, in the hope that they will attain more rapidly and effectively their fullest possible development as individuals and will learn how to live as competent citizens in their society. Elementary school, high school, and college are some of the stages in this controlled process.

Education as a subject field—that is, as a branch of knowledge—is the science which has to do with the principles and practices of teaching and learning. It is also the name given to that curriculum, in institutions of higher education, which consists of professional courses for the preparation of teachers, supervisors, and administrators. Included in these courses are philosophy and history of education (that is, education as a social process), psychology as applied to learning and teaching, curriculum, methods of teaching (how to teach), administration, and supervision.

The following reference sources are designed to answer, in the language of the educator, some of the numerous and specialized questions in this subject field.

REPRESENTATIVE REFERENCE SOURCES IN EDUCATION

Bibliographies, guides, and indexes[10]

Berry, Dorothea M. *Bibliographic Guide to Educational Research.* 2d ed. Metuchen, N.J.: Scarecrow Press, Inc., 1980. Emphasizes basic sources

---

[10] See also Chapter 9, Indexes, and Chapter 13, Bibliographies.

and recently published works; arranged by type of publication, subdivided by subject categories; each title is annotated.

The Education Index. New York: The H. W. Wilson Company, 1929–   . (Monthly, except July and August.) Indexes by author and subject some 330 education periodicals; monographs and yearbooks are also indexed; covers all aspects of education; book review citations are in a separate section of the index.

Dictionaries and encyclopedias

The Encyclopedia of Education. New York: The Macmillan Company and The Free Press, 1971. 10 vols. Intended for all persons concerned with education; gives an overview of education: history, theory, research, philosophy, and structure of education; emphasizes American education.

Good, Carter Victor (ed.). *Dictionary of Education.* 3d ed. New York: McGraw-Hill Book Company, 1973. Defines and explains more than 30,000 professional terms in education and related fields.

Metzel, Harold E. (ed.) *Encyclopedia of Educational Research.* 5th ed. New York: Macmillan Free Press, 1982. 4 vols. Gives the status of research in all aspects of education methods of research including the characteristics of particular groups, such as the gifted and the retarded, computer-assisted instruction, bilingual education, aptitude measurement, etc.

Directories

Accredited Institutions of Post-Secondary Education: 1983–1984. Washington, D.C.: American Council on Education, 1984. Arranged by state; gives information about enrollment, curriculum, degree programs, certification, etc.

American Universities and Colleges, 13th ed. Edited by the American Council on Education. Hawthorne, N.Y.: Walter de Gruyter, 1987. Gives detailed information about 1900 four-year accredited institutions of higher education in the United States: history, admission requirements, fees, educational programs, faculty, enrollment, library, officials, etc.

Cass, James, and Birnbaum, Max. *Comparative Guide to American Colleges.* 13th ed. New York: Harper & Row, Publishers, Incorporated, 1987. Gives admission requirements, curricula, costs, scholarships, regulations: arranged alphabetically by name of the institution.

————. *Comparative Guide to Two-Year Colleges and Career Programs.* New

York: Harper & Row, Publishers, Incorporated, 1976. Lists alphabetically, by state, public community colleges, private junior colleges, and other institutions which offer a two-year degree; gives information about admission, costs, degrees, curricula, training programs.

The College Blue Book. 21st ed. New York: Macmillan Publishing Company, 1987. 5 vols. Gives narrative descriptions of more than 3200 colleges in the United States and Canada covering cost, accreditation, enrollment, faculty, administration, curricula, faculty, scholarships, and other information. More than 10,000 trade and business schools and community colleges are included.

International Handbook of Universities, 10th rev. ed. Edited by the International Association of Universities. Hawthorne, N.Y.: Walter de Gruyter, 1986. Describes in English institutions of higher education in over 100 countries outside the United States and British Commonwealth: administration, faculties, degrees, diplomas, fees, admission requirements.

Peterson's Annual Guides to Graduate Study. Princeton, N.J.: Peterson's Guides, 1976– . 5 vols. (Annual.) Gives an overview of accredited institutions offering graduate work, with a profile of each institution: data on students and programs, housing, financial aid, fields of study, etc.; has separate listing by field of study and institutions offering it, e.g., Humanities and Social Sciences. *Peterson's Annual Guide to Undergraduate Study, 1982–,* gives similar information about two-year and four-year colleges. identifying more than 400 major fields of study and the colleges which offer them.

Handbooks and yearbooks

Commonwealth Universities Yearbook. 1914– . London: Association of Commonwealth Universities, 1914. 4 vols. Presents the essential facts about the history, facilities, organization, staff, and admission requirements of universities in the Commonwealth; arranged by countries.

Requirements for Certification of Teachers, Counselors, Librarians, and Administrators for Elementary Schools, Secondary Schools, Junior Colleges. Chicago: The University of Chicago Press, 1935– . (Annual.) Arranged by state, then by level and positions; gives certification requirements, recommendations of regional and other accrediting associations, information concerning applications.

World of Learning. London: Europa Publications, Ltd., 1947– . (Annual.) 2 vols. Arranged alphabetically by country; gives information about educational, cultural, and scientific organizations all over the world.

Biographical dictionaries[11]

Directory of American Scholars. 8th ed. Edited by Jaques Cattell Press. New York: R. R. Bowker Company, 1982/83. Covers currently active scholars in the United States and Canada.

Examples of professional journals in education[12]

American Community, Technical, and Junior Colleges. Washington, D.C.: The American Council on Education, 1984. Gives detailed information about each college: fees, admission requirements, offerings, faculty, library, and so on.

Educational Leadership. Washington, D.C.: Association for Supervision and Curriculum Development, 1943– . (Monthly, October–May.) Emphasizes curriculum; reports research data to the membership.

Journal of Higher Education. Columbus: Ohio State University Press, 1930– . (Monthly.) A general magazine devoted to issues of interest to higher education; includes book reviews.

NEA Today. Washington, D.C.: National Education Association, 1913– . (Bimonthly.) The official journal of the National Education Association; provides articles of general interest and reports new developments in education; covers all aspects of education. Formerly *NEA Journal* and *Today's Education.*

Phi Delta Kappan. Bloomington, Ind.: Phi Delta Kappa, Inc., 1918– . (Monthly, September–June.) Aims to promote leadership in education at all levels.

Abstract journals

Current Index to Journals in Education. Phoenix, Ariz.: Oryx Press, 1969– . (Monthly.) Covers the periodical literature in education, giving complete citation to the journal in which an article appears; brief annotations (not abstracts) are included when the titles and descriptors do not indicate the content of the article; indexes about 780 education and education-related journals.

Resources in Education, Vol. 1, No. 1, November 1966– . Washington, D.C.: United States Government Printing Office, 1967– . (Monthly.) A

---

[11] See also Chapter 10, Biographical Dictionaries.

[12] See also *Ulrich's International Periodicals Directory*, 27th ed., and *Magazines for Libraries*, 5th ed., edited by Bill Katz and Linda S. Katz.

monthly abstract journal announcing recent report literature related to the field of education; made up of résumés and indexes. The résumés highlight the significant parts of the document and are numbered sequentially in the Document Section by ED number. The ED prefix identifies documents of educational significance selected by ERIC.[13] The contents of each issue are indexed by subject, author, and sponsoring institution. The document résumés (abstracts) give the name of the sponsoring agency of the research project, date, report number, ERIC Document Reproduction Service (EDRS) price, descriptors (subject headings which describe it), brief abstract, educational documents number which is the means of locating it in the ERIC file, availability, and price in microfiche and hard or paper copy.

The source of all subject headings used in the ERIC collection and in indexing *Current Index to Journals in Education* and *Resources in Education* is *The Thesaurus of ERIC Descriptors* (Phoenix, Arizona: Oryx Press, 1980; Annual–), which lists descriptors and synonyms or near synonyms.

Review Questions

CHAPTER 19. THE SOCIAL SCIENCES AND EDUCATION

1. Name the subject fields included in the broad term "the social sciences."
2. Identify two or more titles described in this chapter which a student can consult for information on:

a. Law
b. Political science
c. Economics
d. Black Americans
e. Commerce
f. Social welfare

g. The American Indian
h. The Third World
i. Ethnic groups
j. State governments
k. Individual countries
l. Business

(See also Chapter 12, Yearbooks and Handbooks.)

---

[13] The Educational Resources Information Center (ERIC), a nationwide information network for acquiring, abstracting, indexing, storing, and disseminating significant research reports and projects in the field of education, was established in June 1964 to disseminate educational research results, research-related materials, and other resource information. Sixteen special centers or clearinghouses acquire, evaluate, abstract, and index these report materials and the abstracts in *Resources in Education*. Reports are available in microfiche or paper-copy reproductions from the ERIC Document Reproduction Service, which is part of ERIC's information storage and retrieval system. (ERIC files can be searched by computer.) Many libraries have part or all of the ERIC microfiche collection. It is usually housed in the area where microfilm and other microforms are kept. Each microfiche is filed in a drawer by its identifying ED number (ED 174744, ED 174745, ED 174746, etc.), which is given in the entry in *Resources in Education*. Microfiche must be read with a reader.

3. List one or more sources in education that: define terms, locate journal articles, give information about colleges, give information about study abroad, discuss certification requirements for various positions in education.

4. Discuss ERIC.

CHAPTER

❦ 20 ❦

Language (Philology)

Philology (by derivation, "love of learning" and "love of speech and discourse") is that branch of learning concerned with human speech and what it reveals about humans. The 400 class in the Dewey Decimal Classification is devoted to language class P of the Library of Congress classification includes language and linguistics.

Language as a subject was first studied because it was important in reading and in understanding literature, and emphasis was placed upon the study of Greek, Latin, and Hebrew, since most of the early writing was done in those languages. When the study of language, as such, emerged as a branch of learning during the nineteenth century, it was called "linguistics."

Linguistics, the scientific study of human speech, includes an investigation of the sound, form, and meaning of language and of the relations of one language to another.

The study of language as a branch of knowledge includes:

1. Morphology, the study of the historical development of speech patterns
2. Syntax, the study of the use and forms of the language and of the parts of speech and their various forms
3. Etymology, the study of the origin of words
4. Semantics, the historical and psychological study of meaning and change of meaning of words

In the study of language and linguistics, dictionaries[1] are the major aids,

---

[1] This chapter is concerned with specialized dictionaries of language. See Chapter 7 for a discussion of general word dictionaries.

both the general word dictionaries of a language and dictionaries which provide more than a mere listing of words of a language and their several meanings. The latter include:

1. Dictionaries based on the historical development of words
2. Etymological dictionaries
3. Dictionaries of usage
4. Dictionaries of slang, dialect, and colloquialisms
5. Dictionaries of synonyms and antonyms

In addition to these kinds of dictionaries, there are specialized dictionaries which treat abbreviations, acronyms, eponyms, foreign words and phrases, and pronunciations.

Other types of reference sources useful in the study of language are bibliographies, indexes, general histories of language, biographical dictionaries, and nonbook sources such as tapes and disks.

Useful Reference Sources in Language[2]

BIBLIOGRAPHIES AND GUIDES[3]

Collison, Robert Lewis. *Dictionaries of Foreign Languages*. 2d ed. New York: Hafner Publishing Company, 1971. "A bibliographical guide to both general and technical dictionaries with historical and explanatory notes and references" (subtitle); includes dictionaries of the chief foreign languages; discusses specific dictionaries.

Comrie, Bernard. *The World's Major Languages*. Oxford: Oxford University Press, 1987. A guide to the world's forty major languages; covers languages in general and language families.

Modern Humanities Research Association. *Annual Bibliography of English Language and Literature*. Cambridge: Cambridge University Press, 1921– . (Annual.) Includes books, periodical literature, pamphlets, and references to book reviews; the language section is arranged by subject.

Modern Language Association of America. *MLA International Bibliography of Books and Articles on the Modern Languages and Literatures*. 1921– . (Annual.) 2 vols. Offers a classified list of books and articles on language,

---

[2] See also Chapter 7, Dictionaries.

[3] See also Chapter 9, Indexes, and Chapter 13, Bibliographies.

literature, linguistics, and folklore. Author index follows listings in first volume; second volume is a subject index.

DICTIONARY OF LANGUAGE AS A SUBJECT FIELD

Pei, Mario. *Glossary of Linguistic Terminology*. New York: Columbia University Press, 1966. Includes the historical, descriptive, and geolinguistic terminology, American and European, that has gained acceptance in the field.

DICTIONARIES OF CERTAIN ASPECTS OF LANGUAGE

Abbreviations and acronyms

Barnhart, Robert K. *The Barnhart Dictionary of Etymology*. New York: The H. W. Wilson Company, 1987. Gives information regarding derivation, changes of meanings, earliest dates of borrowing from another language, how a word entered the language and where; includes coined words.

Crowley, Ellen T. (ed.). *Acronyms, Initialisms, and Abbreviations Dictionary*, 11th ed. Detroit: Gale Research Company, 1987. 3 vols. Vol. 1 contains more than 200,000 entries ranging from the time of ancient Rome to the present day; all areas of knowledge are represented; humorous and slang acronyms are included. Vol. 2, *New Acronyms, Initialisms, and Abbreviations*, is the annual supplement. Vol. 3, *Reverse Acronyms, Initialisms, and Abbreviations Dictionary*, companion to Vol. 1, is arranged alphabetically by complete word or term; the acronym is the definition.

De Sola, Ralph (ed.). *Abbreviations Dictionary*. 7th ed. New York: Elsevier, 1986. Defines and explains abbreviations, acronyms, anonyms, and eponyms, contractions, geographical equivalents, historical and mythological characters, initials and nicknames, signs and symbols, slang, and short forms in all areas.

Etymology[4]

Hoad, T. F. (ed.) *The Concise Oxford Dictionary of English Etymology*. Oxford: The Clarendon Press, 1986. Based on *The Oxford Dictionary of English Etymology*; has 19,000 entries, some quotations, and dates when a word entered the language.

---

[4] In etymological dictionaries, definitions as such are not given. The meaning of the word is determined through the etymology.

Klein, Ernest. *A Comprehensive Etymological Dictionary of the English Language*. New York: American Elsevier, 1966–1967. 2 vols. Treats the origin of words and the development of their meanings, thus illustrating the history of civilization and culture; includes many scientific and technical terms and personal and mythological names.

Onions, Charles Talbut, and others (eds.). *The Oxford Dictionary of English Etymology*. New York: Oxford University Press, 1966. Based on the *Oxford English Dictionary*, but brought up to date by recent research; includes some words of United States origin and some proper names; notable for its breadth of coverage, scholarship, and ease of use.

Partridge, Eric (ed.). *Origins*. 4th ed. New York: The Macmillan Company, 1966. Emphasizes civilization rather than science; includes the most common words in modern English.

Foreign words and phrases

Guinagh, Kevin (comp.). *Dictionary of Foreign Phrases and Abbreviations*. 3d ed. New York: The H. W. Wilson Company, 1982. Aims to help students and nonspecialists understand foreign expressions, proverbs, mottoes, etc., which they frequently hear or read; covers phrases in law, philosophy, business, medicine, etc.

Mawson, Christopher Orlando. *Dictionary of Foreign Terms*. 2d ed. Revised and updated by Charles Berlitz. New York: Thomas Y. Crowell Company, 1975. Explains words from more than fifty ancient and modern languages, from a wide variety of fields; the language of each word is identified.

Pei, Mario, and Ramondino, Salvatore. *Dictionary of Foreign Terms*. New York: Delacorte Press, 1974. Explains foreign terms and phrases that English-speaking people encounter in reading or listening; original language, pronunciation, and definition are given for each term; some usage labels are given.

Historical development of words

Craigie, William, and Hulbert, James R. (eds.). *A Dictionary of American English on Historical Principles*. 2d ed. Chicago: University of Chicago Press, 1938–1944. 4 vols. Indicates words which originated in America or which are in greater use here than elsewhere and words which are important in the history of America; follows the plan of *The Oxford English Dictionary*.

A Dictionary of Canadianisms on Historical Principles. Produced by the Lexicographical Centre for Canadian English, University of Victoria, British Columbia. Scarborough, Ont.: W. J. Gage, Ltd., 1967. Modeled after *The Oxford English Dictionary*; covers the period from the sixteenth century to the present; each entry is "substantiated" with dates and quotations from books, periodicals, and newspapers; includes regional, political, historical, and proper names; does not claim that all entries originated in Canada, but all are original or are closely related to Canada.

Mathews, Mitford N. (ed.). *A Dictionary of Americanisms on Historical Principles*. Chicago: University of Chicago Press, 1956. Includes words which have been added to the English language in the United States from colonial times to the present.

_____. *Americanisms: A Dictionary of Selected Americanisms on Historical Principles*. Chicago: University of Chicago Press, 1966. An abridgment of *A Dictionary of Americanisms on Historical Principles*; gives approximately 1000 entries.

Morris, William, and Morris, Mary (eds.). *Dictionary of Word and Phrase Origins*. New York: Harper & Row, Publishers, 1962, 1967, 1971. 3 vols. Explains a variety of additions to the English language from many sources.

_____. *Morris Dictionary of Word and Phrase Origins*. Harper & Row, Publishers, Inc., 1977. To some extent an abridgment of the 3-vol. work by these authors; presents the history of several thousand words and phrases with illustrative examples; some etymologies are given; does not give pronunciation.

Murray, James Augustus Henry, and others (eds.). *The Oxford English Dictionary*. London: Oxford University Press, 1933. 12 vols. and supplement. Presents the historical development of each word which has entered the English language since 1150.

A Supplement to the Oxford English Dictionary. Edited by R. W. Burchfield. Oxford: Clarendon Press, 1972–1986. 4 vols. The four-volume *Supplement* will incorporate the material in the 1933 *Supplement* and will contain all words that came into common use in English during the publication of the *OED*, 1884–1928, and words which have come into use from 1928 to the present. It aims to record the vocabulary of the twentieth century, including literary, scientific, and technical terminology; legal and other professional terminology; and popular, colloquial, and modern slang expressions.

New words

Barnhart, Clarence L., and others (eds.). *The Second Barnhart Dictionary of New English*. New York: Harper & Row, Publishers, Inc., 1980. Records and defines new words in the language, giving the meaning of the word and quotations to show its usage in context; gives pronunciation for difficult words and dates of earliest instance of usage or definition.

Pronunciation

Erlich, Eugene H., and Hand, Raymond. *NBC Handbook of Pronunciation*. 4th ed. rev. and updated. New York: Harper & Row, 1984. More than 21,000 commonly used words and proper names with pronunciation are covered.

Kenyon, John S., and Knott, Thomas A. (eds.). *A Pronouncing Dictionary of American English*. Springfield, Mass.: G. & C. Merriam Company, 1953. Gives pronunciation only, according to the alphabet of the International Phonetic Association; records standard speech.

Lass, Abraham Harold, and Lass, Betty. *Dictionary of Pronunciation*. New York: Quadrangle and The New York Times Book Company, 1976. Lists some 8000 words which are pronunciation problems and gives the recommended pronunciations found in four standard desk dictionaries; the number of dictionaries that recognize each acceptable pronunciation is indicated; includes words of foreign origin.

Sign language

Sternberg, Martin L. A. *American Sign Language: A Comprehensive Dictionary*. New York: Harper & Row, Publishers, Inc., 1981. Has about 5000 word and phrase entries, with a description of each and an illustration of how it is conveyed in English.

Slang, dialect, colloquialisms, idioms, and regionalisms

Berrey, Lester V., and Van Den Bark, Melvin (eds.). *The American Thesaurus of Slang*. 2d ed. New York: Thomas Y. Crowell Company, 1953. A collection of colloquialisms, slang, and vulgarisms arranged according to the ideas which they express; has an alphabetical word index for ease of use.

Cassidy, Frederic G. *Dictionary of American Regional English*. Cambridge, Mass.: Belknap Harvard University Press, 1985– . The first of a projected five-volume work; aims to record English as it is spoken in the United States, covering regional usage, dialect, colloquialisms, and ethnic words; includes illustrative examples, definition, pronunciation, alternative forms, and places where the word is used; selected maps show where the word or term is used. Vol. I: A–C.

Cowie, A. P., and others. *Oxford Dictionary of Current Idiomatic English*. New York: Oxford University Press, 1975–1983. 2 vols. Treats parts of speech, phrases, clauses, sentences, and idioms.

Green, Jonathan. *The Dictionary of Contemporary Slang.* New York: Stein & Day, 1985. Emphasis is on post-1945 words and terms, British and American; gives definitions, part of speech, country of origin, users of the word or term, including authors.

Longman Dictionary of Contemporary English. London: Longman, 1978. Designed to help the foreign learner of English; covers the most common words and idiomatic phrases in use; gives examples of usage, pronunciation, concise definitions, and part of speech; gives sources (for example, American English, African English); gives British and American pronunciations; illustrated.

Partridge, Eric. *A Dictionary of Slang and Unconventional English.* 8th ed. Edited by Paul Beall. New York: Macmillan Publishing Company, 1984. "Colloquialisms and catch-phrases, solecisms and catch-phrases, nicknames and vulgarisms" (subtitle). Emphasis is on British English.

Wentworth, Harold, and Flexner, Stuart B. (comps. and eds.). *Dictionary of American Slang.* 2d supplemented ed. New York: Thomas Y. Crowell Company, 1975. First published in 1960, and reprinted in 1967 with a 48-page supplement; this edition retains all words in the two earlier editions and adds about 1500 new slang words that have become current since 1967; gives brief definition of each term, and multiple meanings if appropriate; notes the group which uses the term; gives synonyms and antonyms. *New Dictionary of American Slang,* edited by Robert L. Chapman (Harper & Row, 1986), is a revised edition of Wentworth and Flexner.

Synonyms and antonyms

Hayakawa, S. I. (comp.). *Funk & Wagnalls Modern Guide to Synonyms and Related Words.* New York: Funk & Wagnalls Company, 1968. In more than 1000 essays or articles, discusses, defines, compares, and contrasts over 6000 synonyms and related words in the context of the American 1960s; gives concise definitions and illustrative quotations.

Roget's International Thesaurus. 4th ed. Revised by Robert L. Chapman. New York: Thomas Y. Crowell Company, 1977. Lists about 250,000 words and phrases arranged in categories by their meanings; reflects modern vocabulary.

Roget's II: The New Thesaurus. By the editors of *The American Heritage Dictionary of the English Language.* Boston: Houghton Mifflin Company, 1980. Arranged alphabetically; groups synonyms by precise meanings with definitions; gives illustrative examples of usage.

Webster's Collegiate Thesaurus. Springfield, Mass.: G. & C. Merriam Company, Publishers, 1976. Alphabetically arranged; has some 20,000 entries; each entry is defined briefly, with an illustrative phrase if needed; definition is followed by a group of exact synonyms, a group of related words, and a group of contrasted words and antonyms.

Webster's New Dictionary of Synonyms. Springfield, Mass.: G. & C. Merriam Company, Publishers, 1978. "A dictionary of discriminated synonyms with analogous and contrasted words" (subtitle); has illustrative quotations from old and new authors.

Usage

Copperud, Roy H. *American Usage and Style: The Consensus.* New York: Van Nostrand Reinhold Company, 1980. Compares the opinions of nine authorities regarding words, phrases, and usage.

Follett, Wilson. *Modern American Usage: A Guide.* Edited and completed by Jacques Barzun in collaboration with Carlos Baker and others. New York: Hill & Wang, 1966. Arranged in dictionary format; explains words and phrases, giving recommended forms of usage; articles vary in length; treats matters of style.

Fowler, H. W. *A Dictionary of Modern English Usage.* 2d ed. Revised by Ernest Gowers. Oxford: Clarendon Press, 1965. Gives definitions of terms, sometimes with disputed spellings and plurals; brief essays on use and misuse of words and expressions; reflects the author's personal opinions; many new articles; modernized and brought up to date in light of current usage; some terms dropped; new ones added.

Morris, William, and Morris, Mary. *Harper Dictionary of Contemporary Usage.* 2d ed. New York: Harper & Row, Publishers, Incorporated, 1985. Treats idioms, slang words, regionalisms, spelling and pronunciation; articles range in length from a few sentences to several pages; opinions of a panel of expert writers and speakers are cited on certain points; aims to direct attention to incorrect or awkward oral or written language, but does not prescribe usage.

Wiener, E. S. C. *The Oxford Guide to English Usage.* Oxford: Clarendon Press, 1983. Provides simple and direct guidance regarding the formation and use of English words—pronouns, spelling, grammar, meaning, etc.; highlights "correct and acceptable standard British English" (preface.)

BIOGRAPHICAL DICTIONARIES[5]

Directory of American Scholars. 8th ed. Vol. III: *Foreign Languages, Linguistics, and Philology.* Edited by the Jaques Cattell Press. New York: R. R. Bowker Company, 1982. Includes living persons in the field of language.

[5] See also Chapter 10, Biographical Dictionaries.

EXAMPLES OF PROFESSIONAL JOURNALS[6]

American Speech, A Quarterly of Linguistic Usage. University, Ala.: University of Alabama Press, 1925–   . (Quarterly.) Provides general and scholarly studies of English language in North America; covers dialect, current usage, structural linguistics, phonetics, dialects, geography, semantics, names, and vocabulary.

Modern Language Journal. Madison, Wis.: University of Wisconsin Press, 1916–   . (Quarterly, September–May.) Published by the National Federation of Modern Language Teachers Association; devoted to methods, pedagogical research, and topics of interest to all language teachers.

Modern Language Quarterly. Seattle: University of Washington, 1940–   . (Quarterly.) Contains critical studies of literary works and forms in English, Romance, and Germanic languages; covers use of language and form in literary works; gives book reviews.

PMLA. New York: Modern Language Association of America, 1884–   . (Six times a year.) The journal of MLA; presents scholarly and critical articles, professional news and notes, and bibliography. The abbreviation PMLA stands for Publications of the Modern Language Association.

Studies in Philology. Chapel Hill: University of North Carolina Press, 1906–   . Reports research in the classical and modern languages and literatures.

Review Questions

CHAPTER 20. LANGUAGE (PHILOLOGY)

1. Discuss language as a subject field.
2. Name the kinds of dictionaries useful in the study of language. Give an example of each kind.
3. Review Chapter 7. How do the dictionaries in this chapter differ from those discussed in Chapter 7?
4. Name one dictionary that is devoted to each of the items listed in your answer to Question 2, Chapter 7.

---

[6] See also *Ulrich's International Periodicals Directory*, 27th ed., and *Magazines for Libraries*, 5th ed., edited by Bill Katz and Linda S. Katz.

CHAPTER

❧ *21* ❧

Science and Technology

The word "science," deriving from a Latin word which means "to learn" or "to know," is in its broadest sense synonymous with learning and knowledge, and in general usage it means an organized body of knowledge. In a more restricted meaning, science is organized knowledge of natural phenomena and of the relations between them. Sciences are commonly classified as exact or descriptive. Exact sciences are those characterized by the possibility of exact measurement—for example, physics. Descriptive sciences are those which have developed a method of description or classification that permits precise reference to the subject matter—for example, zoology.

The 500 class of the Dewey Decimal Classification System, class Q in the Library of Congress classification, is assigned to pure sciences and includes mathematics, astronomy and allied sciences, physics, chemistry and allied sciences, earth sciences, paleontology, anthropology and biological sciences, botanical sciences, and zoological sciences.

Technology—applied science—is concerned with the tools (machines, instruments) and the techniques (methods, ways) for carrying out the plans, designs, etc., created by science. It has been defined as "the totality of the means employed to provide objects necessary for human sustenance and comfort."[1]

Technology (applied science) is placed in the 600 class, which comprises the medical sciences, engineering and allied operations, agriculture and agricultural industries, domestic arts and sciences, business and related enterprises, chemical technology, manufactures, and buildings. The Library

---

[1] *Webster's Seventh New Collegiate Dictionary* (Springfield, Mass.: G. & C. Merriam Company, Publishers, 1967), p. 905.

of Congress classification devotes parts of classes R, S, and T to these areas.

Books in science and technology become outdated more quickly than those in other subject fields, and the student who seeks material on a topic in any of these areas must consult periodicals, abstract journals,[2] and original sources—such as papers read at scientific meetings, reports, and patent applications—for the latest information. In addition to these sources, there are reference books designed to provide answers to the many questions which arise in this broad subject area. Among the most useful kinds of reference sources are bibliographies and guides, professional journals, abstract journals, indexes, handbooks, dictionaries and glossaries (both English and foreign-language), encyclopedias, yearbooks, directories, biographical dictionaries, and general histories.

The importance of frequently consulting the bibliographies in periodicals and abstract journals and the library catalog in order to keep up with new materials in these rapidly changing fields cannot be overemphasized.

Useful Reference Sources in Science and Technology

BIBLIOGRAPHIES[3]

Antony, Arthur. *Guide to Basic Information Sources in Chemistry.* New York: John Wiley & Sons, Inc., 1979. Arranges information sources by type with concise annotations; has a chapter on computer search strategy; includes nonprint, textbooks, and monographs; for students from freshman to graduate level.

Malinowsky, H. Robert, and Richardson, Jeanne M. *Science and Engineering Literature: A Guide to Reference Sources.* 3d ed. Littleton, Colo.: Libraries Unlimited, 1980. Arranged by subject, describes the nature of the various fields of science and engineering; offers discussions of basic types of scientific literature; annotates a selective list of sources in these areas; gives attention to computer-searchable data bases; energy, environment, and other important recent topics are covered.

---

[2] An abstract journal lists and provides digests or summaries of periodical articles and other literature. Abstracts may be in the original language in which the article appeared, or they may be translated into English or another language.

[3] See also Chapter 13, Bibliographies.

Scientific and Technical Books and Serials in Print, New York: R. R. Bowker Company, 1981– . (Annual.) Lists by author, title, and subject titles in print in all areas of the physical and biological sciences, engineering, and technology; the fourth edition lists some 18,000 periodicals by subject and title.

Walford, A. J. (ed.). *Guide to Reference Materials.* Vol. I: *Science and Technology.* 4th ed. London: The Library Association, 1980. Lists reference works in pure and applied science and technology; covers topics of recent interest (oil, drugs, computers, and astronautics); international in scope but with emphasis on items published in Britain.

Ward, Dedrick C., and others. *Geologic Reference Sources.* Metuchen, N.J.: Scarecrow Press, 1981. Covers general information sources, bibliography, abstracting services, and current awareness services of interest to the geological sciences; gives some annotations; includes a regional section with maps.

GUIDES

Bottle, R. T. (ed.). *The Use of Chemical Literature,* 3d ed. London: Butterworth & Company (Publishers), Ltd., 1979. Covers primary sources, abstracts, translations, dictionaries, monographs, tables, patent literature, and government publications; gives information about libraries and their use.

———— and Wyatt, H. V. (eds.). *The Use of Biological Literature.* 2d ed. (Information Sources for Research and Development.) Hamden, Conn.: Archon Books, 1971. Includes primary sources, translations, patents, abstracts in general and by specific subjects such as botany, zoology, ecology, genetics; treats use of libraries in research.

Chen, Ching-Cheh. *Scientific and Technical Information Sources.* Cambridge, Mass.: MIT Press, 1987. Presents a classified list of print and nonprint sources—guides, dictionaries, treatises, etc.—some with brief annotations.

Dick, Elie M. *Current Information Sources in Mathematics: An Annotated Guide to Books and Periodicals; 1960–1972.* Littleton, Colo.: Libraries Unlimited, Inc., 1973. Lists and describes books published in English during the period indicated; arranged by subject with author and subject indexes; includes list of important mathematics periodicals.

Smith, Roger, and others. *Guide to the Literature of the Life Sciences.* 9th ed. Minneapolis: Burgess Publishing Company, 1980. Offers material for

research in the biological sciences and suggestions for finding and using
it; gives an introductory discussion of the topics related to the life
sciences; includes information on the use of the library.

INDEXES[4]

Applied Science and Technology Index. New York: The H. W. Wilson Company,
1958– . (Monthly except July.) Indexes by subject more than 300
periodicals in aeronautics, automation, physics, chemistry, engineering,
industrial and mechanical arts, computer technology, energy, electricity
and electronics, and related fields. Author listing of citations to book
reviews follows main body of index.

The Biological and Agricultural Index. New York: The H. W. Wilson Company, 1964– . (Monthly except August.) Indexes by subject 200 periodicals in the field of agriculture, biology, and related areas; includes
book reviews in a separate section.

Engineering Index, 1906– . New York: Engineering Information, Inc., 1982.
(Annual.) International in scope; indexes literature in more than 2700
publications, including professional and trade journals, publications of
engineering societies, technical and scientific associations, government
agencies, conference proceedings, and selected books.

General Science Index. New York: The H. W. Wilson Company, 1978– .
(Monthly, except June and December; annual cumulation.) Indexes by
subject more than 100 general science periodicals published in the English language covering pure and applied science; each issue contains an
index to book reviews.

Index Medicus. Washington, D.C.: National Library of Medicine, 1960– .
(Monthly.) Published in various forms and by various publishers since
1879. A comprehensive index to the world's medical literature; indexes
completely or selectively 2300 biomedical journals by subject and name;
cumulated annually into the *Cumulated Index Medicus*; journal articles are
cited under the subject headings which represent the most important
concepts discussed; all citations are stored in the computerized bibliographic data base of the National Library of Medicine.

Technical Book Review Index. Compiled and edited in the Technology Department, Carnegie Library of Pittsburgh. (Monthly, except July and August.) New York: Special Libraries Association, 1933– .

---

[4] See also Chapter 9, Indexes.

DICTIONARIES—*SCIENCE*

Barnhart, Robert. *Hammond Barnhart Dictionary of Science*. Maplewood, N.J.: C. S. Hammond & Company, 1986. An aid to students in their beginning study of the physical and biological sciences; defines terms in all areas of the sciences.

Bynum, William F., and others (eds.). *Dictionary of the History of Science*. Princeton, N.J.: Princeton University Press, 1981. Explains the major ideas and concepts in western natural science developments over the last five centuries; also considers ideas important to natural science in antiquity, the Middle Ages, and nonwestern cultures; philosophical and metaphysical bases of science, historiography, and methods of scientific process are also treated.

Challinor, John. *A Dictionary of Geology*. 6th ed. Edited by Anthony Wyatt. New York: Oxford University Press, 1986. Aims to give a critical and historical review of the subject; defines some 1500 terms, giving both meaning and usage; illustrative quotations showing usage are from geological literature.

Holmes, Sandra. *Henderson's Dictionary of Biological Terms*. 9th ed. New York: Van Nostrand Reinhold Company, 1979. Defines about 22,500 terms, giving brief, concise definitions; includes the derivation of the term; explains acronyms.

James, Glenn, and James, Robert C. (eds.). *James & James Mathematics Dictionary*. 4th ed. New York: Van Nostrand Reinhold Company, 1976. Definitions range from terms in high school algebra and geometry to more advanced university topics in topology and analysis; designed for use by persons with some background in the field; includes brief biographical entries.

Lapedes, Daniel N. (ed.). *McGraw-Hill Dictionary of the Life Sciences*. New York: McGraw-Hill Book Company, 1976. Defines more than 20,000 terms in the biological sciences and related disciplines; includes many recent terms; illustrated.

————. *McGraw-Hill Dictionary of Scientific and Technical Terms*. 3d ed. New York: McGraw-Hill Book Company, 1984. Provides more than 100,000 definitions, each definition identified with a field of science or technology; electronics, computer science, physics, and chemistry are emphasized; includes brief biographies of about 1000 Nobel Prize winners or persons associated with laws and phenomena defined in the dictionary; has many illustrations; shows mathematical signs and symbols and international graphic symbols.

_____. *McGraw-Hill Dictionary of Physics and Mathematics*. New York: McGraw-Hill Book Company, 1978. Defines some 20,000 terms in physics, mathematics, and related disciplines; uses basic vocabulary and current and specialized terminology; illustrated.

Leftwich, A. W. *A Dictionary of Zoology*. 3d ed. Princeton, N.J.: D. Van Nostrand Company, 1973. For students as well as naturalists; includes brief, concise definitions of the principal phyla and classes of animals as well as a large number of orders, suborders, and families.

Little, R. John, and Jones, C. Eugene. *A Dictionary of Botany*. New York: Van Nostrand Reinhold Company, 1980. Defines some 5500 botanical terms.

Sax, N. Irving, and Lewis, Richard J. *Hawley's Condensed Chemical Dictionary*. 11th ed. New York: Van Nostrand Reinhold, 1987. Defines and discusses many thousands of chemical entities, phenomena, and terms.

Stenesh, J. *Dictionary of Biochemistry*. Philadelphia: Interscience Publishers, a division of John Wiley & Sons, Inc., 1975. Has some 12,000 entries covering terms in biochemistry and related fields.

Thewlis, J. *Concise Dictionary of Physics and Related Sciences*. 2d ed. New York: Pergamon Press, 1979. Emphasizes short definitions of terms from physics and related fields such as astronomy, astrophysics, meteorology, geophysics, physical chemistry, etc.; intended for college-level students, teachers, and educated nonspecialists.

_____. *The Encyclopaedic Dictionary of Physics*. New York: Pergamon Press, 1961–1963. 9 vols. Supplements I and II, 1966, 1967. An international work; presents the whole of physics and its related subjects; brief to lengthy articles, each complete in itself; provides bibliographies for further study; Vol. 9 is a multilingual glossary; annual supplements.

Thomson, Sir Arthur L. (ed.). *A New Dictionary of Birds*. New York: McGraw-Hill Book Company, 1964. Worldwide in scope; designed for both British and North American readers; provides long articles as well as short articles which define terms; includes bibliography; intended for both the general reader and the ornithologist; many illustrations in color and black and white.

DICTIONARIES—*TECHNOLOGY*

Black's Medical Dictionary. 34th ed. Edited by William A. R. Thompson. London: Adam and Charles Black, 1984. The standard British dictionary of terminology; includes sections on drugs and new subjects in medicine.

Blakiston's Gould's Medical Dictionary. 4th ed. New York: McGraw-Hill Book Company, 1979. Defines terms used in all branches of medicine and allied sciences; provides charts and anatomical tables; for students and practitioners.

Campbell, Robert J. *Psychiatric Dictionary*. 5th ed. New York: Oxford University Press, 1981. Includes terminology from psychiatry and related sciences; gives pronunciation, illustrations, quotations, and some bibliography.

Chandor, Anthony. *The Facts on File Dictionary of Microcomputers*. New York: Facts on File, Inc., 1981. Gives brief definitions of 2500 common terms in the field of microcomputers.

De Vries, Louis. *French-English Science and Technology Dictionary*. 4th ed. Revised and enlarged by Stanley Hochman. New York: McGraw-Hill Book Company, 1978. Includes 4500 terms; emphasizes new developments in electronics, automotive technology, astronautics.

———— and Hermann, T. M. (eds.). *English-German Technical and Engineering Dictionary*. 2d ed., revised and enlarged. New York: McGraw-Hill Book Company, 1966. For the engineer, research worker, translator, and student; offers over 225,000 terms; includes new words in the fields of nuclear physics, space flight, and plastics.

Dorland's Illustrated Medical Dictionary. 26th ed. Philadelphia: W. B. Saunders Company, 1985. Frequently revised; provides broad coverage of the field; gives pronunciations; claims that it is not just a record of usage but maintains "certain standards of etymological propriety and selection." *Dorland's Medical Dictionary, Shorter Edition* (1980) is an abridgment.

Graf, Rudolf F. *Modern Dictionary of Electronics*, 6th ed. New York: Howard W. Sams & Co., 1984. Includes new terms in special fields; has special pronunciation guide; includes most widely used symbols and abbreviations; features popular type of writing.

Hunt, V. Daniel. *Energy Dictionary*. New York: Van Nostrand Reinhold Company, 1979. Provides brief definitions of some 4000 terms in energy and in a variety of fields relating to energy production and use; has diagrams, charts, and other illustrations.

Markus, John. *Electronics Dictionary*. 4th ed. New York: McGraw-Hill Book Company, 1978. Provides easy-to-understand and up-to-date definitions of some 17,000 terms used in solid-state electronics, television, radio, computers, satellite communications, etc.

Melloni's Illustrated Medical Dictionary. 2d ed. Baltimore: The Williams & Wilkins Company, 1985. Defines 25,000 health science terms; has more than 2000 drawings.

Rosenberg, Jerry M. *Dictionary of Computers, Data Processing and Telecommunications.* New York: John Wiley & Sons, Inc., 1984. Defines terms; explains symbols, acronyms, and abbreviations, giving general and specialized meanings.

Sippl, Charles J. *Computer Dictionary.* 4th ed. Indianapolis: Howard W. Sams, 1985. Defines words, terms, concepts.

Spencer, Donald D. *Computer Dictionary for Everyone.* 3d ed. New York: Charles Scribner's Sons, 1985. Defines some 3000 terms in language for the layperson; includes information about persons important in the development of computers.

Stedman's Medical Dictionary. 24th ed. Baltimore: The Williams & Wilkins Company, 1982. "A vocabulary of medicine and its allied sciences with pronunciation and derivation" (subtitle); includes biographical sketches of persons important in the history of medicine.

ENCYCLOPEDIAS—*SCIENCE AND TECHNOLOGY*

Above and Beyond: The Encyclopedia of Aviation and Space Science. Chicago: New Horizons Publications, Inc., 1967–1969. 14 vols. Covers the full range of topics related to aviation and space from the earliest mythology into the predictable future; aims to be the world's first complete encyclopedia of aviation and space; includes biographies.

Besançon, Robert M. (ed.). *The Encyclopedia of Physics.* 2d ed. New York: Van Nostrand Reinhold Company, 1974. Provides short introductory articles on physics, the history of physics, measurements, symbols, and terminology; has general articles on the major areas of physics.

The Cambridge Encyclopaedia of Astronomy. By the Institute of Astronomy at the University of Cambridge. New York: Crown Publishing Company, 1977. Presents a broad survey of astronomy, covering stars, star systems, and galaxies, past and present; gives information on the latest astronomical findings; has a glossary.

The Cambridge Encyclopedia of Life Sciences. Edited by Adrian Friday and David S. Ingram. Cambridge: Cambridge University Press, 1985. Covers modern biology and related fields; numerous photographs and drawings, many in color.

Encyclopedia of Bioethics. New York: The Free Press, 1978. 4 vols. A comprehensive source of information on ethical and social issues in the life sciences, medicine, health care, and the health professions; covers such ethical and legal problems as abortion, genetics, organ transplantation, sterilization, medical malpractice, and privacy; discusses basic concepts and principles, ethical theories, religious traditions, value questions, norms of right conduct, history of medical ethics, and subject fields related to bioethics; provides bibliographies and an index.

Fairbridge, Rhodes W. *The Encyclopedia of World Regional Geology*. Part I: *Western Hemisphere*. New York: John Wiley & Sons, Inc., 1975. Includes Antarctica and Australia; gives geologic and geomorphic data by continent, region, country, and island group; for persons with a background in the subject.

Gray, Peter (ed.). *The Encyclopedia of the Biological Sciences*. 2d ed. New York: Van Nostrand Reinhold Company, 1970. Aims to provide succinct and accurate information for biologists in those fields in which they are not experts; defines and explains subjects; has lengthy articles; gives biographical information on some individuals in the field.

Groves, Donald G., and Hunt, Lee M. *Ocean World Encyclopedia*. New York: McGraw-Hill Book Company, 1980. Presents recent oceanographic research relating to the physics, geophysics, chemistry, and biology of the world's oceans: covers the geography of the ocean, the ocean floor, plant and animal life, and waves and currents; includes information about important oceanographers and organizations.

Grzimek's Encyclopedia of Ecology. Edited by Bernhard Grzimek. New York: Van Nostrand Reinhold Company, 1977. Covers almost every concept pertinent to ecology, including pesticides, atomic energy, and oxygen distribution.

Hora, Bayard. *The Oxford Encyclopedia of Trees of the World*. New York: Oxford University Press, 1981. Covers a wide range of the most significant trees of the world; discusses the anatomy and morphology of trees and ecology of forest regions; explains the importance of certain trees in their geographical area; gives information on cultivation, history, and commercial use; maps, photographs, other illustrative materials, many in color.

Hurlbut, C. S., Jr. (ed.). *The Planet We Live On: An Illustrated Encyclopedia of the Earth Sciences*. New York: Harry N. Abrams, Inc., 1976. Covers all aspects of the earth sciences—geology, meteorology, and oceanography—as well as lunar science; has many drawings, photographs, and diagrams.

Lapedes, Daniel (ed.). *McGraw-Hill Encyclopedia of the Geological Sciences*. New York: McGraw-Hill Book Company, 1980. Covers geology, geochemistry, geophysics, and aspects of oceanography and meteorology which are essential to understanding the materials, processes, composition, and physical characteristics of the solid part of the earth; has photographs, maps, graphs, drawings, and diagrams.

Larousse Encyclopedia of the Animal World. Edited by A. R. Waterston. New York: Larousse and Company, Inc., 1975. Surveys the animal kingdom from protozoans to mammals; treats each order, class, or genus and gives typical species; has 1000 photographs.

Lerner, Rita G., and Trigg, George L. (eds.). *Encyclopedia of Physics.* Reading, Mass.: Addison-Wesley Publishing Company, Inc., 1981. Covers the major areas of physics and subdivisions and interfaces between physics and other sciences; illustrated; gives bibliographical references for each article.

McGraw-Hill Encyclopedia of Science and Technology. 6th ed. New York: McGraw-Hill Book Company, 1987. 20 vols. Presents factual, basic data in all the physical sciences, earth sciences, life sciences, and engineering; describes recent developments and advances in all fields of science including astronomy and space technology, computers and electronics, communications, aeronautical engineering, energy, genetics, medicine, psychology, printing, industrial engineering, and many others; for students and scholars. Available on CD-ROM.

Newman, James R. (ed.). *The Harper Encyclopedia of Science.* Rev. ed. New York: Harper & Row, Publishers, 1967. 4 vols. Intended for the nonspecialist and planned as a work of moderate length, covering almost every aspect of pure and applied science, including scientific thought, history, and achievement; provides long articles; includes biographical sketches of leading scientists; has many illustrations; gives a bibliography in the final volume.

Parker, Sybil P. (ed.). *McGraw-Hill Encyclopedia of Energy.* 2d ed. New York: McGraw-Hill Book Company, 1980. Covers energy consumption, energy reserves, world energy, energy choices, economic and social aspects of energy, and protecting the environment.

————. *McGraw-Hill Encyclopedia of Environmental Science.* 2d ed. New York: McGraw-Hill Book Company, 1980. Offers articles on environmental protection, environmental analysis, precedents for weather extremes, urban planning, strip mining, noise pollution, water conservation, forests, and forestry.

————. *McGraw-Hill Encyclopedia of Ocean and Atmospheric Sciences.* New York: McGraw-Hill Book Company, 1980. Covers marine resources, weather modification, atmospheric pollution, and satellites; arranged alphabetically; illustrated.

Todd, David Keith (ed.). *The Water Encyclopedia, A Compendium of Useful Information on Water Resources.* Port Washington, N.Y.: Water Information Center, 1970. Gives a variety of information on water resources from many sources; presents facts, statistics, information regarding climate, hydrology, surface and ground water, resources agencies, water use, water quantity, and pollution control presented in tabular form; the only text is explanatory notes and footnotes.

Van Nostrand's Scientific Encyclopedia. 6th ed. Edited by D. M. Considine. New York: Van Nostrand Reinhold Company, 1983. Covers all science and technology; provides clear definitions, well-written articles, many illustrations and diagrams; has more than 7000 entries and some bibliographies.

Williams, Roger J., and Lansford, Edwin M., Jr. (eds.). *The Encyclopedia of Biochemistry.* New York: Reinhold Publishing Corporation, 1967. Provides explanatory information and broad discussions for the biochemist, more technical and detailed information for the specialist; serves as an introduction to a much larger body of literature, bibliographies follow articles; brief biographical information on famous biochemists.

HANDBOOKS

Burington, Richard Stevens. *Handbook of Mathematical Tables and Formulas.* 5th ed. New York: McGraw-Hill Book Company, 1973. A quick reference source of mathematical information, including a large collection of the most frequently needed tables.

Considine, Douglas M. (ed.). *Energy Technology Handbook.* New York: McGraw-Hill Book Company, 1977. Gives data in all areas of energy production where progress can be expected in the next few years; emphasizes scientific and engineering aspects; discusses projects from all over the world; has bibliographies.

Gray, Asa. *Gray's Manual of Botany.* 8th ed. New York: American Book Company, 1950. Corrected printing, 1970. Identifies the flowering plants and ferns of the central and northeastern United States and nearby Canada. Centennial edition of a standard handbook.

Helms, Harry (ed.). *The McGraw-Hill Computer Handbook.* New York: McGraw-Hill Book Company, 1983. Addressed to the nonexpert; covers the history of computers, hardware, software, computer languages, voice recognition, robots, and other topics.

Howard, Neale E. *The Telescope Handbook and Star Atlas.* Rev. 2d ed. New York: Thomas Y. Crowell Company, 1975. Describes celestial phenomena; gives photographs and diagrams of astronomical instruments; identifies and locates 239 stars; designed for amateur astronomers.

Kreider, J. F., and Kreith, F. (eds.). *Solar Energy Handbook*. New York: McGraw-Hill Book Company, 1981. "Covers the history of solar technology, solar law, solar design, wind power and many more aspects of solar energy; uses charts, conversion tables, bibliographies."

Lange's Handbook of Chemistry. Edited by John A. Dean. 13th ed. New York: McGraw-Hill Book Company, 1985. A compilation of facts, data, tabular material, and experimental findings; provides ready access to every aspect of chemistry; for students and professionals.

Loftness, Robert L. *The Energy Handbook*. 2d ed. New York: Van Nostrand Reinhold, 1984. Covers energy resources, technology, and policies; has maps, tables, charts, and a glossary.

Perry, Robert H. (ed.). *Engineering Manual*. 3d ed. New York: McGraw-Hill Book Company, 1976. For students, engineers, and technical people in general; covers standard fields of engineering in individual chapters.

The Peterson Field Guide Series. Boston: Houghton Mifflin Company, 1934– . Under the editorship of Roger Tory Peterson; each title treats a specific subject, such as birds, shells, butterflies, mammals, rocks and minerals, animal tracks, ferns, trees and shrubs, reptiles and amphibians, wildflowers, stars and planets; usually regional in coverage; useful for identification purposes; illustrated. *A Field Guide to the Birds* (1980) is the latest work in the series.

"Putnam's Nature Field Books." New York: G. P. Putnam's Sons, 1928– . This series includes separate volumes on specific scientific subjects. Titles include *Field Book of American Wild Flowers*, by F. S. Mathews; *Field Book of the Stars*, by W. T. Olcott; and *Field Book of Common Rocks and Minerals*, by F. B. Loomis.

Rickett, Harold William (ed.). *Wildflowers of the United States*. New York: McGraw-Hill Book Company, 1966–1973. 6 vols. in 14. Prepared in cooperation with the New York Botanical Gardens; provides full-color photographs of thousands of wildflowers, most of them shown in their natural habitats; gives both Latin and common names. Vol. I: *The Northeastern States* (2 vols.). Vol. II: *The Southeastern States* (2 vols.). Vol. III: *Texas* (2 vols.). Vol. IV: *The Southwestern States* (3 vols.). Vol. V: *The Northwestern States* (2 vols.). Vol. VI: *The Central Mountains and Plains* (3 vols.). *Index*. 1975.

Walker, Ernest P. *Walker's Mammals of the World*. By Ronald M. Nowac and John L. Paradiso. 4th ed. Baltimore: Johns Hopkins University Press, 1983. 2 vols.

YEARBOOKS[5]

McGraw-Hill Year Book of Science and Technology. New York: McGraw-Hill Book Company, 1961– . (Annual.) Planned as an annual supplement to the *McGraw-Hill Encyclopedia of Science and Technology*; summarizes the significant events and advances of the previous year in every area of science and technology and serves to keep the *Encyclopedia* up to date.

U.S. Department of Agriculture. *Yearbook of Agriculture*. Washington, D.C.: Government Printing Office, 1894– . Covers a specific subject in each issue, such as soil, water, food, or trees.

U.S. Department of Interior, Bureau of Mines. *Minerals Yearbook*. Washington D.C.: Government Printing Office, 1933– . Reviews performance and developments in the nation's mineral industries; includes statistical summaries.

BIOGRAPHICAL DICTIONARIES[6]

American Men and Women of Science: Physical and Biological Sciences. 16th ed. Edited by Jaques Cattell Press. New York: R. R. Bowker Company, 1986. 8 vols. Gives biographical information on American and Canadian men and women now working and teaching in the physical, biological, and engineering sciences. On-line access to this data base has been available since 1981.

Dictionary of Scientific Biography. Published under the auspices of the Council of Learned Societies. New York: Charles Scribner's Sons, 1970–1981. 14 vols. Vol. XV, *Supplement*, 1977; Vol. XVI, *Index*, 1981. Describes and evaluates the lives of more than 5000 scientists from all regions and periods; does not include living persons; gives biographical information and information on the contributions of each person in relation to other scientists; each biography has a bibliography of works by and about the biographee. *Concise Dictionary of Scientific Biography* (1981) is an abridgment of the basic work.

---

[5] Most of the societies in the subject fields issue a yearbook—e.g., *The Yearbook of Mathematics*. Some encyclopedias issue a science supplement—e.g., *Science Year*, issued to supplement *World Book Encyclopedia* (1965–). Other yearbooks and annuals provide information on activities in the fields of science and technology during the preceding year. These titles are examples of yearbooks which treat subdivisions of science and technology.

[6] See also Chapter 10, Biographical Dictionaries.

McGraw-Hill Modern Scientists and Engineers. New York: McGraw-Hill Book Company, 1980. 3 vols. Contains 1140 biographies of scientists and engineers from the 1920s to the present—living and not living.

Ogilvie, Marilyn. *Women in Science.* Cambridge, Mass.: MIT Press, 1986. Provides information about women who made a contribution to science from antiquity through the nineteenth century.

ATLASES

Audouze, Jean, and Israel Guy (eds.). *The Cambridge Atlas of Astronomy.* Cambridge: Cambridge University Press, 1985. Presents what is currently known about the universe in text and illustrations, color and black and white.

Cuff, David J., and Young, William J. *The United States Energy Atlas.* New York: The Free Press, A Division of Macmillan Publishing Company, 1981. Uses maps, photographs, charts, diagrams, and tables to locate America's energy sources; gives comprehensive and comparative coverage to each energy source; has a glossary of energy terms, bibliographies, and an index.

Our Magnificent Earth: A Rand McNally Atlas of Earth Resources. Chicago: Rand McNally & Company, 1979. Arranged in six sections: the nature of resources, the resources of people, energy, living resources, minerals, and planning for tomorrow; explains major topics related to the earth's resources; combines text and illustrations—photographs, charts, maps, diagrams.

The Rand McNally Atlas of the Oceans. Chicago: Rand McNally & Company, 1977. Gives a comprehensive survey of the ocean regions; the birth and evolution of oceans, marine life, and minerals.

EXAMPLES OF PROFESSIONAL JOURNALS IN SCIENCE AND TECHNOLOGY[7]

American Chemical Society Journal. Washington, D.C.: American Chemical Society, 1879– . (Fortnightly.) Reports significant research in all branches of chemistry; has a section on short preliminary studies of importance; gives book reviews.

American Journal of Physics. College Park, Md.: 1933– . (Monthly.) Published by the American Association of Physics Teachers; represents the

---

[7] See also *Ulrich's International Periodicals Directory*, 27th ed., and *Magazines for Libraries*, 5th ed., edited by Bill Katz and Linda S. Katz.

entire field; reports on new techniques and apparatus; includes some abstracts; gives book reviews.

American Journal of Public Health. Washington, D.C.: American Public Health Association, 1911– . (Monthly.) Covers all aspects of public health; written for the expert but has information of interest to nonexperts; discusses current issues in health; gives book reviews.

American Mathematical Monthly. Washington, D.C.: Mathematical Association of America, 1894– . (Ten times a year.) The official journal of the association; aimed at the college-level mathematics student; presents papers and notes, including reports of research; includes book reviews.

Geological Society of America. *Bulletin.* Boulder, Colo.: Geological Society of America, 1888– . (Monthly.) The official publication of the society; concerned with original research on any facet of geology, including geochemistry, geophysics, mineralogy, etc.; has long and short articles; illustrated.

JAMA: The Journal of the American Medical Association. Chicago: American Medical Association, 1848– . (Weekly.) The official journal of the association; reviews current research; reports advances in the field of medical science; gives selected abstracts of world's medical literature; gives information on current topics of interest to the medical profession; includes news, views, and reviews of the profession.

Journal of Geology. Chicago: University of Chicago Press, 1893– . (Bimonthly.) Concerned with original studies in all aspects of geology; some issues are devoted to a single subject; has book reviews; international in scope.

Natural History. New York: American Museum of Natural History, 1900– . (Monthly.) Provides a popular approach to many topics of interest to nature lovers, including conservation, anthropology, geography, and astronomy; authoritative articles are written in semipopular style; has many photographs.

Nature. London: Macmillan Journals, Ltd., 1869– . (Three weekly editions.) A British publication; represents all branches of science; gives essay and review articles by leading scientists and some studies on original research; provides both general and specialized treatment; includes book reviews.

Scientific American. New York: Scientific American, 1845– . (Monthly.) Reports scientific and technical advances and theories; for both general readers and specialists; has many illustrated articles; gives book reviews.

Sky and Telescope. Cambridge, Mass.: Sky Publishing Corporation, 1941– (Monthly.) For beginners in astronomy; features articles by experts; includes information on telescope accessions, observations, celestial calendars, etc.; has news notes.

ABSTRACT JOURNALS[8]

Biological Abstracts. Philadelphia: Biological Abstracts, 1926– . (Semi-monthly.) Covers the world's biological research literature in agriculture, genetics, behavioral sciences, and other related fields, including periodical publications, books, government reports, and reports of conferences; is the major abstracting source for the biological sciences; entries are arranged under broad subject headings with many subdivisions.

Chemical Abstracts. Washington, D.C.: American Chemical Society. 1907– . (Weekly.) Provides abstracts from about 12,000 journals covering fifty languages, patents from twenty-five countries, and theses, books, conference proceedings, and government reports; makes available some 240,000 abstracts annually; not confined to chemistry but covers all scientific and technical literature; reports new chemical information from patent literature; covers all scientific and technical papers; now on machine-readable tape for computer searching.

Mathematical Reviews. Providence, R.I.: American Mathematical Society, 1940– . (Monthly.) Abstracts and reviews mathematical literature appearing in some 1200 journals and books, conference proceedings, and translations grouped under general subject headings; international in scope.

Pollution Abstracts. Bethesda, Md.: Cambridge Scientific Abstracts, 1970– . (Bimonthly.) Divided into chapters by subject (such as air, fresh water, land, noise pollution) or by type of document cited (such as government documents, patents); includes books, journals, papers, government reports.

Science Abstracts. London: Institution of Electrical Engineers 1898– . (Monthly.) Includes physics abstracts, electrical and electronics abstracts, and computer and control abstracts; covers journals, papers, books, and conference proceedings; arranged by classified subject headings; available on magnetic tape for computer searches.

Review Questions

CHAPTER 21. SCIENCE AND TECHNOLOGY

1. Examine Class Q in the Library of Congress Classification System (p. 58) to see the large subdivisions in the Science class. Find one or more titles in this chapter which treat each of those subdivisions.

---

[8] This is just a sample; there are abstract journals in every major area of science and technology.

2. See the subdivisions of Classes R, S, and T on pp. 58–59. Name a
   title in this chapter that is devoted to each of the following: medicine,
   agriculture, electronics, engineering, pollution, computers, the
   environment.

The Fine Arts

Art—the word is derived from the Latin *ars*—is any skill or aptitude which enables its possessor to perform in a superior manner. This meaning of the word covers (1) the fine arts, which express ideas, emotions, and experiences in beautiful or significant forms; (2) the useful arts, which are both utilitarian and artistic; (3) the decorative arts, which adorn rather than create; and (4) the recreational arts, which afford relaxation and amusement.

The fine arts, as a branch of knowledge, are those arts (skills or aptitudes) concerned with creating, producing, or expressing what is beautiful, imaginative, or appealing for its own sake, rather than for some utilitarian purpose. Traditionally, the fine arts include music, painting, sculpture, dance, drama, architecture, and poetry.

In the fine arts class of the Dewey Decimal Classification System (700), all the above-named fine arts are included except poetry. Landscape and civic arts, drawing and decorative arts, prints and printmaking, photography, and recreation are also placed in the 700 class. In the Library of Congress classification, M is music and N is fine arts. Recreation is placed in the G class (GV).

Works of art—that is, paintings, sculpture, musical scores, dramatic productions, etc.—constitute the primary source materials in the fine arts subject field. There are, however, many reference sources designed to aid the student in understanding and appreciating works of art; the artists who produced them; the technical terminology of the several areas; the historical backgrounds of schools, movements, and trends; and the actual techniques employed. Those reference aids include bibliographies, guides and catalogs, indexes to periodical literature and to paintings and illustrations, dictionaries and encyclopedias, biographical dictionaries, handbooks, histories, and professional journals.

Useful Reference Sources in the Fine Arts

PAINTING, SCULPTURE, ARCHITECTURE, AND DECORATIVE ARTS

Bibliographies, guides, and indexes[1]

Appel, Marsha (ed.). *Illustration Index*. 4th ed. Metuchen, N.J.: Scarecrow Press, 1980. Indexes photographs, paintings, drawings, and diagrams in major periodicals, 1972–1976; arranged by subject; includes wildlife, furniture, art works, and pictures of individuals. *Illustration Index V: 1977–1981*. Methuen, N.J.: Scarecrow Press, 1984.

Arntzen, Etta, and Rainwater, Robert (comps.). *Guide to the Literature of Art History*. Chicago: American Library Association, 1981. An update and revision of Chamberlin's *Guide to Art Reference Books* (1959); organizes and evaluates the literature of art history—the basic reference works and sources for advanced research; annotates more than 4000 sources, including general reference sources, bibliographies, directories, encyclopedias, handbooks, primary sources, histories, periodicals, and serials; includes basic monographs on each of the arts arranged by period and region.

The Art Index. New York: The H. W. Wilson Company, 1929– . (Quarterly.) Indexes more than 200 selected art journals, museum publications, domestic art publications, and foreign journals by author and subject; includes fine arts and applied arts; citations to book reviews are arranged alphabetically by author in a separate section of the index.

British Humanities Index. London: Library Association, 1962– . (Quarterly; annual cumulations.) Index to 400 British journals covering architecture, art, cinema, sports and games, language, law, music, politics, television, and theater.

Clapp, Jane. *Sculpture Index*. Metuchen, N.J.: Scarecrow Press, Inc., 1970–1971. 2 vols. Indexes pictures of sculpture in some 950 art publications; traces sculpture from prehistoric times to the present; for each work, gives the present location of the sculpture, dimensions, materials of construction, and picture sources; Vol. I covers Europe and the contemporary Middle East; Vol. II covers the Americas, the Orient, Africa, the Pacific, and the Classical world.

Ehresmann, Donald L. *Applied and Decorative Arts: A Bibliographic Guide to Basic Reference Works, Histories, and Handbooks*. Littleton, Colo.: Libraries Unlimited, 1977. Includes both scholarly and popular works written in

---

[1] See also Chapter 9, Indexes, and Chapter 13, Bibliographies.

western European languages from 1875 to 1975; is annotated; includes works on ceramics, toys, furniture, folk art, and ornament.

————. *Fine Arts: A Bibliographic Guide to Basic Reference Works, Histories, and Handbooks.* 2d ed. Littleton, Colo.: Libraries Unlimited, 1979. Annotates a basic list of more than 1600 titles published in western European languages between 1930 and 1978; includes only works which treat one or more of the fine arts; covers oriental as well as western art; arranged by geographical regions.

Ellis, Jessie Croft. *Index to Illustrations.* Boston: F. W. Faxon Company, 1967. Indexes paintings, people, places, and symbols in books and in some periodicals; does not include nature illustrations.

Turner, Pearl. *Collectors Index.* Westwood, Mass.: F. W. Faxon Company, Inc., 1980. Provides information on how to collect, maintain, display, and determine the value of numerous collectible items; lists collectible items alphabetically with page reference to books published between 1972 and 1981; covers a wide range of collectibles, including those of long-standing interest as well as recent interest, such as comic books.

Dictionaries and encyclopedias

Adeline, Jules. *The Adeline Art Dictionary.* Translated from the French, with a supplement of new terms, by Hugo G. Beigel. New York: Frederick Ungar Publishing Company, 1966. A republication of the *Adeline Art Dictionary* with a supplement of new terms, gives brief, clear definitions and explanations; many illustrations; includes terms in architecture, heraldry, and archaeology.

Baigell, Matthew. *Dictionary of American Art.* New York: Harper & Row, Publishers, 1980. Provides information about American painters, sculptors, printmakers, and photographers, as well as about movements in American art from the sixteenth century to the present. Emphasis is on artistic achievement rather than biographical information.

Encyclopedia of American Art. New York: E. P. Dutton & Company, Inc., 1981. Gives a summary of American art and artists from pre-Revolutionary times to the present—painting, sculpture, architecture, prints, photography, folk arts, decorative arts, and contemporary handicrafts; covers styles, materials, and techniques; arranged alphabetically; lists some museums.

Encyclopedia of World Art. New York: McGraw-Hill Book Company, 1959–1968. 15 vols. Includes biographies of artists; has monographic treatments of periods, movements, and areas of art; gives discussions of types, media, technology, concepts, and problems of art; provides bibliographies.

Fleming, John, and Honour, Hugh. *Dictionary of Decorative Arts*. New York: Harper & Row, Publishers, Incorporated, 1977. A guide to the decorative arts of the west from the Middle Ages to the present; emphasizes European and American art but gives attention to China, Japan, Turkey, and Persia; covers all forms of art; defines and explains stylistic and technical terms; has many illustrations.

The Focal Encyclopedia of Photography. Rev. ed. New York: McGraw-Hill Book Company, 1977. 2 vols. Covers new techniques, new subjects, new terminology; includes some statistical, historical, geographical, and biographical information; discusses the major developments in the field; provides practical information for both professional and amateur.

Garner, Philippe (ed.). *The Encyclopedia of Decorative Arts, 1890–1940*. New York: Van Nostrand Reinhold, 1979. Arranged by country; reviews the major styles and influences of the period covered; includes major categories of decorative arts (furniture, glass, ceramics, metal, and graphic arts); relates the decorative arts to other arts and events of each period covered.

Gouring, Lawrence (ed.). *The Encyclopedia of Visual Art*. Englewood Cliffs, N.J.: Prentice-Hall, 1983. 2 vols. Vol. I: *History of Art*; Vol. II: *Biographies*.

Harris, Cyril M. (ed.). *Dictionary of Architecture and Construction*. New York: McGraw-Hill Book Company, 1975. Provides clear definitions of current basic terminology in architecture and construction; has many illustrations.

————. *Historic Architecture Sourcebook*. New York: McGraw-Hill Book Company, 1977. Defines more than 5000 terms in both eastern and western architecture covering some 5000 years; has many line drawings.

McGraw-Hill Dictionary of Art. New York: McGraw-Hill Book Company, 1969. 5 vols. Gives worldwide coverage of concepts, styles, periods, movements, and works of art; includes biographies.

Praeger Encyclopedia of Art. New York: Praeger Publishers, Inc., 1971. 5 vols. Aims to provide a comprehensive and authoritative reference guide for students and general readers to the history of world art; includes biographies, chronological surveys, and articles on periods, styles, and schools; gives articles on civilizations for which no artists' names are known.

Savage, George. *Dictionary of Antiques*. New York: Praeger Publishers, Inc., 1970. Emphasizes style and fashion in art; has articles on almost every aspect of American and European decorative art; gives definitions for terms and explains techniques; provides biographical information on individual artisans; designed to help readers recognize fakes in antiques; includes bibliographies.

Stevenson, George A. *Graphic Arts Encyclopedia*. 2d ed. New York: McGraw-Hill Book Company, 1979. Provides information on terms, techniques, processes, concepts, equipment, and methods in the graphic arts profession; covers electronic text processing, copying machines, and other recent developments; has illustrations, tables, and charts.

Torbet, Laura (ed.). *The Encyclopedia of Crafts*. New York: Charles Scribner's Sons, 1980. 4 vols. Provides basic information on the terminology, history, tools and materials, techniques, and processes of fifty major crafts from all over the world; has many illustrations.

Walker, John A. *Glossary of Art, Architecture and Design Since 1945*. London: Clive Bingley, 1977. Covers contemporary art terminology with emphasis on painting, sculpture, and architecture; groups and styles are discussed; international in scope but emphasizes Anglo-American terminology.

Wilkes, Joseph A. (ed.). *Encyclopedia of Architecture: Design, Engineering and Construction*. New York: John Wiley & Sons, 1987– . Vol. 1– . (In progress.) Covers construction, materials, design, planning, and energy considerations; includes biography and history of architectural building types; has many illustrations and tables.

Yarwood, Doreen. *The Encyclopedia of World Costume*. New York: Charles Scribner's Sons, 1978. Portrays costume and costume-related topics from the ancient world to the present in text and illustrations; covers various historical periods and geographical areas; gives the history and development of each garment as well as the forms and designs of that garment.

Handbooks

Osborne, Harold (ed.). *The Oxford Companion to Art*. Oxford: Clarendon Press, 1970. "Nonspecialist introduction to the fine arts" (Preface); has only introductory articles; includes visual arts, but excludes arts of the theater and cinema; covers all parts of the world from earliest times to the present; includes brief historical articles; some bibliographies are given.

————. *The Oxford Companion to Twentieth Century Art*. New York: Oxford University Press, 1982. Covers the entire range of twentieth century art; includes architects and photographers if their work is related to other art forms.

The Oxford Companion to the Decorative Arts. Oxford: Clarendon Press, 1975. Some 1000 illustrated articles written by experts cover prehistoric crafts and technologies to modern times; includes some biographies; gives information on schools, styles, processes, and ornamentation; emphasis is on the western world.

Biographical dictionaries and directories[2]

American Art Directory. 49th ed. New York: R. R. Bowker Company, 1982. (Biennial.) Includes art associations and museums, periodicals, scholarships, art schools, and people and places in United States and Canadian art.

Cederholm, Theresa A. (comp. and ed.). *Afro-American Artists: A Bio-bibliographical Directory*. Boston: Boston Public Library, 1973. Provides biographical information on some 2000 American artists, identifies media used, titles of works, and locations of permanent collections.

Cummings, Paul. *A Dictionary of Contemporary American Artists*. 5th ed. New York: St. Martin's Press, 1988. Gives personal data and bibliographical references for further study on contemporary painters, sculptors, and printmakers; has black and white illustrations.

_____. *Fine Arts Market Place*. 3d ed. New York: R. R. Bowker Company, 1977. Gives information about art associations, exhibitions, organizations, suppliers, services, dealers, publishers, auction houses, suppliers of art materials, etc.

Emanuel, Muriel (ed.). *Contemporary Architects*. New York: St. Martin's Press, 1980. Provides detailed information on about 600 contemporary architects of international reputation, including landscape architects and structural engineers: biographical information; a chronological sketch of constructed works or projects; illustration of a significant work; a bibliography of books and articles by and about the architect; an essay about his or her career; some photographs.

Macmillan Encyclopedia of Architects. New York: Macmillan/Free Press, 1982. 4 vols. Biographies cover more than 2450 architects from ancient to recent times, giving information about their training, careers, and influence; has a glossary of technical terms; black and white illustrations.

Marks, Claude. *World Artists 1950–1980*. New York: The H. W. Wilson Company, 1984. Presents 312 artists who have been influential in the post–World War II period: life, work, and methods; includes painting, sculpture, graphic media; lists collections of each artist's work.

Larousse Dictionary of Painters. New York: Larousse & Company, 1981. Gives biographical information about more than 500 important western paint-

[2] See also Chapter 10, Biographical Dictionaries.

ers from medieval times to the present; includes an evaluation of their work, the museums which have their paintings, and examples of each artist's work, most of them in color.

Norman, Geraldine. *Nineteenth-Century Painters and Painting: A Dictionary.* Berkeley, Calif.: University of California Press, 1977. A biographical dictionary of painters and a historical survey of painting of the period; painting schools, movements, styles, and important institutions are covered.

Richards, J. M. (ed.). *Who's Who in Architecture from 1400 to the Present.* New York: Holt, Rinehart and Winston, Inc., 1977. Covers the period from the early Renaissance to the present, emphasizing the west; other areas are included; both factual and critical articles are provided; has many illustrations.

Rubinstein, Charlotte S. *American Women Artists: From Early Indian Times to the Present.* Boston: G. K. Hall, 1982. Gives biography and criticism of leading women painters and sculptors. Black and white illustrations.

Watson-Jones, Virginia. *Contemporary American Women Sculptors.* Phoenix, Ariz.: Oryx Press, 1986. Treats some 328 American women sculptors briefly; gives personal information, including education, collections, awards, exhibitions, and media.

Who's Who in American Art. 17th ed. Edited by the Jaques Cattell Press. New York: R. R. Bowker Company, 1986. (Revised biennially.) Gives biographies of American and Canadian artists including professional painters, sculptors, illustrators, graphic artists, executives, collectors, patrons, scholars, and critics.

Examples of professional journals[3]

Art Bulletin. New York: College Art Association of America, 1913– . (Quarterly.) Contains articles for students of art history written by faculty members of the association and covering all facets and periods of fine arts.

Art in America. New York: Art in America, Inc., 1913– . (Bimonthly.) International in scope; emphasis is on contemporary art; includes some historical articles; covers painting, sculpture, architecture, design, and photography.

---

[3] See also *Ulrich's International Periodicals Directory*, 27th ed., and *Magazines for Libraries*, 5th ed., edited by Bill Katz and Linda S. Katz.

MUSIC

Music, according to *The Oxford English Dictionary*, is "that one of the fine arts which is concerned with the combination of sounds with a view of beauty of form and the expression of emotion; . . . the science of the laws or principles (of melody, harmony, rhythm, etc.) by which the art is regulated."[4]

The literature of music covers works on music as a whole or a part; the music of various nations and peoples; the technical aspects of music (theory, notation, tone, and harmony); the history of music and musicians; musical form and the means of executing it (instrument or voice, group or individual); the types of music (for example, jazz, folk songs, and Greek music); critical studies of music and musicians; musical scores; biographical information on performers, composers, and lyricists; and the teaching of music.

There are many reference sources which are designed to aid in the study, interpretation, understanding, and appreciation of music. Some of these are: bibliographies, guides, indexes, dictionaries, encyclopedias, handbooks, biographical dictionaries, professional journals, and many kinds of nonbook sources. (See Chapter 14 for a discussion of nonbook information sources.)

Bibliographies, guides, and indexes[5]

Cohn, Arthur. *Recorded Classical Music; A Critical Guide to Compositions and Performances.* New York: Macmillan Publishing Company, 1981. Describes and evaluates the best recordings of classical music; arranged alphabetically by composer; gives one or more recommended recordings with commentary for each one.

Duckles, Vincent Harris (comp.). *Music Reference and Research Materials: An Annotated Bibliography.* 3d ed. New York: The Free Press of Glencoe, Inc., 1974. Points out and describes the resources of the field with emphasis on dictionaries, encyclopedias, histories, chronologies, bibliographies of music and music literature, guides to research methods in musicology, and catalogs of major music libraries and collections throughout the world; does not include biographical material.

Horn, David (comp.). *The Literature of American Music in Books and Folk Music Collections: A Fully Annotated Bibliography.* Metuchen, N.J.: Scarecrow Press, Inc., 1977. Aims to include all English-language material— scholarly, historical, or popular—and a sample of books in other languages.

---

[4] *The Oxford English Dictionary*, VI, 1933, 782.

[5] See also Chapter 9, Indexes, and Chapter 13, Bibliographies.

Music Index. Detroit: Information Coordinators, Inc., 1949– . (Monthly; annual cumulations.) A subject and author guide to current music periodical literature; indexes more than 400 periodicals treating various aspects of the music field; book reviews are listed under that heading.

Shapiro, Nat (ed.). *Popular Music, An Annotated Index of American Popular Songs.* 10 vols. New York: Adrian Press, 1964–1985. Aims to provide selective annotated lists by decades of significant American popular songs, giving discussions of the decades in question and, for each song, information about the composer, lyricist, current publisher, recordings, film or stage show in which it was introduced, and performers associated with it. Volumes 7–10 published by Gale Research Company, 1984–1985.

Dictionaries

Ammer, Christine. *Harper's Dictionary of Music.* New York: Harper & Row, Publishers, Incorporated, 1972. Defines the most commonly used musical terms; gives material on music history and biographical material about composers; emphasizes popular music; includes information about musical forms and musical instruments.

Arnold, Denis (ed.). *The New Oxford Companion to Music.* Oxford: Oxford University Press, 1983. 2 vols. International in coverage; treats careers and achievements of musicians, the history of music in various countries, individual works, instruments, forms of music, music theory, and other topics. Emphasis is on classical music.

Everyman's Dictionary of Music. 5th ed., revised and enlarged. Compiled by Eric Blom, revised by Jack Westrup and others. New York: St. Martin's Press, 1972. Aims to provide "the maximum amount of information possible in a limited space" (Preface); includes living composers and composers not living, but does not include all composers; defines terms, identifies works, and gives musical illustrations.

Fink, Robert, and Ricci, Robert. *The Language of Twentieth Century Music: A Dictionary of Terms.* New York: Schirmer Books, a Division of Macmillan, Inc., 1975. Defines basic terminology in current use by composers and performers in computer music, electronic music, jazz, film music, rock, etc.

Griffiths, Paul. *The Thames and Hudson Encyclopaedia of 20th Century Music.* London: Thames & Hudson, 1986. International in scope; presents contemporary musical subjects such as ensembles, instruments, techniques, biography; arranged chronogically 1901–1985.

Hitchcock, Wiley, and Sadie, Stanley (eds.). *The New Grove Dictionary of*

American Music. New York: Grove's Dictionaries of Music, 1986. All aspects of specifically American music are included: jazz, popular, folk, serious, regional, ethnic, American composers and performers, music periodicals, etc. Has illustrations and musical notations.

Kennedy, Michael. *The Oxford Dictionary of Music.* New York: Oxford University Press, 1985. Provides articles on composers, performers, and other persons in music; gives brief definition or identification of terms, titles of works, types of music and instruments; covers new developments in music.

The New Grove Dictionary of Music and Musicians. Edited by Stanley Sadie. New York: Macmillan Publishing Company, 1980. Distributed by Grove's Dictionaries of Music. 20 vols. Both a dictionary and an encyclopedia; includes all types of music and performers up to the present; explains terms, concepts, forms, and genres; gives brief and lengthy critical biographies; covers nonwestern music; offers many illustrations (musical notations, facsimiles of manuscripts, and pictures of composers); has extensive bibliographies.

Picerno, Vincent J. *Dictionary of Musical Terms.* Brooklyn: Haskell House Publishers, Ltd., 1976. Gives simple definitions of contemporary musical terms in all languages; does not give biographical information; intended for college students taking undergraduate courses in music and for nonspecialists; gives pronunciation and brief definition of terms; has a selected annotated bibliography.

Randel, Don Michael (ed.). *The New Harvard Dictionary of Music.* Cambridge, Mass.: Belknap, Harvard University Press, 1986. Brings the previous editions by Apel up to date and expands coverage of recent music, including jazz and rock; covers music of some ninety countries and regions, instruments from earliest times to the present, and history and theory of music.

Rosenthal, Harold, and Warrock, John. *The Concise Dictionary of Opera.* 2d ed. New York: Oxford University Press, 1979. Covers the development of opera throughout the world; includes explanation of terminology, plots of major operas, and information about composers and performers; has bibliographies.

Sadie, Stanley (ed.). *The New Grove Dictionary of Musical Instruments.* New York: Grove's Dictionaries of Music, 1984. 3 vols. Based on *The New Grove Dictionary of Music*; covers instruments of classical and modern Western music and their makers, non-Western music, and folk instruments.

Scholes, Percy A. (ed.). *The Concise Oxford Dictionary of Music.* 2d ed. Edited by John Owen Ward. New York: Oxford University Press, 1964. For the layman; illustrated; gives brief information on composers, musical compositions, performances, and terminology. Rev. ed. by Michael Kennedy, 1980.

Tudor, Dean. *Popular Music: An Annotated Guide to Recordings*. Littleton, Colo.: Libraries Unlimited, 1984. Includes old and contemporary popular music with annotation and discographic information.

Vinton, John (ed.). *Dictionary of Contemporary Music*. New York: E. P. Dutton & Company, Inc., 1974. Covers stylistic and technical aspects of concert music in the western tradition of the present day and of the last several decades; gives biographical information and list of works for some 1000 composers who were living after 1930; provides survey articles on technical and special topics of current importance in music.

Encyclopedias

Ewen, David. *The New Encyclopedia of the Opera*. New York: Hill and Wang, Inc., 1971. Gives stories of the most significant operas in detail; others are given briefly; identifies characters of operas; gives passages from operas, history of opera, some biographies, and literary sources of operas.

Feather, Leonard G., and Gitler, Ira. *The Encyclopedia of Jazz in the Seventies*. New York: Horizon Press, 1977. Covers the period 1966–1976; examines all forms of jazz; includes biographical information and bibliography.

Nite, Norm N. *Rock On: The Illustrated Encyclopedia of Rock 'n' Roll*. Updated ed. New York: Harper & Row, Publishers, Incorporated, 1982. Vol. I: *The Solid Gold Years*. Provides brief biographical and career information on the popular recording artists of the 1950s, 1960s, and 1970s. Vol. II: *The Modern Years, 1964–Present* (1978). Offers the same coverage for the period 1964–1978.

Orrey, Leslie (ed.). *The Encyclopedia of Opera*. New York: Charles Scribner's Sons, 1976. Contains information on a limited number of operas and persons concerned with their production: composers, librettists, singers, conductors, and designers; includes operatic characters and opera companies; includes terminology; has some entries for musical comedies and their composers; illustrated.

Stambler, Irwin (ed.). *Encyclopedia of Pop, Rock, and Soul*. New York: St. Martin's Press, 1974. Covers individual groups, terms, types of music, and events; gives biographical information on persons and some critical evaluations; includes year-by-year listings of Gold Record Awards from 1965 to 1973.

————. *Encyclopedia of Popular Music and Rock*. Rev. ed. New York: St.

Martin's Press, 1973. Presents popular music from 1925, the people responsible for it, and its effects on modern life; gives definitions, biographical information, and synopses of musicals; lists award winners.

———— and Landon, Grelun. *Encyclopedia of Folk, Country and Western Music.* 2d ed. New York: St. Martin's Press, 1983. Emphasizes biographical information on current and past performers; defines terms; describes instruments; gives some historical background; includes items of general interest in this field.

Thompson, Oscar (ed.). *The International Cyclopedia of Music and Musicians.* 11th ed. Edited by Bruce Bohle. New York: Dodd, Mead & Company, 1985. Provides definitions, bibliography, biography, synopses of opera plots, and pronunciation of names; has short articles and lengthy discussions; international in scope, but has strong emphasis on American music and the American scene.

Handbooks

Cross, Milton, and Kohrs, Karl. *The New Milton Cross: More Stories of the Great Operas.* New York: Doubleday & Company, Inc., 1980. Reviews seventy widely performed operas act by act, aria by aria.

Ewen, David. *All the Years of American Popular Music.* Englewood Cliffs, N.J.: Prentice-Hall, Inc., 1977. Attempts to cover every style and field of popular music from colonial days to rock musicals; includes brief biographies of composers, lyricists, and librettists.

Fuld, James J. *The Book of World-famous Music—Classical, Popular and Folk.* Rev. and enlarged ed. New York: Crown Publishers, Inc., 1971. Gives information about many hundreds of the best-known musical compositions from twenty-five countries; includes music and words of songs, date of first appearance, and brief biographical information for composer, librettist, and lyricist; traces each melody to its original printed source; gives first line of music and words of each work in original key.

Geiringer, Karl. *Instruments in the History of Western Music.* 3d ed. New York: Oxford University Press, 1978. Explains the development of instruments and the relationship of instruments to artistic trends; discusses the musical trends of a period and the instruments in use (construction, manufacturers, and composers who used them); has drawings and photographs.

Haggin, B. H. (ed.). *The New Listener's Companion and Record Guide.* 5th ed. New York: Horizon Press, 1978. Gives critical evaluation, meaning of music, music producers, forms, and analyses of works.

Kobbé, Gustav. *The New Kobbé's Complete Opera Book.* Edited and revised by the Earl of Harewood. New York: G. P. Putnam's Sons, 1976. Traces the development of opera; gives stories of more than 300 operas; gives brief notes on composers; includes old and modern works; arranged chronologically, subdivided by country and within each country arranged by dates of the composers; includes musical examples.

Marcuse, Sibyl. *A Survey of Musical Instruments.* New York: Harper & Row, Publishers, Incorporated, 1975. Offers historical and technical information on the musical instruments of the world, tracing the development of individual instruments from their origin to the present; quotations from scholarly works and bibliographical references are given.

Martin, George. *The Opera Companion to Twentieth-Century Opera.* New York: Dodd, Mead & Company, Inc., 1979. Gives a synopsis of seventy-eight twentieth-century operas; translates key words in foreign-language operas; discusses personalities and aspects of twentieth-century opera.

Sandberg, Larry, and Weissmann, Dick. *The Folk Music Sourcebook.* New York: Alfred A. Knopf, Inc., 1976. Lists and analyzes significant folk and folk-based music and performers; gives wide coverage, including the blues, North American Indian music, and Chicano music; has lists of songbooks, instructional books, records, musical instruments, films, periodicals, videotapes, and music festivals.

The Simon and Schuster Book of the Opera: A Complete Reference Guide, 1597 to the Present. New York: Simon & Schuster, Inc., 1977. Arranges 777 operas chronologically by premiere date; gives composer, librettist, original plot source, and synopsis of each opera; provides illustrations, some in color.

Slonimsky, Nicolas. *Music since 1900.* 4th ed. New York: Charles Scribner's Sons, 1971. Presents chronologically the occurrences of musical importance in Europe and North America from January 1, 1900, through July 20, 1969; includes information on composers and their works and other items of musical interest; covers electronic music and instruments; includes a glossary. *Supplement to Music Since 1900.* By Nicolas Slonimsky. 1986. Brings coverage to 1985.

Zalkind, Ronald. *Contemporary Music Almanac, 1980/81.* New York: Schirmer Books, a division of Macmillan Publishing Company, 1980. A guide to rock music and the people who make it; covers history, events, awards, concerts, performers, trends, and business.

Biographical dictionaries[6]

Anderson, E. Ruth (comp.). *Contemporary American Composers: A Biographical Dictionary.* 2d ed. New York: G. K. Hall & Co., 1982. Gives brief biographical information for some 4000 composers born in 1870 or later who did the major part of their work in the United States; includes

---

[6] See also Chapter 10, Biographical Dictionaries.

information about career, compositions, professional positions, awards, etc.

Baker's Biographical Dictionary of Musicians. 7th ed. Edited by Nicolas Slonimsky. New York: Macmillan Publishing Company, 1984. Gives up-to-date information on the lives and works of performers, composers, critics, librettists, publishers, instrument makers, scholars, conductors, musicologists, and patrons of music; includes lists of works and selective bibliographies; indicates pronunciation of words and names; covers some American popular music. *The Concise Baker's Biographical Dictionary of Musicians*, 1987.

Ewen, David (comp. and ed.). *Great Composers, A Biographical and Critical Guide: 1300–1900.* New York: The H. W. Wilson Company, 1966. Supplies detailed biographical, historical, and analytical information on 198 composers of the past whose works are significant in the development of music; includes lesser masters and composers. *Composers since 1900* (1969) and *Composers since 1900: First Supplement* (1981), companion volumes, bring the coverage of composers up to date. The *First Supplement* contains biographies of forty-seven composers who have attained prominence since 1969, including traditional composers as well as composers experimenting with electronic and other modern types of music.

————. *Great Men of American Popular Song.* Englewood Cliffs, N.J.: Prentice-Hall, Inc., 1970. Tells the "history of American popular song through the lives, careers, achievements, and personalities of its foremost composers and lyricists from William Billings of the Revolutionary War to Bob Dylan" (subtitle).

————. *Musicians Since 1900.* New York: The H. W. Wilson Company, 1978. Gives detailed biographical information about 432 performing artists; includes photographs and bibliographical references; has a classified list of performers by instrument or voice; has articles about music and musicians; gives critical reviews of recordings of all kinds of music—classical, folk, jazz, and pop.

Examples of professional journals[7]

High Fidelity. New York: ABC Leisure Magazines, Inc., 1951– . (Monthly.) Covers current music performances, music, and performing artists; has articles about music and musicians; gives critical reviews of recordings of all kinds of music—classical, folk, jazz, and pop.

The Musical Quarterly. New York: G. Schirmer, Inc., 1915– . (Quarterly.)

[7] See also *Ulrich's International Periodicals Directory*, 27th ed., and *Magazines for Libraries*, 5th ed., edited by Bill Katz and Linda S. Katz.

Aims to present the best musical thought throughout the world; publishes research in the field of serious music; gives reviews of recordings and musical examples.

THE PERFORMING ARTS

The performing arts include dance in its various forms; dramatic and musical theater; motion picture films; television productions; writers, directors, composers, producers, performers, and choreographers; drama; and the history of each medium. The original performances are primary sources in the performing arts.

Reference materials (secondary sources) which are designed to aid in studying, understanding, and appreciating the performing arts include dictionaries, encyclopedias, handbooks, biographical dictionaries, and professional journals.

Bibliographies, guides, and indexes[8]

The Art Index. (See p. 253.)

Humanities Index. New York: The H. W. Wilson Company, 1974– . Includes opera, ballet, drama, television, and film reviews; lists important persons in various fields under appropriate subject headings.

Epstein, Lawrence S. (ed.). *A Guide to Theatre in America.* New York: Macmillan Publishing Company, 1985. Gives addresses of people, companies, and organizations associated with the theater, such as foundations, schools, colleges, and theater groups; arranged by state and city.

Performing Arts Books 1876–1981. New York: R. R. Bowker Company, 1981. A subject bibliography of works published or distributed in the United States in all areas of the performing arts between 1876 and 1981; covers radio, music, dance, television, theater, film, opera, circus, and other forms.

Salem, James M. (comp.). *A Guide to Critical Reviews.* New York: Scarecrow Press, Inc. Part I: *American Drama, 1909–1969*, 2d ed., 1973; Part II: *The Musical, 1909–1974*, 2d ed., 1976; Part III: *Foreign Drama, 1909–1977*, 2d ed., 1979; Part IV: *The Screen Play from The Jazz Singer to Dr. Strangelove*, 2 vols., 1971, *Supplement I*, 1982. Each gives a checklist of reviews.

---

[8] See also Chapter 9, Indexes, and Chapter 13, Bibliographies.

Dictionaries and encyclopedias

Bordman, Gerald. *American Musical Theatre: A Chronicle*. New York: Oxford University Press, 1978. Covers the period 1866–1978; gives a season-by-season account of the Broadway stage; includes a brief summary of the plot of each musical covered, together with its major credits and comments on its place in the history of the musical; the appendix covers major figures in the theater.

Bronner, Edwin. *The Encyclopedia of the American Theatre, 1900–1975*. Rev. ed. Cranbury, N.J.: A. S. Barnes & Company, 1980. Gives brief information about every major theatrical presentation on and off Broadway in this century: author, director, New York opening date, theater, number of performances, cast, and excerpt from a review; does not include musicals.

Brown, Les. *The New York Times Encyclopedia of Television*. New York: Quadrangle/The New York Times Book Company, Inc., 1977. Covers the history of television, personalities, technology, regulations, networks, cable TV, pay TV, public television, and legal cases; gives evaluative comments.

Chujoy, Anatole, and Manchester, P. W. *The Dance Encyclopedia*. Rev. ed. New York: Simon and Schuster, 1967. Covers history, dances, and dancers.

Clarke, Mary, and Vaughan, David (eds.). *The Encyclopedia of Dance and Ballet*. New York: G. P. Putnam's Sons, 1977. Discusses ballet and contemporary dance, especially of the twentieth century; traces the development of the major ballet companies; describes more than 300 ballets and modern dance works; gives biographical information on the choreographers, composers, designers, and dancers who created them; has numerous photographs and a glossary of terms.

Esslin, Martin (ed.). *The Encyclopedia of World Theater*. New York: Charles Scribner's Sons, 1977. Based on the German *Friedrichs Theaterlexikon* (1969); covers all facets of the theater; many strictly German-oriented articles have been removed and more English and American articles added; gives biographies and definitions of literary characters; illustrated.

Green, Stanley. *Encyclopedia of the Musical Film*. New York: Oxford University Press, 1981. Gives brief plot outlines and credits; provides factual information about singers, actors, actresses, songs, and awards.

————. *Encyclopedia of the Musical Theatre*. New York: Dodd, Mead & Company, 1976. Gives brief information on plots, casts, and background of about 200 musicals; has short biographies of composers, lyricists, librettists, performers, directors, choreographers, and producers; gives a list of awards through 1975.

Koegler, Horst. *The Concise Oxford Dictionary of Ballet*. 2d ed. New York: Oxford University Press, 1982. Covers all aspects of ballet for the past four centuries (ballets and their sources, dancers, choreographers, schools, theaters, companies, cities important to ballet); defines terms; includes information on ethnic, ballroom, and modern dancing.

McGraw-Hill Encyclopedia of World Drama. 2d ed. New York: McGraw-Hill Book Company, 1984. 5 vols. International in scope; gives articles on 910 dramatists and important movements and schools in world drama; has biographical articles; includes critiques of the work of all dramatists listed and synopses of their most important plays.

Terry, Walter. *Ballet Guide*. New York: Dodd, Mead & Company, 1976. Gives background, listings, credits, and description of more than 500 of the world's major ballets.

Wilson, G. B. L. *A Dictionary of Ballet*. 3d ed. New York: Theatre Arts Books, 1974. Emphasizes dance in English-speaking countries, with special emphasis on classical ballet; covers individual ballets, dancers, steps, technical terms.

Handbooks

Bawden, Liz Anne. *The Oxford Companion to Film*. New York: Oxford University Press, 1977. A guide to feature films; gives information about the art of films; has biographies of actors, actresses, directors, and producers; provides histories of major film companies and discussions of movements and genres; includes some critics; gives history of films in each country.

Bordman, Gerald. *The Oxford Companion to American Theatre*. New York: Oxford University Press, 1984. Arranged in dictionary style, with brief articles; covers social history of the theater, personalities, schools of acting, companies, plays, musical and nonmusical films, foreign plays, and theater-related subjects, both well known and obscure.

Halliwell, Leslie. *Halliwell's Film Guide*. 3d ed. New York: Charles Scribner's Sons, 1982. Provides information about some 12,000 sound and silent feature films from the United States and the United Kingdom and some from other countries released up to 1980; arranged alphabetically; for each film, gives a quality rating, country of origin, release date, running time, cast credits, author, producer, music credits, and a brief annotation.

Hardy, Phil. *The Film Encyclopedia.* New York: William Morrow, 1983–1984. 2 vols. Vol. I: The Western; Vol. II: Science Fiction. Both volumes give synopses, credits, review of each film; arranged alphabetically by decade. Additional volumes will cover comedy, romance, horror, musicals, and war epics.

Hirschhorn, Clive. *The Hollywood Musical.* New York: Crown Publishers, 1981. Lists in chronological arrangement every Hollywood film released from 1927 to 1980, giving information about title songs, performers, composers, directors, and producers; includes some black-and-white stills.

Hartnoll, Phyllis (ed.). *The Oxford Companion to the Theatre.* 4th ed. New York: Oxford University Press, 1983. Provides information on every aspect of the theater; deals with the theater in all ages and in all countries; includes new playwrights and players.

McDonagh, Don. *The Complete Guide to Modern Dance.* New York: Doubleday & Company, Inc., 1976. Traces modern dance from the last decade of the nineteenth century to the present; gives biographies of individual artists and describes their more outstanding performances and the works they created; describes dancers in terms of their worth and variety of approaches; gives stories of modern dances; lists the choreography of each artist.

The Simon and Schuster Book of the Ballet. New York: Simon & Schuster, 1979. A complete guide from 1581 to the present.

Biographical dictionaries[9]

Notable Names in the American Theatre. Clifton, N.J.: James T. White & Company, 1976. A new and revised edition of *The Biographical Encyclopedia & Who's Who of the American Theatre*; gives biographical sketches of those important in the American theater as performers, writers, directors, producers, etc; includes awards, premieres, information about theater groups, and theater buildings.

Directory of American Scholars. 8th ed., Vol. II. *English, Speech, and Drama.* Edited by the Jaques Cattell Press. New York: R. R. Bowker Company, 1982. Provides information about the education, positions, research, publications, etc., of persons in these fields.

Who's Who in the Theatre. 17th ed. Edited by Ian Herbert. Detroit: Gale Research Company, 1981. 2 vols. Vol. I, *Biographies*, gives biographical

---

[9] See also Chapter 10, Biographical Dictionaries.

information for actors, actresses, directors, playwrights, and other persons associated with the English-speaking stage. Volume 2, *Playbills*, covers the period 1976–1979 for Broadway, off-Broadway, London, Stratford-on-Avon, and Stratford, Ontario.

Examples of professional journals[10]

Dance Magazine. New York: Dance Magazine, Inc., 1926– . (Monthly.) A general-coverage dance magazine; includes all aspects of the dance, national and international (costumes, schools, dance companies, and tours); gives information about choreographers, dancers, and various kinds of dance (ballet and modern, ethnic and variety dancing).

Drama Review. Cambridge, Mass.: MIT Press, 1956– . (Quarterly.) Provides articles about new trends in drama; includes short plays; international coverage; has illustrations and photographs.

SPORTS AND RECREATION

Art, meaning "any skill or aptitude which enables the possessor to perform in a superior manner," includes sports and other forms of recreation.

There are reference sources which are useful for both the participant and the spectator in studying and understanding the numerous sports and games. They include encyclopedias, dictionaries, handbooks, and periodical publications.

Encyclopedias, dictionaries, and handbooks

Arlott, John (ed.). *The Oxford Companion to World Sports and Games.* New York: Oxford University Press, 1975. Traces the development of specific sports; introduces the sports that are played in national or international competition; explains the way a sport is played; gives a digest of the rules of each game, line drawings and diagrams, and action photographs; provides information on prominent players, teams, and stadiums; traces the historical development of each sport; intended to help the reader understand a sport when watching it for the first time.

The Baseball Encyclopedia. 6th ed. New York: Macmillan Publishing Company, Inc., 1985. Provides statistical information on all aspects of professional baseball from the 1870s to 1984: special achievements, awards, records, teams and players, all-star games, World Series, etc.

---

[10] See also *Ulrich's International Periodicals Directory.* 27th ed., and *Magazines for Libraries,* 5th ed., edited by Bill Katz and Linda S. Katz.

Cuddon, J. A. *The International Dictionary of Sports and Games.* New York: Schocken Books, 1979. Includes well-known sports and games and many that are not well known; covers history, rules, definitions, equipment, associations, and awards of each sport and game; mentions important figures in the various sports.

Hickok, Ralph. *New Encyclopedia of Sports.* New York: McGraw-Hill Book Company, 1977. Gives full information on more than 100 sports; includes related topics; has many illustrations.

Hollander, Zander (ed.). *The Modern Encyclopedia of Basketball.* 2d rev. ed. New York: Doubleday & Company, Inc., 1979. A comprehensive record of basketball with emphasis on the period since 1930; includes history, all forms of the game, records of professional players, and the Olympics; has some biographies.

Menke, Frank G. *The Encyclopedia of Sports.* 6th rev. ed. New York: A. S. Barnes and Co., Inc., 1978. Gives information about the background of sports, rules, records, players, and awards; covers nearly eighty sports.

Neft, David S., and Cohen, Richard M. *The Sports Encyclopedia: Baseball.* 6th ed. New York: St. Martin's Press, 1985. Covers facts and figures for American and National League baseball through 1984. Arranged by year, beginning with 1876.

Treat, Roger. *The Encyclopedia of Football.* 14th rev. ed. Edited by Pete Palmer. New York: A. S. Barnes and Co., Inc., 1976. Gives comprehensive coverage of football, with complete AFL, NFL, and AAFC records; has Hall of Fame information; includes the 1975–1976 season.

Webster's Sports Dictionary. Springfield, Mass.: G. & C. Merriam Company, 1976. Defines briefly and concisely terms used in the principal sports of the English-speaking countries; gives common sports abbreviations, specifications for playing fields, and discussions of sports equipment, officials' signals, and scoring; has many drawings.

Examples of professional journals[11]

Journal of Physical Education and Recreation. Washington, D.C.: American Association for Health, Physical Education, and Recreation, 1930– . (Monthly, September–June.) Covers physical education and related areas, such as dance, intramural sports, athletics; gives some history.

Sports Illustrated. Chicago: Time, Inc., 1954– . (Weekly.) Covers all the usual spectator sports; includes information about sports personalities, sports records, news of interest; has many illustrations.

---

[11] See also *Ulrich's International Periodicals Directory*, 27th ed., and *Magazines for Libraries*, 5th ed., edited by Bill Katz and Linda S. Katz.

Review Questions

CHAPTER 22. THE FINE ARTS

1. What subjects are included in the fine arts?
2. Look at Class 700 of the Dewey Decimal System, p. 48–49, and Classes GV, M, and N in the Library of Congress Classification System, p. 57–58. Name one title that treats each of the classes in the 700s. Name one title for each of the classes given in GV, M, and N.
3. What are the primary sources in the fine arts?
4. Name the kinds of fine arts materials—book and nonbook—which your library provides. What facilities or types of equipment are available for using these materials? Which nonbook fine arts materials are circulated?
5. Name several kinds of fine arts materials that a student can use in preparing an assignment; in making a class presentation.
6. Identify a source that will give information on:
   a Musical instruments
   b Classical music
   c Popular recording artists
   d Electronic music
   e Ballet companies
   f Opera
   g The World Series

CHAPTER

❧ 23 ❧

Literature

Any discussion of reference and information sources in the field of literature must be prefaced by a definition and a delimiting of the term "literature."

In its broadest sense, "literature" includes all preserved writings. In a more limited but still general denotation, it is the total written works of a people, such as the literature of America or the literature of England. It is also the name given to all writings upon a particular subject, such as the literature of geography, the literature of education, or the literature of history.

Specifically and as a subject area, literature is that class of writing which is notable for imaginative and artistic qualities, form, or expression. The forms of literature are poetry, drama, prose fiction, and essay. The Dewey Decimal class assigned to literature is 800. In the Library of Congress classification, literature and language share class P.

Reference sources in the field of literature are more numerous than in any other subject field. There are materials which cover all forms of literature, and there are materials in each of the literary genres, such as poetry, drama, and fiction.

Since each source is designed to serve a particular purpose, the representative titles listed below are grouped according to the purposes they serve and the kinds of questions they answer. Distinguishing features are noted with the bibliographical entry.

Bibliographies[1] and Guides

Bibliographies and guides in literature, as in other areas of knowledge, are designed to locate and evaluate the literature of a field. They may group works according to form, such as poetry, drama, fiction, or essay; they may be complete and include all works; or they may be selective, listing only a part of the literature. Not all bibliographies and guides do all these things.

Altick, Richard Daniel, and Wright, Andrew. *Selective Bibliography for the Study of English and American Literature*. 6th ed. New York: Macmillan Publishing Company, Inc., 1979. Provides a guide to a highly selective group of materials for research; includes more than 600 items; lists, does not annotate.

Bateson, Frederick Wilse, and others (eds.). *A Guide to English and American Literature*. 3d ed. New York: Gordian Press, Inc., 1976. Formerly *A Guide to English Literature*; now includes American literature and American authors; arranged chronologically according to periods; intended for the serious student of English literature.

Blanck, Jacob (comp.). *Bibliography of American Literature*. New Haven: Yale University Press, 1955–1983. Vols. 1–8. (In progress.) A selective bibliography limited to the past 150 years of American literature; describes but does not evaluate; arranged chronologically.

Fiction Catalog. 11th ed. New York: The H. W. Wilson Company, 1986. An annotated list of more than 500 of the best new and established English language fiction titles including literary classics and recent popular works; has author, title, and subject index.

Gohdes, Clarence Louis Frank, and Marovitz, Sanford E. *Bibliographical Guide to the Study of the Literature of the U.S.A.* 5th ed. Completely revised and enlarged. Durham, N.C.: Duke University Press, 1984. Lists types and sources of bibliography, biography, and other materials on forms and periods of the literature of the United States; includes allied fields such as folklore, theater, history, literature on or by racial and other minority groups, and materials on methods of research; gives sources on the book trade, publishing, and areas of literary study, e.g., women's studies.

Handbook of Latin American Studies. Gainesville: University of Florida Press, 1976–   . (Annual.) Publisher varies. A guide to books published in the Latin American countries, excluding science and technology, with criti-

---

[1] See also Chapter 13, Bibliographies.

cal notes; in two parts: *Humanities* and *Social Sciences*, published in alternate years.

Leary, Lewis Gaston. *Articles on American Literature 1950–1967*. Compiled with the assistance of Carolyn Bartholet and Catharine Roth. Durham, N.C.: Duke University Press, 1970. Based on the quarterly checklists of articles appearing in *American Literature*; supplements author's volume which covered articles from the first half of the century (1900–1950), published in 1954. Continued by *Articles on American Literature: 1968–1975*. Compiled by Lewis Leary with John Auchard. Durham, N.C.: Duke University Press, 1979.

The Literary History of the United States. Edited by Robert E. Spiller and others. *Bibliography Supplement II*. Edited by Richard M. Ludwig. New York: The Macmillan Company, 1972. Covers the period 1958–1970.

The Literary History of the United States Bibliography. Edited by Robert E. Spiller and others. New York: The Macmillan Company, 1963. This is Vol. 2 of *The Literary History of the United States*. Edited by Robert E. Spiller and others. 3d ed., rev. New York: The Macmillan Company, 1963. 2 vols. Classifies literature by author, period, and literary type; describes and evaluates. A 4th ed., rev., was published in 2 vols. in 1974.

Ludwig, Richard M., and Nault, Clifford, A. J. (eds.). *Annals of American Literature*. New York: Oxford University Press, 1986. Arranges American literature chronologically, with social history, journals, and foreign literature in a parallel column; gives year by year and alphabetically by author the most influential works of fiction, poetry, drama, and nonfiction published; examines related contributing facts, such as current events and prominent works published abroad as well as in America.

Mainiero, Lina (ed.). *American Women Writers: A Critical Reference Guide from Colonial Times to the Present*. New York: Frederick Ungar Publishing Company, Inc., 1979–1982. 4 vols. Provides bio-bibliographical and critical information about American women writers from colonial times to 1981, including writers in many subject areas.

Modern Humanities Research Association. *Annual Bibliography of English Language and Literature*. Cambridge: Cambridge University Press, 1920– . (Annual.) Lists books, pamphlets, and periodical articles in English and American literature with references to reviews of works; arranged chronologically.

Modern Language Association of America. *MLA International Bibliography of Books and Articles on the Modern Languages and Literatures*. 1921– . (Annual.) A classified list of books, articles, and monographs covering general literatures, criticism, linguistics, folklore, and other related topics; lists materials in English and in foreign languages.

Reardon, Joan, and Thorsen, Kristine A. *Poetry by American Women, 1900–1975: A Bibliography.* Hamden, Conn.: Scarecrow Press, 1979. Lists some 9500 separately published volumes of poetry by more than 5500 American women between 1900 and 1975.

Rubin, Louis D., Jr. (ed.). *A Bibliographical Guide to the Study of Southern Literature* (Southern Literary Studies). Baton Rouge: Louisiana State University Press, 1969. Aims to be "a compilation of some of the most useful materials available for the student who would begin work in the field of Southern literary study" (Preface); gives discussions of general topics and historical periods and 100 selected writers; covers folklore, drama, popular literature, and local color; gives a checklist of aids to the study of each area. *Southern Literature, 1968–1975*, compiled by the Committee on Bibliography of the Society for the Study of Southern Literature (Boston: G. K. Hall, 1978), contains the annotated entries from the annual checklists published in the spring issue of the *Mississippi Quarterly*.

Stapleton, Michael. *The Cambridge Guide to English Literature*. Cambridge: Cambridge University Press, 1984. Gives factual information about authors, major works, literary terms, subjects, and periods; articles are brief; arranged alphabetically. Includes English writing of all English-speaking countries.

Watson, George (ed.). *The Concise Cambridge Bibliography of English Literature, 600–1950*. 2d ed. Cambridge: Cambridge University Press, 1965. Lists books (and a few articles) about some 400 English writers; includes significant works by and about each writer; provides a concise statement of the bibliography of all periods of English literature through the early twentieth century; includes only writers native to or mainly resident in the British Isles.

_____ . *The New Cambridge Bibliography of English Literature*. Cambridge: Cambridge University Press, 1969–1977. 5 vols. Covers works by and about authors in both primary and secondary sources; covers belles lettres, philosophy, book publication, religion, history, travel, education, sports, newspapers, and magazines; the location of manuscripts and papers of some authors is given; Vol. V, *Index*, compiled by J. D. Pickles, 1977. Supersedes *The Cambridge Bibliography of English Literature*, edited by F. W. Bateson (1941, 4 vols.), and *Supplement*, A.D. *600–1900*, ed. by George Watson (1957). *The Shorter New Cambridge Bibliography of English Literature*, edited by George Watson (1981), is based on the 5-vol. work.

Indexes[2]

An index in the field of literature locates an article in a periodical or locates a poem, quotation, fairy story, play, essay, or other work in an anthology. Since the person seeking information does not always know the title and the author of a poem, play, or essay, a means of locating these items by subject is also necessary. It may be necessary to locate quotations by means of key words. The following indexes provide some or all of these kinds of listings; they are representative of the indexes available.

Chapman, Dorothy. *Index to Poetry by Black American Women*. Westport, Conn.: Greenwood Press, 1986. Provides information about black women poets from 1746 to the present. First of a two-volume work.

Essay and General Literature Index. New York: The H. W. Wilson Company, 1934– . (Semiannual.) Indexes by author and subject collections of essays and other collected works in many areas, particularly in the humanities and the social sciences; emphasizes literary criticism; indexes only twentieth-century publications, but includes authors of all ages and nationalities. (See Figure 9.6, p. 124.)

Granger's Index to Poetry. 8th ed. New York: Columbia University Press, 1986. Indexes by first line, title, author, and subject the poems appearing in 406 major anthologies published as early as 1900 through June 1985. Covers many new and current topics.

Humanities Index. New York: The H. W. Wilson Company, 1974– . (Quarterly.) Indexes by author and subject 295 English language periodicals in the humanities; includes poems, short stories, and other fiction in the periodicals as well as essays.

Ottemiller's Index to Plays in Collections. 6th ed., revised and enlarged. Edited by John M. Connor and Billie M. Connor. Metuchen, N.J.: Scarecrow Press, Inc., 1976. Indexes by author and title plays which appear in collections published from 1900 through early 1975.

Play Index. New York: The H. W. Wilson Company, 1953–1987. 6 vols. Covers plays published from 1949 to 1986, including plays in collections; single plays; radio, television, and Broadway plays; and plays for children and young adults. Gives plot, cast, set, and other information; lists plays under author, title, and subject.

Short Story Index. New York: The H. W. Wilson Company, 1953– . (Annual since 1974; five-year cumulations.) Indexes by author, title, and

---

[2] See also Chapter 9, Indexes.

subject short stories in more than 8000 collections published from 1900 to 1983 and 3000 stories in periodicals published between 1974 and 1983.

Sutton, Roberta B. *Speech Index*, 4th ed., revised and enlarged. New York: Scarecrow Press, 1966. Indexes world-famous orations and speeches for various occasions found in more than 250 collected works; covers works published through 1965; three *Supplements* cover the period 1966–1980.

Book Reviews[3]

A book review is a notice, usually in a periodical publication, of a current book or play. Its purpose is to tell enough about the work under consideration to enable the reader to decide whether or not to read it. Therefore, it describes the subject matter, discusses the method and technical qualities, and may examine its value or usefulness when it is compared with similar works. A book review may be only descriptive; it may also be critical and evaluative. Among the sources of book reviews are the book review sections of newspapers, notably *The New York Times Book Review*; professional and scholarly journals which review materials in specific subject fields, for example, *The American Historical Review*; trade publications, which announce and sometimes promote newly published books (see Chapter 13, Bibliographies); and bibliographies in the subject fields. The sources below cover book reviews in several fields and in several kinds of publications.

Book Review Digest. New York: The H. W. Wilson Company, 1905– . (Monthly except February and July.) Indexes reviews of books published or distributed in the United States, Britain, and Canada which appear in more than eighty periodicals and journals; each book reviewed is entered by author, with a descriptive note; gives citations to all reviews (which appear in the periodicals indexed) and excerpts from selected reviews; indicates the number of words in the review; has a title and subject index in each issue and a cumulated subject and title index every five years, covering the preceding five-year period. (See Figure 9.5, p. 119.)

Book Review Index. Detroit: Gale Research Company, 1965– . (Bimonthly; annual cumulations.) An index to reviews appearing in more than 300 periodicals (both magazines and newspapers) including the major adult and children's book reviewing media and many special-interest maga-

---

[3] See also Chapter 9, Indexes.

zines; gives book title, name, date, and pages of the publication in which the review is located; does not give excerpts from the reviews. Since 1976, has a title index.

An Index to Book Reviews in the Humanities. Vol. 1, No. 1, March, 1960– . Detroit: Philip Thomson, 1960– . (Quarterly; annual cumulation. Since 1963, annual.) Indexes reviews appearing in English in some 700 periodicals, American and foreign; does not include theology and archaeology; does not give excerpts from reviews.

Nineteenth Century Readers' Guide to Periodical Literature. New York: The H. W. Wilson Company, 1944. 2 vols. Indexes by author, subject, and illustrator fifty-one periodicals published in the 1890s. Includes book reviews.

Dictionaries and Encyclopedias

Dictionaries and encyclopedias of literature define words and phrases; identify references to fictional, mythical, and legendary places, characters, and events; explain the historical, geographical, social, economic, and cultural backgrounds of literature; provide biographical and critical information about authors and their works; and in some cases give pronunciation, summaries of plots, and bibliographical references. Some useful dictionaries and encyclopedias of literature follow.

DICTIONARIES

Beckson, Karl, and Ganz, Arthur (eds.). *Literary Terms: A Dictionary.* New York: Farrar, Straus, and Giroux, Inc., 1975. Defines and illustrates terms from poetry, drama, criticism, fiction, and rhetoric; identifies literary movements.

Bédé, Jean-Albert, and Edgerton, William B. *Columbia Dictionary of Modern European Literature.* 2d ed., revised and enlarged. New York: Columbia University Press, 1980. Covers the period from the end of the nineteenth century to the present; gives biographical and critical discussions of authors and overviews of the various national literatures, arranged alphabetically; provides brief biographies.

Cuddon, J. A. (ed.). *A Dictionary of Literary Terms.* Rev. ed. Garden City, N.Y.: Doubleday & Company, Inc., 1976. Covers technical terms, forms of literature, movements, well-known phrases, styles, and themes; has illustrative examples; gives sources for further reading; includes some foreign terms.

Eagle, Dorothy (ed.). *Concise Dictionary of English Literature*. New York: Oxford University Press, 1970. Covers authors, literary terms, characters, works, and recently established authors, notes scholarly developments and research since the 1939 edition.

Hammond, N. G. L., and Scullard, H. H. (comps.). *The Oxford Classical Dictionary*. 2d ed. Oxford: Clarendon Press, 1970. Revised in light of new discoveries and recent scholarship; covers ancient Greek and Roman periods; includes archaeology, geography, history, literature, mythology, philosophy, religion, and science; arranged alphabetically by topic; includes bibliographies.

Reed, Joyce M. H. (ed.). *The Concise Dictionary of French Literature*. New York: Oxford University Press, 1976. An abridgment and updated version of the *Oxford Companion to French Literature* (1959); reflects developments since 1959; gives essential facts on writers, works, forms, genres, and trends that have influenced French literature.

Shaw, Harry (ed.). *Dictionary of Literary Terms*. New York: McGraw-Hill Book Company, 1972. Defines, explains, and illustrates more than 2000 literary terms, references, and allusions likely to be encountered by the general reader in any kind of literature, including magazines, newspapers, plays, and television programs.

ENCYCLOPEDIAS

Cassell's Encyclopedia of World Literature. Rev. and enlarged ed. Edited by J. Buchanan-Brown. New York: William Morrow & Company, Inc., 1973. 3 vols. Provides general articles on literary genres, movements, and terms; brief histories of national literature and biographical articles; aims to cover all periods and peoples.

Gassner, John, and Quinn, Edward (eds.). *The Reader's Encyclopedia of World Drama*. New York: Thomas Y. Crowell Company, 1969. Emphasizes drama as literature, not as theater; does not include entries on actors or theatrical troupes; includes all countries; gives biographies and criticism of playwrights, plots of plays, articles on genres, and historical surveys of national drama.

Klein, Leonard S. (ed.). *Encyclopedia of World Literature in the 20th Century*. New ed. New York: Frederick Ungar Publishing Company, Inc., 1981–1984. 4 vols. Contains essays on national literature; critical articles on individual writers; covers more than eighty-five Asian and African literatures; has pictures, bibliographies, and an index.

Hochman, Stanley (ed.). *McGraw-Hill Encyclopedia of World Drama*. 5th ed. New York: McGraw-Hill Book Company, 1984. 5 vols. An international reference work; includes articles on theatrical subjects, terms, movements, and styles; covers national and ethnic theaters and theater companies; for works of major dramatists, gives critique, synopsis, and biography; has bibliographies, illustrations, and photographs.

Preminger, Alex, and others (eds.). *Princeton Encyclopedia of Poetry and Poetics.* Enlarged ed. Princeton, N.J.: Princeton University Press, 1974. Covers the full range of poetry from oral tradition to the latest trends (history, theory, technique, and criticism); international in scope; provides entries on the history of each major body of world poetry.

Handbooks

Handbooks provide short, concise answers to questions about literary authors, terminology, works, and trends; movements affecting literature; and events, places, and characters referred to in literature. The Oxford Companions, which are listed below, provide these kinds of information, although each volume may vary in points of emphasis. The other handbooks listed provide some or all of the types of information mentioned above.

Benét's *Reader's Encyclopedia.* 3d ed. New York: Harper & Row, Publishers, 1987. Covers all nations and all peoples; explains literary expressions and terms; identifies literary schools and movements, plots, and characters; gives information on musical compositions, works of art, writers, philosophers, scientists and musicians; treats myths, legends, and folklore; lists recipients of major literary awards; covers both classic and contemporary literature.

Brewer's Dictionary of Phrase and Fable. Rev. ed. Edited by Ivor H. Evans. New York: Harper & Row, 1981. Emphasizes the unusual; includes words which are not in the traditional dictionary; defines, identifies, and explains words, phrases, and allusions in nonfiction, folklore, and legend; gives pronunciation for some words; universal in scope.

Burke, W. J., and Howe, Will D. (eds.). *American Authors and Books.* 3d rev. ed. Revised by Irving Weiss and Anne Weiss. New York: Crown Publishers, 1972. Has articles on authors, books, periodicals, newspapers, publishing firms, literary societies, regions, and locations in the United States; primarily about authors and their works; secondarily about aspects of American literature; covers all types of writing, including western and detective stories; limited to the United States; covers the period 1940–1970.

Campbell, Oscar James, and Quinn, Edward G. (eds.). *The Reader's En-*

cyclopedia of Shakespeare. New York: Thomas Y. Crowell Company, 1966. A comprehensive view of Shakespearean criticism from Shakespeare's time to about 1964; provides convenient reference to persons, places, literary works, and other subjects relevant to Shakespeare.

Deutsch, Babette. *Poetry Handbook: A Dictionary of Terms*. 4th ed. New York: Funk & Wagnalls Company, 1974. Defines and explains literary terms; arranged alphabetically.

Drabble, Margaret. *The Oxford Companion to English Literature*. 5th ed. New York: Oxford University Press, 1985. Broad in scope; provides information about classical allusions in literature; gives biographical and background material; identifies characters; offers brief synopses of literary topics, institutions, and movements. Appendices include treatment of censorship, the English copyright law, and the calendar.

Feder, Lillian (ed.). *Crowell's Handbook of Classical Literature*. New York: Thomas Y. Crowell Company, 1964. Aims to help people interested in Greek and Roman civilization understand and enjoy classical literature; provides summaries, definitions, and factual material on authors, myths, and places; gives critical commentaries.

Frye, Northorop, and others (eds.). *The Harper Handbook to Literature*. New York: Harper & Row, Publishers, 1984. Defines literary terms and phrases; covers forms, styles, movements, and periods.

Hart, James David. *The Oxford Companion to American Literature*. 5th ed. New York: Oxford University Press, 1983. Provides biographical information on American authors; gives summaries of American literary works: novels, poems, essays, short stories, and plays; discusses movements and events that influenced American literature; presents literary and social history of America from 1578 to 1982 in chronological listing in parallel columns.

Harvey, Paul, and Heseltine, Janet E. (eds.). *The Oxford Companion to French Literature*. New York: Oxford University Press, 1961. Surveys French literary life from the emergence of the vernacular to 1939.

Hathorn, Richmond Y. (ed.). *Crowell's Handbook of Classical Drama*. New York: Thomas Y. Crowell Company, 1967. Gives synopses of plays, biographical information on dramatists, short articles on dramatic forms, criticisms, mythology, and other topics; includes lost and fragmentary works.

Holman, Hugh, and Harmon, William. *A Handbook to Literature*. 5th ed. New York: Macmillan Company Publishers, 1986. A comprehensive dictionary of terminology and literary history and criticism; defines and explains terms, words, phrases, and movements peculiar to English and American literature. Emphasizes terminology related to literary study.

The Penguin Companion to World Literature. New York: McGraw-Hill Book Company, 1971. 4 vols. The four volumes cover English literature; European literature; American literature; and classical, oriental, and African literature. Includes biography and critical evaluation of work, plots, and bibliography for each entry.

Salzman, Jack. *The Cambridge Handbook of American Literature.* Cambridge: Cambridge University Press, 1986. Treats the major landmarks in American literature; covers 500 authors from Henry Adams to the present; includes novels, plays, poetry, and historical narratives; emphasis is on authors; includes literary movements and literary magazines; gives chronological tables of American history and literature.

Toye, William (ed.). *The Oxford Companion to Canadian Literature.* New York: Oxford University Press, 1983. Surveys periods of literature and ethnic literature (e.g., Indian, Yiddish); covers literary genres—fiction, drama, poetry, folklore, science fiction; includes writers of French and French Canadian literature; provides literary and historical background; gives attention to the period since World War II.

Literature in Collections (Anthologies)

BOOK DIGESTS

Magill, Frank N. (ed.). *Masterpieces of World Literature in Digest Form.* Series 1–4. New York: Harper & Brothers, 1952–1969. Emphasizes poetry and philosophical works; has some essay-type reviews; is universal in scope.

————. *Masterplots.* Rev. ed. Story editor, Dayton Koehler. Englewood Cliffs, N.J.: Salem Press, 1976. 12 vols. "2,010 plot stories and essay reviews from the world's fine literature" (subtitle); begun in 1949; now covers more than 1000 authors; arranged alphabetically by title, gives plot summaries and essay-reviews of each; identifies form, author, period, type of plot, locale, date of first publication, principal characters, and themes; gives an evaluation of the work; poems, philosophy, and speeches have essay-reviews only.

Weiss, Irving, and Weiss, Anne de la (comps. and eds.). *Thesaurus of Book Digests 1950–1980.* New York: Crown Publishers, 1981. Offers plot summaries of 1700 important works published in English from 1950 to

1980; covers fiction, nonfiction, plays and poetry; arranged alphabetically by title; gives some evaluative comment.

Books of Quotations

Books of quotations provide (1) quotations on a subject for speeches or papers and (2) the correct wording and source of a given quotation. There are many collections of quotations; each one includes some quotations omitted in others, and thus they supplement each other. The usefulness of a book of quotations depends on (1) the kinds of quotations included, (2) the kind of reference provided (name of author, work from which the quotation is taken, collection in which it can be located, with page, stanza, or line), and (3) the ways each quotation is indexed (author, title, subject, first line, key word). Some useful collections of quotations follow.

Bartlett, John. *Familiar Quotations*. 15th ed., revised and enlarged; 125th anniversary ed. Edited by Emily Morison Beck and the staff of Little, Brown and Company. Boston: Little, Brown and Company, 1980. "A collection of passages, phrases and proverbs traced to their sources in ancient and modern literature." (Subtitle.) Arranged by author chronologically by birth dates; quotations arranged under author chronologically; key-word index; includes quotations from many contemporary authors.

Bohle, Bruce. *The Home Book of American Quotations*. New York: Dodd, Mead & Company, 1967. Companion volume to Stevenson's *Home Book of Quotations*; emphasizes distinctly American subjects and American writers and speakers who have commented on them; quotations are exclusively American and chiefly contemporary; sources are American or deal specifically with America.

Magill, Frank Northen. *Magill's Quotations in Context*. New York: Harper & Row, Publishers, 1966. 2 vols. Offers quotations of prose, poetry, and proverbs from all periods of western literature in context, with emphasis on English and American writers; arranged alphabetically with historical background information. Second Series, 1969.

The Oxford Dictionary of English Proverbs. 3d ed. Revised by F. P. Wilson. Oxford: Clarendon Press, 1970. Arranged alphabetically; gives dated uses in chronological order. *Concise Oxford Dictionary of English Proverbs*. Edited by J. A. Simpson. 1983.

The Oxford Dictionary of Quotations. 3d ed. New York: Oxford University Press, 1979. A comprehensive collection of quotations from English and foreign authors; thousands of new quotations reflecting recent events and writers have been added, including quotations from politicians and public figures; arranged alphabetically by author with an extensive key-word index.

Portnow, Elaine. *The Quotable Woman from Eve to 1799*. New York: Facts on File, 1985. Gives noteworthy quotations from women from the beginning to 1799; arranged chronologically; gives brief biographical information about the more than 800 women quoted. *The Quotable Woman, 1800–1981* (1982) gives similar material covering that period.

Stevenson, Burton Egbert (ed.). *The Home Book of Quotations, Classical and Modern*. 10th ed. New York: Dodd, Mead & Company, 1967. Includes classical and modern selections; provides quotations from important contemporary figures; arranged alphabetically by subject.

Tripp, Rhoda T. (ed.). *International Thesaurus of Quotations*. New York: Thomas Y. Crowell Company, 1970. Arranges 16,000 brief quotations under subject; about one-third of the quotations are from the twentieth century; original sources are given when known.

Biographical Dictionaries[4]

General encyclopedias, biographical dictionaries, handbooks, and histories of literature provide much information on the lives and works of authors. In addition to these sources, there are biographical dictionaries which are devoted exclusively to authors.

Contemporary Authors. Detroit: Gale Research Company, 1962– . (4-vol. cumulations.) Vols. 1 to 121 in print, 1987; aims to be an up-to-date source of bio-bibliographical information on authors in many fields and of many nationalities; includes little-known authors.

Dictionary of Literary Biography. Detroit: Gale Research Company, 1978– . A multivolume series; each volume treats a specific literary movement or period in bio-critical essays; gives personal and career information and discussion of all major works. Arranged alphabetically. 58 volumes had been published by 1987.

Grant, Michael. *Greek and Latin Authors: 800 B.C.–A.D. 1000*. New York: The H. W. Wilson Company, 1980. Gives biographical sketches of 376 authors from Homer to the Middle Ages; includes information about the

---

[4] See also Chapter 10, Biographical Dictionaries.

author's life, description of the titles and contents of the work, and critical commentary on the work; has bibliographical references.

Kunitz, Stanley J., and Colby, Vineta (eds.). *European Authors 1000–1900: A Biographical Dictionary of European Literature.* New York: The H. W. Wilson Company, 1967. Contains 967 biographies of European authors representing thirty-one different literatures; gives both biographical and critical information on each author; includes some portraits; lists principal works translated into English.

———— and Haycraft, Howard (eds.). *American Authors: 1600–1900.* New York: The H. W. Wilson Company, 1938. Presents some 1300 biographies of American authors, including politicians, religious leaders, educators, and professional persons, with lists of principal works, biographical and critical sources, and 400 portraits.

———— and ————. *British Authors before 1800.* New York: The H. W. Wilson Company, 1952. Gives biographies of authors from the beginning of English literature to Cowper and Burns with lists of principal works by and about each author; includes 220 portraits.

———— and ————. *British Authors of the Nineteenth Century.* New York: The H. W. Wilson Company, 1936. Contains more than 1000 biographies of British authors from William Blake to Aubrey Beardsley, with lists of principal works, biographical and critical sources, and some portraits of authors.

———— and ————. *The Junior Book of Authors.* 2d ed., revised. New York: The H. W. Wilson Company, 1951. Covers the lives of writers and illustrators of books for young readers from Lewis Carroll and Louisa M. Alcott to the present time. Companion volumes are *More Junior Authors* (1963), *Third Book of Junior Authors* (1972), *Fourth Book of Junior Authors & Illustrators* (1978), *Fifth Book of Junior Authors & Illustrators*, 1983.

———— and ————. *Twentieth Century Authors.* New York: The H. W. Wilson Company, 1942. Gives biographical information about more than 1800 authors throughout the world whose works have been published in English; includes a list of books by and about each author and a portrait. *First Supplement*, edited by Stanley J. Kunitz (1955), adds about 700 authors who have become prominent since 1942.

Rush, Theressa Gunnels, and others. *Black American Writers Past and Present: A Biographical and Bibliographical Dictionary.* Metuchen, N.J.: Scarecrow Press, Inc., 1975. 2 vols. Covers the period from the early eighteenth century to the present; gives brief biographical information, list of works, some quotations from the author, references to critical materials on the author; lists more than 2000 authors including writers from Africa and the West Indies who live or publish in the United States.

Wakeman, John (ed.). *World Authors, 1950–1970*. New York: The H. W. Wilson Company, 1975. Provides biographical and evaluative information on about 1000 authors, most of whom came to prominence between 1950 and 1970; international in coverage, includes not only imaginative writers but historians, critics, theologians, philosophers, scientists, and journalists whose works have a wide audience. *World Authors: 1970–1975* (edited by John Wakeman, 1979) supplements the earlier work and adds more than 300 writers who have become prominent in the years covered. *World Authors, 1975–1980* (edited by Vineta Colby, 1985) adds 379 authors who have become prominent since 1975.

Reference Histories[5] and Criticism

Literary criticism is concerned with the description, analysis, comparison, and evaluation of works of literature. There are various sources of critical articles: indexes to periodical literature (under the heading "literary criticism"), indexes to newspapers; indexes to collected works, general bibliographies (under literary criticism), bibliographies in the field of literature, biographical works which provide critical commentary or list sources of critical works, bibliographies which treat literary criticism exclusively, and histories of literature.

REFERENCE HISTORIES

The Cambridge History of American Literature. New York: G. P. Putnam's Sons, 1917–1921. 4 vols. Gives trends, evaluation, and extensive bibliographies.

The Cambridge History of English Literature. London: Cambridge University Press, 1907–1927. 15 vols. Emphasizes movements in English literature, influence of foreign literature on the literature of England, and bibliographies.

Elliott, Emory (ed.). *Columbia Literary History of the United States*. New York: Columbia University Press, 1987. Surveys the literature of the United States from prehistoric cave narratives to the 1980s; treats authors, literary movements, and forms of writing; covers all aspects of literature.

Sampson, George. *The Concise Cambridge History of English Literature*. 3d ed. Revised by R. C. Churchill. Cambridge: Cambridge University Press, 1970. Has sections on Indian, Canadian, Australian, and South African literature; has a new chapter on the United States from the colonial

[5] See p. 187.

period to Henry James, giving attention to the relations between American and British literature and the ways each has influenced the other.

CRITICISM

American Writers. New York: Charles Scribner's Sons, 1974. 6 vols. *Supplement*, 1979. 2 vols. A collection of 155 articles of literary criticism covering authors from the seventeenth century to the present; gives information about the author's life, style, and genre, and an analysis and evaluation of his or her works; includes poets, novelists, essayists, playwrights, short story writers, and philosophers.

Coleman, Arthur, and Tyler, Gary R. *Drama Criticism.* Denver: Alan Swallow, 1966, 1971. 2 vols. A checklist of interpretation of English and American plays in a variety of journals published since 1940.

Combs, Richard E. *Authors: Critical and Biographical References.* Metuchen, N.J.: Scarecrow Press, Inc., 1971. "A guide to 4,700 critical and biographical passages in books" (subtitle); includes a large number of books published in the past twenty-five years.

Contemporary Literary Criticism. Edited by Sharon R. Gunton. Detroit: Gale Research Company, 1972–   . A continuing series, provides lengthy excerpts from current criticism of major authors and playwrights now living (or deceased since 1960); 25 vols. in print in 1987.

Curley, Dorothy Nyren, and others. *Modern American Literature (A Library of Literary Criticism).* 4th enlarged ed. New York: Frederick Ungar Publishing Company, 1969. 3 vols. An index to hundreds of critical books, essays, articles, and reviews dealing with works of some 300 important twentieth-century American poets, novelists, dramatists, essayists; includes excerpts from the criticism. Vol. IV: *Supplement* to the 4th ed., 1976. *Second Supplement*, compiled by Paul Schlueter and others, 1985.

Eddleman, Floyd Eugene (comp.). *American Drama Criticism: Interpretations 1890–1977.* 2d ed. Hamden, Conn.: Shoestring Press, 1979. "Lists interpretations of American plays published 1890–1977 in books, periodicals, and monographs." (Preface.) *Supplement One*, 1984.

Eichelberger, Clayton L. (comp.). *A Guide to Critical Reviews of United States Fiction 1870–1910.* Metuchen, N.J.: Scarecrow Press, Inc., 1971. Lists reviews from thirty American and English periodicals, including some regional sources, of the period covered. Vol. II, 1974.

Gerstenberger, Donna (comp.). *The American Novel: A Checklist of Twentieth Century Criticism on Novels Written since 1789.* Chicago: The Swallow Press, 1970. 2 vols. Vol. I: *The American Novel 1789–1959;* Vol. II:

Criticism Written 1960–1968. Does not include reviews; is a listing by novelist of critical writings on particular works.

Inge, Thomas, and Others (eds.). *Black American Writers: Bibliographical Essays.* New York: St. Martin's Press, Inc., 1978. 2 vols. Identifies and evaluates bibliographies, editions, manuscript material, biographies, and criticism for major black American writers.

Kearney, Elizabeth, and Fitzgerald, Louise S. (comps.). *The Continental Novel: A Checklist of Criticism in English, 1900–1966.* Metuchen, N.J.: Scarecrow Press, Inc., 1968. Lists criticism from books and periodicals of the period covered. *1967–1980,* edited by Louise Fitzgerald, 1983.

Kuntz, Joseph M., and Martinez, Nancy E. *Poetry Explication: A Checklist of Interpretation Since 1925 of British and American Poems, Past and Present.* 3d ed. Boston: G. K. Hall, 1980. Indexes poetry explications in collected works and literary periodicals.

Davis, Lloyd. *Contemporary American Poetry: A Checklist.* Metuchen, N.J.: Scarecrow Press, 1980. Lists interpretations of poetry of British and American writers published in America. *Second Series,* 1973–1982.

Luce, T. James (ed.). *Ancient Writers: Greece and Rome.* New York: Charles Scribner's Sons, 1982. 2 vols. Introduces the Classical writers in clear nontechnical style; covers the entire Classical Age.

Magill, Frank Northen (ed.). *Magill's Bibliography of Literary Criticism.* Englewood Cliffs, N.J.: Salem Press, 1979. 4 vols. "Selected sources for the study of more than 2,500 outstanding works of Western literature." (Subtitle.) Emphasizes criticism published in the 1960s and 1970s, including criticism of novels, plays, and poems; also includes works of all literary periods; arranged alphabetically by author.

Palmer, Helen H. *European Drama Criticism 1900–1975.* Hamden, Conn.: The Shoe String Press, Inc., 1977. A checklist of criticism in books and periodicals in English and foreign languages; extends coverage through 1975.

————— and Dyson, Anne Jane (comps.). *English Novel Explication: Criticisms to 1972.* Hamden, Conn.: Shoe String Press, Inc., 1972. A checklist of critical articles arranged alphabetically by author and then by novel; lists criticism from 1957 to 1972 which is found in books and journals. *Supplement I* to 1975, edited by Peter Abernethy and others. *Supplement II,* 1981; *Supplement III,* 1986.

Scott-Kilvert, Ian (ed.). *British Writers.* New York: Charles Scribner's Sons, 1979–1984. 8 vols. A survey of major British writers from Langland and Chaucer to the present; gives for each author a biographical sketch, survey and evaluation of the author's principal works, and a bibliography of works by and about the author. *Supplement I*, 1987, adds writers who have become prominent during the period 1950–1980.

Stade, George, and others. *European Writers*. New York: Charles Scribner's Sons, 1983–   . Thirteen volumes are projected by 1988; gives biographical sketches and plot summaries; emphasis is on criticism; examines events which influenced an author; covers Middle Ages to the twentieth century.

Temple, Ruth Z., and Tucker, Martin (eds.). *Modern British Literature (A Library of Literary Criticism)*. New York: F. Ungar Publishing Co., 1966. 3 vols. Presents over 400 twentieth-century British and Commonwealth authors, giving excerpts from criticism of their works found in British and American sources; includes bibliography of author's works. Vol. IV, 1975.

Todd, Janet. *A Dictionary of British and American Women Writers 1660–1800*. Totowa, N.J.: Rowman and Allanheld, 1985. In bio-critical essays, provides information on 500 women writers, their achievements and place in literary history.

Tucker, Martin (ed.). *The Critical Temper: A Survey of Modern Criticism on English and American Literature from the Beginnings to the Twentieth Century*. New York: Frederick Ungar Publishing Co., 1969. 3 vols. Gives a view of the best twentieth-century criticism; shows wide range of thought within the criticism; gives excerpts from criticism and bibliographical references. Vol. IV (1979) adds criticism published during the past ten years.

Walker, Warren S. *Twentieth Century Short Story Explication*. 3d ed. Hamden, Conn.: The Shoe String Press, Inc., 1977. A bibliography of explications published in books, monographs, and periodicals; explications are listed alphabetically by critic's name; coverage is through 1975. *Supplement I to Third Edition*, 1980. *Supplement II*, 1984.

Yearbooks

American Literary Scholarship. 1963–   . Durham, N.C.: Duke University Press, 1963–   . (Annual.) Reviews the year's work in American literature.

Year's Work in English Studies. London: English Association, 1921–   . (Annual.) Surveys studies of English literature appearing in books and periodicals published in Britain, Europe, and America; includes material on the English language and on American literature.

Examples of Professional and Literary Journals[6]

American Literature: A Journal of Literary History, Criticism and Bibliography.
Durham, N.C.: Duke University Press, 1929–   . (Quarterly.) Published with the cooperation of the American Literature Section of the
Modern Language Association, gives research articles on history, criticism, and bibliography of American literature; includes critical book
reviews; reports dissertations completed or under way and research in
progress.

Poetry. Chicago: Modern Poetry Association, 1912–   . (Monthly.) Publishes
work of poets from the least-known to the best-established; offers essays
on poetry and critical reviews of books about poetry.

Sewanee Review. Sewanee, Tenn.: University of the South, 1892–   . (Quarterly.) The oldest literary magazine in the United States; contains original fiction, poetry, book reviews, essays, and recent criticism on literary
figures.

Abstract Journal

Abstracts of English Studies. Calgary, Alberta: University of Calgary Press,
1958–   . (Four times a year, September–June.) Contains abstracts of
articles on English and American literature from both American and
foreign journals; each issue has a subject index.

Review Questions

CHAPTER 23. LITERATURE

1. Explain the general meaning of the word "literature." Explain the
   word "literature" as a subject field.
2. Name and give an example of each type of information source in the
   field of literature. What purpose does each type serve?

---

[6] See also *Ulrich's International Periodicals Directory*, 27th ed., and *Magazines for Libraries*, 5th ed.,
edited by Bill Katz and Linda S. Katz.

INFORMATION SOURCES IN THE SUBJECT FIELD

3. Name a source that will:
   a Give the plot of a play
   b Give a chronology of American literature
   c Help locate a quotation from a public figure
   d Help locate criticism of an American novel
   e Identify American women writers
4. Review pp. 123–124. What is an anthology?
5. Read the complete entry from *Essay and General Literature Index*, p. 124.

CHAPTER

🐚 24 🐚

History and Geography

History

The discovery of writing and the beginnings of the measurement of time made possible the preservation of temple records which form the first historical annals.[1]

History is that area of study which is concerned with the recording of past events and with the interpretations of the relationships and significance of these events. It is divided into ancient, medieval, and modern, and each of these divisions may be subdivided geographically, as the history of medieval Europe or the history of modern England. History can be subdivided further into its economic, cultural, social, political, military, and literary aspects. The history class of the Dewey Decimal Classification System, 900, includes geography. G is assigned to geography in the Library of Congress classification; C, D, E, and F are the classes assigned to history and its subdivisions.

Many of the general reference sources—encyclopedias, dictionaries, handbooks, atlases, gazetteers, indexes, and bibliographies—provide material in the field of history. There are, however, specialized reference materials that have been prepared for the primary purpose of aiding students of history. They include bibliographies, guides, indexes, encyclopedias, chronologies, handbooks, dictionaries, historical atlases, general histories, and professional journals.

---

[1] T. R. Glover, "Historiography: Antiquity," *Encyclopaedia of the Social Sciences*, VII (1932), 368.

REPRESENTATIVE REFERENCE SOURCES IN HISTORY

Bibliographies, guides, and indexes[2]

America: History and Life. Santa Barbara, Calif.: American Bibliographical Center of ABC-Clio, 1964– . (Quarterly.) *Part A: Article Abstracts and Citations* offers abstracts and citations of articles on the history and culture of the United States and Canada from prehistoric times to the present from more than 2000 serial publications in 30 languages. *Part B: Index to Book Reviews* is an index to book reviews in more than 100 journals published in the United States and Canada. *Part C: American History Bibliography* lists books, articles, and dissertations. *Part D: Annual Index.* Parts A, B, and C are available on-line through the DIALOG service.

Freidel, Frank (ed.). *Harvard Guide to American History.* Rev. ed. Cambridge: Belknap Press of Harvard University, 1974. 2 vols. A selection of the more important works; covers research methods and materials, biographies, general histories, and histories of special subjects; includes political science, constitutional, and economic history; intended for the intelligent general reader, student, and scholar.

Frey, Linda, and others. *Women in Western European History.* Westport, Conn.: Greenwood Press, 1982–1984. 2 vols. V. I: *Antiquity to the French Revolution.* V. II: *19th and 20th centuries.* "A select chronological, geographical, and topical bibliography" (subtitle). Lists more than 17,000 citations from books and articles covering major topics relating to women, such as marriage, politics, education, and religion; *First Supplement*, 1986, adds more than 6500 citations from books and articles from the United States and foreign countries.

Harrison, Cynthia E. *Women in American History. A Bibliography.* Vol. II. Santa Barbara, Calif.: ABC-Clio, 1986. Covers periodical literature in history and related sources from 1976–1984, listing articles relating to women in such areas as Women and Religion, Women and Politics, Women and Education.

Library of Congress, Reference Division. *A Guide to the Study of the United States of America.* Washington, D.C.: Government Printing Office, 1960. "[Introduces] representative books reflecting the development of American life and thought" (subtitle). *Supplement 1956–1965.* 1976. Most of these titles are annotated.

---

[2] See also Chapter 9, Indexes, and Chapter 13, Bibliographies.

Paetow, Louis John. *A Guide to the Study of Medieval History*. Rev. ed. Prepared under the auspices of the Medieval Academy of America. New York: Kraus Reprint Corporation, 1959. Lists general books useful in the study of medieval history; provides readings to accompany the study of major areas of medieval history; gives some critical notes. *Literature of Medieval History 1930–1975: A Supplement to Louis John Paetow's A Guide to the Study of Medieval History.* Compiled and edited by Gray Cowan Boyce. Millwood, N.Y.: Kraus International Publications, 1981. 5 vols.

Social Sciences Index. (See p. 211.)

Dictionaries and encyclopedias

Carruth, Gorton. *The Encyclopedia of American Facts and Dates.* 8th ed. revised. New York: Harper & Row, Publishers, 1987. Presents some 15,000 facts and dates arranged by subject in chronological order from A.D. 986 through July 6, 1986; includes events in four fields of interest: politics and government, literature and the arts, sciences, and sports.

Champion, Sara. *A Dictionary of Terms and Techniques in Archaeology.* New York: Facts on File, Inc., 1980. Explains terms dealing with artifact analysis and classification, soil analysis, ceramics, excavation, stone tools, dating methods, and other techniques; has many illustrations.

Daniel, Glyn (ed.). *The Illustrated Encyclopedia of Archaeology.* New York: Thomas Y. Crowell Company, 1977. Treats the ancient cultures of the middle east, the far east, Africa, Australia, and the Americas from the Stone Age to the beginnings of modern times; includes information on major sites, key processes, pioneer archaeologists, technical terms, and allied sciences.

Dictionary of American History. Rev. ed. New York: Charles Scribner's Sons, 1976. 8 vols. Revised and brought up to date, this edition provides coverage of almost all aspects of American history; does not include biographical entries. Vol. 8 is the index. *Concise Dictionary of American History,* 1982.

Dupuy, R. Ernest, and Dupuy, Trevor N. *The Encyclopedia of Military History from 3500 B.C. to the Present.* Rev. ed. New York: Harper & Row, Publishers, 1977. A survey of the history of wars and military affairs; offers a series of narratives on these topics; organized chronologically by period; each period is prefaced by an essay on military trends and followed by a chronological arrangement of events and battles; gives a list of nations that have achieved independence since World War II.

Eggenberger, David. *Dictionary of Battles.* New York: Dover Publishers, Inc.,

1985. Gives accounts of more than 1500 battles from 1479 to the Vietnam War; provides battle maps. Arranged alphabetically.

Grant, Michael. *A Guide to the Ancient World*. New York: The H. W. Wilson Company, 1986. "A dictionary of classical places and names." (Subtitle.) Includes maps.

Kohn, George C. *Dictionary of Wars*. New York: Facts on File, 1986. Concisely describes major human conflicts from 2000 B.C. to the present; gives name of the war, dates, cause, and outcome or significance; alphabetically arranged by key word.

Langer, William Leonard (ed.). *An Encyclopedia of World History, Ancient, Medieval, and Modern Chronologically Arranged*. 5th ed., revised and enlarged. Boston: Houghton Mifflin Company, 1972. Covers all aspects of world history through 1970, including political, social, educational, and cultural events; gives attention to space, scientific, and technological advances; has maps and genealogical tables.

Morris, Richard B. (ed.). *Encyclopedia of American History*. 6th ed. New York: Harper & Row, Publishers, Incorporated, 1982. Cites essential historical facts about American life and institutions in both chronological and topical arrangements from the period of discovery; gives attention to recent developments in science and technology, to minorities and ethnic groups, and to film, dance, and popular music; includes biographical information for 500 notable Americans.

Parrish, Thomas (ed.). *The Simon and Schuster Encyclopedia of World War II*. New York: Simon & Schuster, Inc., 1978. Aims to cover every aspect of the war: issues, strategy, campaigns, battles, intelligence sources, conferences, treaties, ships, airplanes, guns, and persons connected with the war. Has maps and photographs; arranged alphabetically.

Roller, David D., and Twyman, Robert W. *The Encyclopedia of Southern History*. Baton Rouge, La.: Louisiana State University Press, 1979. Arranged alphabetically; treats all aspects of southern history from the first discoveries of the Spanish in the fifteenth century to 1978 (historical events, biographical information, history of each southern state—its art, literature, agriculture, economics, industry, music, folklore, and humor); defines and discusses usage of regional expressions; has maps and tables.

Sherratt, Andres (ed.). *The Cambridge Encyclopedia of Archaeology*. New York: Crown Publishers, 1980. Concentrates on the contributions of archaeology to our knowledge of human culture; covers history and techniques; gives chronologies; has maps and charts.

Stillwell, Richard (ed.). *The Princeton Encyclopedia of Classical Sites*. Princeton, N.J.: Princeton University Press, 1976. Presents more than 2200 articles on the archaeology of Greek and Roman civilization covering the period 750 B.C. to A.D. 565; gives sources for further reading.

Strayer, Joseph R. (ed.). *Dictionary of the Middle Ages.* New York: Charles Scribner's Sons, 1982– . 12 vols. (In progress.) Published under the auspices of the American Council of Learned Societies; covers the intellectual, cultural, philosophical, and socioeconomic accomplishments of western Europe, Byzantium, Islam, and the Slavic world from about 500 to 1500; articles range in length from brief descriptions and definitions to monographic treatment of major medieval subjects; includes biographies; each article has a bibliography. Vols. 1–10 available in 1987.

Handbooks

Dupuy, Trevor Nevitt, and Blanchard, Wendell (eds.). *The Almanac of World Military Power.* 3d ed. New York: T. N. Dupuy Associates in association with R. R. Bowker Company, 1975. Arranged by geographical area; gives information about the military and defense structure of every nation and summaries of factors that affect its military potential; includes maps and a glossary of military terms.

Grun, Bernard. *The Timetables of History: A Horizontal Linkage of People and Events.* New updated ed. New York: Simon and Schuster, 1979. Presents a columnar listing of major events in seven areas for each year from about 5000 B.C. to A.D. 1978; history, literature, theater, religion, philosophy, science and technology, music, and visual arts are represented; emphasis is on the western world.

Johnson, Thomas H., in consultation with Harvey Wish. *The Oxford Companion to American History.* New York: Oxford University Press, 1966. Summarizes lives, events, and places of significance in the founding of the nation; gives attention to social, political, and labor movements; includes the fields of art, science, commerce, education, law, sports and entertainment; provides some bibliographies.

Historical atlases

Atlas of American History. 2d rev. ed. Kenneth T. Jackson, Editor in Chief. New York: Charles Scribner's Sons, 1984. Portrays in maps all facets of American history from the earliest settlement to 1982, including all twentieth-century wars, shifts in population, and recent changes in the political, social, and economic characteristics of the country.

Barraclough, Geoffrey (ed.). *The Times Atlas of World History.* 2d rev. ed. Maplewood, N.J.: Hammond, Inc., and The London Times, 1984. For the general reader and the student; covers world history from the earliest times to the mid-1980s; symbols, color, and other devices are used on maps to show political, social, cultural, and economic development important to each period; each map is accompanied by commentary; has a world chronology and a glossary of names.

Cappon, Lester J., and others (eds.). *Atlas of Early American History: The Revolutionary Era, 1760–1790*. Published for the Newberry Library and Institute of Early American History and Culture. Princeton, N.J.: Princeton University Press, 1976. Covers in maps all aspects of life in the period of the Revolution: political, economic, religious, cultural, demographic, and military.

Coe, Michael, and others (eds.). *Atlas of Ancient America*. New York: Facts on File, 1986. Treats prehistoric people, their behavior, and their culture; provides an introduction to the art and archaeology of North, Middle, and South America; relief maps show site locations, political boundaries, cultural boundaries, etc.; provides text, illustrations.

Ferrell, Robert H., and Natkiel, Richard. *Atlas of American History*. New York: Macmillan Publishing Company, 1987. Covers American history from 1492–1980s in maps and charts, treating events, people, movements, population, international involvements, etc.

Finley, M. I. (ed.). *Atlas of Classical Archaeology*. New York: McGraw-Hill Book Company, 1977. An introduction to classical sites, covers the Greco-Roman world of 1000 B.C. through A.D. 500; describes archaeological sites; has diagrams, maps, and photographs.

Heyden, A. A. M. Van Der, and Scullard, H. H. (eds.). *Atlas of the Classical World*. New York: Thomas Nelson & Sons, 1959. Includes maps, illustrations, and text relating to the religious, economic, military, literary, artistic, and political history of Greece and Rome.

Moore, R. I. (ed.). *Rand McNally Historical Atlas of the World*. Chicago: Rand McNally & Company, 1981. Traces the history of mankind in maps and text; includes middle eastern and oriental cultures as well as western; devotes a special section to the United States; gives an overview of the events which are shown in maps.

Schwartzberg, Joseph E. (ed.). *A Historical Atlas of South Asia*. Chicago: The University of Chicago Press, 1978. Seeks to provide a comprehensive record in maps of the history of South Asia from the Old Stone Age to 1975; includes text, maps, bibliography, and charts; text is keyed to maps.

Shepherd, William R. (ed.). *Historical Atlas*. 9th rev. ed. New York: Barnes & Noble, 1964. Provides maps of world history from 1450 B.C. to the 1960s; new maps since 1929.

Talbert, Richard J. A. *Atlas of Classical History*. New York: Macmillan Publishing Company, 1985. Gives information about cities, battles,

trade, countries, and other areas of ancient history; has maps and illustrations.

Documents

Brownlee, Ian (ed.). *Basic Documents on Human Rights.* Oxford: Clarendon
Press, 1971. Includes documents from 1688 to 1967.

Commager, Henry Steele (ed.). *Documents of American History.* 9th ed. New
York: Appleton-Century-Crofts, 1973. Contains reprints of selected
original documents designed to illustrate the course of American history
starting with the age of discovery, arranged chronologically. 2d ed.
1981.

Biographical dictionaries³

Directory of American Scholars. 8th ed. Vol. I, *History.* Edited by the Jaques
Cattell Press. New York: R. R. Bowker Company, 1982.

Who Was Who in America, Historical Volume, 1607–1896. Chicago: Marquis—
Who's Who, Inc., 1963. Provides biographical material on more than
13,000 persons from 1607 to 1896; historical and statistical data on
federal government, states, major cities; major American events. Rev.
ed., 1967, adds about 200 biographies.

Reference histories

Cambridge Ancient History. New York: Cambridge University Press,
1929–1939. 12 vols. 5 vols. of plates. 2d–3d ed., 1970–   . (In progress.)

Cambridge Mediaeval History. New York: Cambridge University Press,
1911–1936. 8 vols. 2d ed., 1966–1967–   . (In progress.)

The New Cambridge Modern History. New York: Cambridge University Press,
1957–1975. 13 vols. and atlas volume.

Examples of professional journals⁴

American Heritage: The Magazine of History. Marion, Ohio: American Heritage
Publishing Company, 1949–   . (Bimonthly.) Covers all aspects of
American history, major and minor; social, educational, and cultural
trends; many illustrations in color.

American Historical Review. Washington, D.C.: American Historical Association, 1895–   . (5 per year.) The official journal of the American Historical Association; has scholarly articles based on original research; gives
book reviews.

---

³ See also Chapter 10, Biographical Dictionaries.

⁴ See also *Ulrich's International Periodicals Directory*, 27th ed., and *Magazines for Libraries*, 5th ed.,
edited by Bill Katz and Linda S. Katz.

English Historical Review. London: Longman Group, Ltd., 1886– . (Quarterly.) Covers history of all periods with some emphasis on Great Britain and the British Empire; offers scholarly articles; includes lengthy and critical book reviews.

Journal of American History. Bloomington, Ind.: Organization of American Historians, 1914– . (Quarterly.) Formerly *Mississippi Valley Historical Review*; the scope is almost entirely American; articles include biographical sketches as well as historical theory.

Journal of Modern History. Chicago: University of Chicago Press, 1929– . (Quarterly.) Published in cooperation with the Modern European History Section of the American Historical Association; articles cover European history from the Renaissance to the present; important documents are often published; has book reviews.

The Journal of Negro History. Washington, D.C.: The Association for the Study of Negro Life and History, Inc., 1916– . (Quarterly.) Aims to promote historical research and writing; articles are concerned with black life and history; has book reviews.

Geography

Geography—the term is derived from *geo*, the Greek combining form for "earth," plus *graphia*, "writing"—is the science concerned with the description of the earth's surface, its form and physical features, its natural and political subdivisions, and its climate, products, and population. Geography is frequently divided into mathematical, physical, and political geography.

In addition to atlases and gazetteers, which are recognized as being essential aids in the study of geography, there are bibliographies of, and indexes to, the literature of geography, dictionaries of place names and terminology, and guidebooks which provide descriptive material and maps not usually found in gazetteers and atlases.

REPRESENTATIVE REFERENCE SOURCES IN GEOGRAPHY[5]

Bibliographies, guides, and indexes[6]

Brewer, J. Gordon. *The Literature of Geography: A Guide to Its Organization and Use*. Hamden, Conn.: Linnet Books, The Shoe String Press, Inc., 1973. Discusses geographical literature and describes and evaluates individual

[5] See also Chapter 11, Atlases and Gazetteers.

[6] See also Chapter 9, Indexes, and Chapter 13, Bibliographies.

reference and research materials in the various categories: bibliographies, handbooks, histories, periodicals, government publications, etc.

Lock, Clara B. M. *Geography and Cartography: A Reference Handbook.* Hamden, Conn.: Linnet Books, The Shoe String Press, Inc., 1976. A revision of two earlier works; gives short articles on geographers (not living), societies, organizations, schools of geography, and journals, atlases, and other geographical sources.

Social Sciences Index. (See p. 211.)

Atlases[7]

The Bartholomew/Scribner Atlas of Europe: A Profile of Western Europe. New York: Charles Scribner's Sons, 1974. Uses text, diagrams, maps, and graphs to present a comprehensive picture of the eighteen countries of western Europe; gives statistical information on business and industry, economic conditions, transportation, trade, and other topics in addition to the physical-political maps.

Glassborow, Jilly, and Freemen, Gillian. *Atlas of the United States.* New York: Macmillan Publishing Company, 1986. Using maps, compares the states with one another; other thematic maps show population, climate, personal wealth, land use, and other topics; maps are accompanied by text; twenty-five maps are devoted to the nation as a whole comparing it with the rest of the world in such areas as health care, military expenditures, food production and consumption.

The New York Times Atlas of the World. In collaboration with the Times of London. New ed. New York: Times Books, 1980. Gives information about the origin and geology of the earth, climate, vegetation, trade and industry, use of energy, development of tourism, pollution and its effect on environment, minerals, and density and growth of population; most of the maps are by John Bartholomew & Son, Ltd., Edinburgh.

Rand McNally Commercial Atlas and Marketing Guide. Chicago: Rand McNally & Company, 1876– . (Annual.) Gives general information about each state in the United States and the territories and possessions regarding agriculture, communications, manufacturing, population, business centers, transportation, distance; covers the United States, Canada, and the world; has maps, tables, etc.

The Times Atlas of the World. Comprehensive 6th ed. New York: Times Books, 1980. Covers world physiography, oceanography, climatology, vegetation, air routes, and population density and distribution; includes

---

[7] See also pp. 140–142.

information on each country; maps by John Bartholomew & Son, Ltd., Edinburgh.

Gazetteers

For a discussion of gazetteers and examples, see pp. 139, 142.

Dictionaries, encyclopedias, and handbooks

British Association for the Advancement of Science. Research Committee. *A Glossary of Geographical Terms*. 3d ed. Edited by L. Dudley Stamp and Audrey N. Clark. London: Longman, 1979. Gives agreed-upon definitions and sources of definitions; includes references to origin and to current use and misuse; uses quotations from original and standard sources to clarify several meanings of a term. Includes foreign and new terms in geography.

Harder, Kelsie B. (ed.). *Illustrated Dictionary of Place Names, United States and Canada* (Hudson Group Book). New York: Van Nostrand Reinhold Company, 1976. Has more than 15,000 place names, including towns, villages, cities, counties, states, provinces, parks, and historic sites.

The International Geographic Encyclopedia and Atlas. Boston: Houghton Mifflin Company, 1979. Gives geographical locations and statistics as well as economic, educational, and cultural information; indicates pronunciation of words; does not define terms; has a 64-page atlas.

Monkhouse, F. J. (ed.). *A Dictionary of Geography*. 2d ed. London: Edward Arnold, 1970. Covers terms relating to landforms, oceanography, climate, soil, vegetation, archaeology, and cartography.

Rand McNally and Company. *The Earth and Man*. Chicago: Rand McNally & Company, 1976. Describes the planet Earth; discusses the preservation of the environment; uses colored illustrations to show the history of the earth and its present condition; includes diagrams, text, and maps.

Rand McNally Encyclopedia of World Rivers. Chicago: Rand McNally & Company, 1980. Locates and describes 1750 rivers which have made a contribution to man's progress and development (selection based on length of the river, natural beauty, and importance); for each river, includes the source, length, tributaries, dams, and history; combines maps and text; arranged by country.

Schmieder, Allen A., and others. *A Dictionary of Basic Geography*. Boston: Allyn and Bacon, Inc., 1970. Covers basic geographic terminology needed for an understanding of general geography; includes a brief, basic annotated bibliography.

Stewart, George R. *American Place Names: A Concise and Selective Dictionary for the Continental United States of America*. London: Oxford University

Press, 1970. Has 12,000 American place names; gives derivation, state, historical, geographical, or other interpretation of the name; includes unusual names.

Guidebooks

Other sources of geographical information are guidebooks. Produced by local or state chambers of commerce, state development commissions, local historical societies, travel bureaus, airlines, railroads, hotels, commercial publishers, and other sources, they are designed for the tourist and traveler, to attract trade and industry, or for purposes of historical record or local interest. They include certain types of information not found in gazetteers or atlases, such as maps of small towns and areas; places of strictly local or historical interest; and information about schools, churches, hotel accommodations, communications, transportation, and natural resources. If guidebooks are produced locally, they reflect the local interpretation of the social, economic, cultural, industrial, and other advantages of a given area.

Guidebooks are available from the local, state, or national agencies which are responsible for industrial development and tourism; from historical societies, tourist bureaus, and book stores; and from commercial publishers. Examples of guidebooks are:

The American Guide Series. Prepared by the Federal Writers' Project of the Works Progress Administration, 1937–1949. Reprinted and distributed by various publishers. Includes guides to each state and to many cities and regions, giving basic economic, historical, and sociological information about each one.

Baedeker Handbook for Travellers. Various publishers, 1828– . Published in English, French, and German editions, these handbooks cover Europe, North and South America, Egypt, and the near east, giving information useful to the sightseeing traveler.

Fodor's Modern Guides. Edited by Eugene Fodor. New York: David McKay Company, Inc., 1953– . Cover Europe, Asia, South America, Japan, and other areas, giving information useful to the sightseeing traveler.

Examples of professional journals[8]

Association of American Geographers. *Annals.* Washington, D.C.: Association of American Geographers, 1911– . (Quarterly.) Provides a scholarly approach to any geographical subject—human, historical,

---

[8] See also *Ulrich's International Periodicals Directory*, 27th ed., and *Magazines for Libraries*, 5th ed., edited by Bill Katz and Linda S. Katz.

economic, or cultural—in articles by professional geographers; illustrated with maps, photographs, tables, and charts; includes abstracts of papers given at professional meetings.

Economic Geography. Worcester, Mass.: Clark University, 1925–   . (Quarterly.) For geographers, economists, generalists in education and the professions; covers economic and urban geography; gives maps, tables, black-and-white illustrations, and book reviews.

Geographical Review. New York: American Geographical Society, 1913–   . (Quarterly.) Offers scholarly articles on all aspects of geography, historical and current; includes illustrations, maps, and charts; gives book reviews.

Historical Abstracts. Santa Barbara, Calif.: ABC-Clio, 1955–   . (Quarterly.) Publisher varies. "Abstracts more than 20,000 articles appearing in some 2000 journals published worldwide in history, the social sciences, and related humanities." *Beginning with Vol. 3 (1910) added listing of new books.* Part A: Modern Historical Abstracts; Part B: Twentieth Century Abstracts, 1914–present. Indexed by subject.

Review Questions

CHAPTER 24. HISTORY AND GEOGRAPHY

1. Examine Class 900, p. 49, and Classes C, D, E, F, and G, pp. 56–57. Name the large subdivisions in History; in Geography.

2. Which titles in this chapter would provide information on each of the areas included in the 900 class?

3. Which of the sources described in this chapter would be useful to the student in a class in the history of the United States; European history; archaeology?

4. Explain the usefulness of atlases in the study of history.

5. What is the difference between a gazetteer and a dictionary of geography?

PART

5

Using Library Resources for a Research Paper

CHAPTER

25

The Undergraduate Research Paper

The word "research" means "search, inquiry, pursuit" and comes from the French *rechercher*, "to seek again."

The true research paper involves not only studious inquiry into a subject but also critical and exhaustive investigation of that subject for the purpose of revising accepted conclusions concerning it in the light of facts uncovered by the investigation.

It may be said that elementary research begins when the first encyclopedia the student consults fails to provide the information which is needed to answer a question or to carry out an assignment, and it becomes necessary to consult several sources.

In general, the college research paper on the undergraduate level is an exposition, designed to present the results of the student's inquiry into, or investigation of, a chosen subject.

The undergraduate-level research paper—sometimes called a "term paper"—may be one of several kinds.

1. It may be a report which relates facts for the purpose of informing the reader or of showing progress over a period of time.
2. It may be a report, based on the student's investigations, which analyzes an event, a situation, or a period.
3. It may be a thesis,[1] that is, a paper which states and maintains by argument a position or a proposition.
4. It may be a thesis taking the form of presentation and evaluation of facts for the purpose of persuading or recommending.

---

[1] "Thesis" is also the name given to a dissertation presented by a candidate for an academic degree, usually the M.A. or M.S. degree.

The successful completion of any research paper depends upon the careful investigation of a subject; the ability to choose and evaluate materials and to take clear, well-documented notes; an understanding of the purpose and forms of footnotes and bibliography; and clear, logical, and orderly development and presentation of facts in keeping with the purpose of the paper.

Procedure

Some of the basic steps in writing a research paper are listed below.

1. Select a subject. In making the choice of a topic, consider the following factors:
   a Is this a subject of sufficient interest to you that you can make it interesting to your readers?
   b Can you study it seriously in the length of time allotted for writing the paper?
   c Can you cover it adequately in the number of words prescribed by your instructor?
   d Is it likely that you will find sufficient material on it to write a paper, or is it too new, too highly specialized, or too limited in appeal to have received coverage in books, newspapers, magazines, or other sources?
2. Restrict your subject if the topic you have chosen is too broad or too general for the assigned paper.
   a Look in the library catalog under your subject and read the subject headings immediately following to see how that subject is subdivided. Notice the subject headings listed at the bottom of each card to find further subdivisions and related headings. For example, if you are looking for material on the general topic "music," you may find in the catalog:

Music

Music, American

Music, American—Discography

Music as a profession
   See Music—Vocational guidance

Music festivals

Music, Gipsy
   See Folk Music—Gipsy

Music, National

Music, Popular (songs, etc.)

Musical fiction

Musical instruments, Electronic

b Find the subject in a periodical index; notice subdivisions; e.g.:[2]

Music	Musical performance
Music, Black	*See* Music—Performance
See Black music	Musicians
Music festivals	*See also*
Music in advertising	Orchestras
Musical instruments	Rock Musicians
Musical instruments, Electronic	

c See how a general encyclopedia index subdivides your subject.[3]

Music	Music box
Acoustics	Music festivals
Band	Music history
Computers	Musical comedy
Dance	Musical Instruments: Types
Folk	Musical theater
Jazz	
Rhythm	

d You may restrict your topic according to a period of time or geographical location or according to historical, social, cultural, or political significance; for example:

Music in Colonial America
The Contribution of Music to Media Production
Military Marches
Music in Television Commercials
The Influence of the Computer on Music

e In the following list of subjects, notice the progression from general to specific:

Music
National music

National music—United States
Music for national holidays
Music for the Fourth of July
Yankee Doodle Dandy

3. Choose the phase of your subject that you wish to investigate.
4. Determine the chronological period in which your subject falls.
5. Decide upon the purpose of your paper.
   a Is it to inform?
   b Is it to show progress?
   c Is it to analyze an event, a situation, or a period?
   d Is it to persuade and recommend?
6. Make a tentative statement of your thesis or purpose—that is, the proposition you will attempt to defend, clarify, or develop. For example, "Monasticism was of major importance in the preservation and development of literature during the Middle Ages," or "The printing press hastened the era of discovery and exploration."
   a Analyze your thesis as to the subject areas it includes or touches: geography, sociology, economics, history, literature, politics.
   b Decide what kinds of sources will provide the information you will need to write your paper.
      (1) Primary sources[4]—interviews, questionnaires, letters, diaries, manuscripts, memoirs
      (2) Secondary sources—books, journals, encyclopedias, other reference books, and nonbook materials.
7. Begin your preliminary search for material. In the preceding chapters, reference sources have been discussed, with emphasis upon their usefulness in providing material on a subject. Since subject headings are the key to the library catalog, the indexes, and most reference books, it is necessary, before using any of these sources, to determine the headings under which your subject may be listed.[5]
   a Consult the library catalogs and indexes to find the books and other materials in your library in which your subject, or any relevant phase of it, is discussed. Read the entire card or citation carefully to see what the source covers, the amount and kind of illustrative material it includes, the bibliographical references provided, the number of topics treated, and the topic which is given the greatest emphasis. Study the subject headings and *see* references as indica-

---

[4] Primary sources are those materials which have not been interpreted by another person. Secondary sources are materials which have been reported, analyzed, or interpreted by other persons.

[5] See pp. 71–73.

tions of other subjects which will lead to material. For example, if your subject is "folk music," some of the headings under which you will find material are:

Folk Music	Country music
See also	*See also*
Folk dance music	Bluegrass music
Folk-songs	Fiddle tunes
Folk dancing	Gospel music
Folk-lore	Guitar—Methods (country)
Folk music, American	Country and Western music
See also Country music	Country musicians
Folk music, French	
Folk music, Gipsy	

b Take the class number or numbers, and browse in these sections of the stacks, looking at the tables of contents and the indexes of books which may be helpful.

c Consult a printed bibliography or guide to find material on your subject which may not be listed in the library catalog, such as parts of books, pamphlets, and reports.

d Use a general dictionary for general definitions; use a subject dictionary for specialized definitions and terminology.

e Find an overview of your topic in a general encyclopedia, and then consult a subject encyclopedia for technical and specialized information. Consult the bibliography at the end of the article for additional readings and the index volume for other headings under which to look; remember that an encyclopedia is *only* the starting point.

f Use general and subject indexes to find recent material in periodicals and to find selections in collected works.

g Consult a handbook for statistical information or for identification of allusions to persons, events, dates, and legendary or mythological figures.

h Look up important persons connected with your subject in a biographical dictionary.

i Establish geographical locations and facts with the aid of an atlas or a gazetteer.

j Consult nonbook sources—microforms and visual and audiovisual materials—for information on your subject; you may want to use pictures, slides, or other forms to illustrate, clarify, or support points you wish to make in your paper.

k Look for current information and statistics in government publications, especially on topics in the social sciences, history, education,
and the sciences.

l Use primary sources whenever possible.

It is essential that you use a variety of sources in order to obtain a broad
view of your subject; to see its various aspects; to discover the factors
which influenced or contributed to it; to know the individuals, groups,
or organizations associated with it; to become acquainted with current
thinking as well as with past opinion regarding it; and to have some
understanding of the terminology of the field in question.

7. Begin preliminary reading

   a Read a background or overview article in a textbook or in a history
of the subject.

   b Examine a general article in an encyclopedia.

   c Read a popular article in a periodical.

   d Skim through the material at first.

   e Make brief notes of references for later serious reading, giving
adequate information for finding these references easily.

8. As you examine material, make a tentative bibliography of the materials
which you think you will use. (See Figure 25.1.)

   a Make the bibliography on cards.

      (1) Use cards of uniform size.

      (2) Use a separate card for each bibliographical reference.

   b Give basic information for each reference.

      (1) Author

      (2) Title

      (3) Facts of publication

      (4) Page or pages on which the information you are using can be
found

   c Include a brief descriptive statement of each work, indicating the
content and its usefulness for your subject.

9. Make a tentative outline of the major divisions of your paper. A
possible outline of the major topics in a paper on "The Music Festival in
the United States" is as follows:

   I   Definition and origin of the music festival

   II Beginnings in the United States

      A Nineteenth century

      B Early twentieth century

   III Development in the United States since the 1960s

      A Sponsors

      B Themes

      C Artists, performers

      D Seasons

Ref
ML
160
N4

New Oxford History of Music. Vol. X:
    The Modern Age 1890-1960. London:
    Oxford University Press, 1974.

    The background of music in the United
States during the period 1918-1960 is
discussed on pp. 569-574.

Vinton, John. "Change of Mind."
    Music Review, XXXV (November, 1974),
    301-318.

    Discusses changes in music in the
19th and 20th centuries.

Ref
ML
113
F8

Fuld, James J. The Book of World-
    Famous Music —Classical, Popular
    and Folk. Revised and enlarged edition.
    New York: Crown Publishers, 1971.

    Gives information about many hundreds of
the best known musical compositions.

FIGURE 25.1
Sample bibliography cards.

    IV   Popularity
       A Number
       B Locations
       C Attendance
    V   Contribution to the cultural life in the United States

10. Begin serious reading.
11. Take notes. (See Figure 25.2.)
    a The kinds of notes you may take include:
       (1) A restatement, in your own words, of the thought or thoughts of an author. It is important that in your paraphrase you do not lose the meaning of the original statement when you take it out of context.
       (2) A direct quotation, copied exactly, including punctuation. Any omission must be indicated by an ellipsis (. . .); any interpolation must be indicated by brackets ([ ]). Credit for a quotation must be given in a footnote.[6]
       (3) A critical or evaluative comment about a book or a person.
    b Use cards for your notes.
       (1) Use cards of uniform size throughout.
       (2) Give complete bibliographical information on the first card for each reference:[7]
          (a) Author's full name
          (b) Complete title
          (c) Imprint: place of publication, publisher, date
          (d) Pages and volume
          (e) Month, day, year, volume, and pages of periodical articles
          (f) Month, day, year, and pages of newspaper articles
    c Use one card for each reference. If more than one card is required to complete a note, number all cards and put the author's last name on all cards after the first.
    d Leave space at the top of the card for the subject headings, which will be the subdivisions of your outline.
12. Formulate your thesis.
    a State it simply, expressing the basic idea which you will develop.
    b Restrict it to one approach to the subject.
    c Avoid using ambiguous words or phrases.
13. Study your notes in order to restrict your subject further.

---

[6] A footnote gives credit for—or explains—a specific part of the text. Failure to give the source for a quotation or a paraphrase in which the language, thoughts, or ideas of another person are used as one's own is plagiarism. (See also pp. 316–318.)

[7] For additional information on nonbook sources, see pp. 161–162.

```
Ref
ML      Thompson, Oscar (ed.).  The International
100         Cyclopaedia of Music and Musicians.
T47         10th ed.  Edited by Bruce Bohle.  New
            York: Dodd, Mead & Company, 1975.


            Before primitive man could speak
        intelligibly, he expressed feelings of
        joy, grief, and fear in bodily movements
        accompanied by rhythmic noises.  (p. 990)
```

```
Ref
N       Encyclopedia of World Art.  New York:
31          McGraw-Hill Book Company, 1959-
E533        1968.  15 vols.

            "Among the most important factors
        that influence the evolution of musical
        instruments are . . . the prevailing
        style of a period and . . . the status
        of technology."  (Vol. X, p. 431)
```

```
Ref
ML      Fink, Robert, and Ricci, Robert.  The
100         Language of Twentieth Century Music:
F55         A Dictionary of Terms.  New York:
            Schirmer Books, A Division of Macmillan,
            1975.

            Useful for brief definitions of terms
        used in contemporary music.
```

F I G U R E 25.2
Sample note cards: (top) restatement or paraphrase; (center) quotation; (bottom) evaluative comment.

14. Make a preliminary detailed outline, either topical or in sentence form. Whatever form you choose, use it throughout your outline.
    a Make sure that your outline is organized in a logical manner, that each division and subdivision receives proper emphasis, and that each part of the outline is in the appropriate relationship to other parts of the outline.[8]
    b Fill in the gaps in your outline by additional reading and note taking.
    c Discard irrelevant material.
15. Remake your outline.
16. Write the first draft of your paper.
17. Use footnotes or endnotes when necessary.
    a Give the source of a direct quotation.
    b Acknowledge the source of an opinion or a discussion which you have paraphrased or of any specific material which cannot be considered common knowledge.
    c Give credit for statistical information, graphs, and charts you have used.
    d Suggest additional reading on a particular point.
    e Add an explanation to clarify or expand a statement in the text of your paper.
    f Make cross references to other parts of your paper.
18. Make a bibliography.
    a Give sources of materials you have used in writing the paper.
    b Suggest additional reading materials.
    c Include an entry for each work mentioned in a footnote.
19. Revise your paper.
20. Evaluate the entire paper, as to clarity of purpose, proper emphasis of important ideas and divisions, elimination of gaps and irrelevant material, accuracy in presenting or in interpreting facts, appropriateness of the choice of words, correctness of grammatical structure and form, unity and coherence in writing, adequacy of documentation, and consistency of bibliographical and footnote form.
21. Write the final draft of your paper.

Footnotes and Bibliography

Footnotes explain or give credit for specific items of information used in the text of the research paper and the exact location of any quotations used;

[8] Show the relationship of subdivisions in an outline (or of items in an enumeration) by indentation and the use of letters and numerals in the following order: I, A, B, 1, a, b, (1), (a), (b), (i).

THE UNDERGRADUATE RESEARCH PAPER

bibliography describes, as a whole, the work or works from which the citations are taken. The forms for footnotes and bibliography—that is, the order of listing the items and the punctuation, capitalization, and underlining of words in the title—vary according to the manual of style[9] which is followed by a college or by a department within a college. Each department may adopt a different form. In general, the variations are not in the items included but in the style in which they are presented. Footnote and bibliographical forms are not the same, and entries for books, periodical and newspaper articles, encyclopedia articles, and special materials differ from each other.

Before writing a research paper, students must understand the forms which they are required to use in making footnotes and bibliography, and they must follow those prescribed forms consistently.

GENERAL RULES FOR FOOTNOTES

In general, footnotes are numbered consecutively and are placed at the bottom of the page, in numerical order. They may be separated from the text by a solid line across the page. However, all footnotes may be placed at the end of the paper in a section for notes.

Arabic numerals are often used as footnote reference indexes, but asterisks and other symbols may be used also. Whatever reference symbol is employed, it must follow the passage to which it refers and must be placed after it (following the punctuation mark if there is one), just above the line.

The first citation of a footnote reference must give complete information in logical order.

1. Author's name (usually not inverted)
2. Title of publication
3. Facts of publication: place, publisher, and date
4. Volume and page numbers
5. Date of periodicals

[9] Among the style manuals which are available are: Kate L. Turabian, *A Manual for Writers of Term Papers, Theses, and Dissertations.* 5th ed. (Chicago: University of Chicago Press, 1987); *The MLA Style Manual,* edited by Walter S. Achtert and Joseph Gibaldi (New York: Modern Language Association of America, 1985); *Webster's Standard American Style Manual* (Springfield, Mass.: Merriam-Webster, Inc., 1985); William Giles Campbell and others, *Form and Style: Theses, Reports, Term Papers,* 6th ed. (Boston: Houghton Mifflin Company, 1982). Look in the library catalog under the subject "report writing" for other manuals of style.

Listed below are examples of one form which may be used in making footnotes:

[1] Ludwig Bieler, *Ireland, Harbinger of the Middle Ages* (New York: Oxford University Press, 1963), p. 24.

[2] Mabel M. Smythe (ed.), *Black American Reference Book* (Englewood Cliffs, N.J.: Prentice-Hall, Inc., 1976), p. 40.

[3] Edwin R. A. Seligman, "What Are the Social Sciences?" *"Encyclopaedia of the Social Sciences*, I (1930), 3–7.

[4] "Phoenicia," *The Encyclopedia Americana*, XXI (1958), 786–788.

[5] Robert Lewis Collison, *Dictionaries of Foreign Languages* (New York: Hafner Publishing Company, 1955), xv, quoted in Jean Key Gates, *Guide to the Use of Libraries and Information Sources*, 5th ed. (New York: McGraw-Hill Book Company, 1983), p. 98.

Usually the complete form of a reference is not repeated after it is first given; a shortened form is used, as follows:

1. When references to the same work follow each other without any other reference in between, use the abbreviation *ibid.*, from the Latin *ibidem*, meaning "in the same place."

[1] Louis B. Wright, *The Cultural Life of the American Colonies, 1607–1763* (New York: Harper & Brothers, 1957), p. 70.

[2] *Ibid.* (*Ibid.* is used in place of full reference and indicates that the source is exactly the same.)

[3] *Ibid.*, p. 87. (In this case, *ibid.* replaces everything except the page number.)

2. An abbreviation may be used in place of the title after a reference has been cited fully, unless there has been more than one reference by the same author. The shortened form would include the author's last name and the abbreviation *op. cit.*, which comes from *opere citato*, meaning "in the work cited."

[1] Charles H. Haskins, *The Rise of Universities* (Ithaca, N.Y.: Great Seal Books, 1957), p. 10.

[2] James W. Thompson, *The Medieval Library* (New York: Hafner Publishing Company, 1957), p. 49.

[3] Haskins, *op. cit.*, p. 40.

GENERAL RULES FOR BIBLIOGRAPHY

There are numerous forms for making a bibliography; there are different forms for government documents and for science, medicine, and other disciplines. (See footnote, p. 317, for titles of some style manuals.) It is necessary to know which form you are required to follow, and it is essential that you follow it consistently throughout your paper. Several principles must be adhered to in any form:

1. All bibliographical entries must be in accord with the purpose of the research paper.
2. All items must be presented accurately, clearly, and logically.
3. The bibliographical form which is prescribed for a given paper must be followed consistently in every entry.

The following items are included in a bibliographical entry:[10]

1. Name of the author
2. Title of the work as it appears on the title page
3. Edition, if it is other than the first
4. Number of volumes in the set, if the entire set is used
5. Place of publication, name of publisher, and date of publication
6. Number of pages in the book and price, if these items are required by the instructor

Bibliographical entries may be grouped according to kind—books, newspapers, periodicals, nonbook sources—or according to the main divisions in the research paper. They are arranged alphabetically within the groups.

Examples: Bibliography and Footnotes

Some examples of one form for making bibliography and footnotes are given below:

BOOKS

One author

Bieler, Ludwig. *Ireland, Harbinger of the Middle Ages.* New York: Oxford University Press, 1963.

[1] Ludwig Bieler, Ireland, *Harbinger of the Middle Ages* (New York: Oxford University Press, 1963), pp. 80–90.

[10] See also p. 161 for additional items for nonbook sources.

Two authors

Brown, James W., and Norberg, Kenneth D. *Administering Educational Media*. New York: McGraw-Hill Book Company, 1965.

[2] James W. Brown and Kenneth D. Norberg, *Administering Educational Media* (New York: McGraw-Hill Book Company, 1965), pp. 100–102.

Several authors

Davis, Cullom, and others. *Oral History: From Tape to Type*. Chicago: American Library Association, 1977.

[3] Cullom Davis and others, *Oral History: From Tape to Type* (Chicago: American Library Association, 1977), pp. 5–7.

Organization or institution as author

American Institute of History and Art. *Hudson Valley Painting, 1700–1750*. Albany, N.Y.: Albany Institute of History and Art, 1959.

[4] American Institute of History and Art, *Hudson Valley Painting, 1700–1750* (Albany, N.Y.: Albany Institute of History and Art, 1959), p. 3.

Edition of an author's work

Deutsch, Babette. *Poetry Handbook: A Dictionary of Terms*. 4th ed. New York: Funk & Wagnalls Company, 1974.

[5] Babette Deutsch, *Poetry Handbook: A Dictionary of Terms*, 4th ed. (New York: Funk & Wagnalls Company, 1974), p. 73.

Author's work edited by another person

Cary, Joyce. *Selected Essays*. Edited by A. G. Bishop. New York: St. Martin's Press, 1976.

[6] Joyce Cary, *Selected Essays*, edited by A. G. Bishop (New York: St. Martin's Press, 1976), p. 60.

Translation

Chastel, André. *The Age of Humanism: Europe, 1480–1530*. Translated by Katherine M. Delavenay and E. M. Gwyer. New York: McGraw-Hill Book Company, 1963.

[7] André Chastel, *The Age of Humanism: Europe, 1480–1530*, translated by Katherine M. Delavenay and E. M. Gwyer (New York: McGraw-Hill Book Company, 1963), p. 40.

Edited work

Smythe, Mabel M. (ed.). *The Black American Reference Book.* Englewood Cliffs, N.J.: Prentice-Hall, Inc., 1976.

[8] Mabel M. Smythe (ed.), *The Black American Reference Book* (Englewood Cliffs, N.J.: Prentice-Hall, Inc., 1976), p. 29.

Volume in a series

Lunt, William Edward. *History of England.* 4th ed. (Harper's Historical Series). New York: Harper & Brothers, 1957.

[9] William Edward Lunt, *History of England,* Harper's Historical Series, 4th ed. (New York: Harper & Brothers, 1957), p. 1.

Multivolume work

McGraw-Hill Dictionary of Art. New York: McGraw-Hill Book Company, 1969. 5 vols.

[10] *McGraw-Hill Dictionary of World Art* (New York: McGraw-Hill Book Company, 1969), vol. 1, pp. 80–85.

Reprint edition

Hansen, Waldemar. *The Peacock Throne: The Drama of Mogul India.* New York: Holt, Rinehart & Winston, 1972; reprint, Delhi, India: Motilal Banarsidass, 1981.

[11] Waldemar Hansen, *The Peacock Throne: The Drama of Mogul India* (New York: Holt, Rinehart & Winston, 1972; reprint, Delhi, India: Motilal Banarsidass, 1981), p. 2.

No author given

Webster's Standard American Style Manual. Springfield, Mass.: Merriam-Webster, 1985.

[12] *Webster's Standard American Style Manual* (Springfield, Mass.: Merriam-Webster, 1985), p. 8.

ARTICLES

Encyclopedia—signed and unsigned

Seligman, Edwin R. A. "What Are the Social Sciences?" *Encyclopaedia of the Social Sciences.* 1930. Vol. I.

[13] Edwin R. A. Seligman, "What Are the Social Sciences?" *Encyclopaedia of the Social Sciences,* I (1930), 3–7.

"Phoenicia." *The Encyclopedia Americana.* 1958. Vol. XXI.

[14] "Phoenicia," *The Encyclopedia Americana,* XXI (1958), 786–788.

Periodical article—magazine

Trippett, Frank. "The Weather: Everyone's Favorite Topic." *Time,* February 6, 1978, 76–77.

[15] Frank Trippett, "The Weather: Everyone's Favorite Topic," *Time,* February 6, 1978, 76–77.

Periodical article—journal

Dodson, Carolyn. "CD-ROMs for the Library." *Special Libraries* 78 (Summer 1987): 191–194.

[16] Carolyn Dodson, "CD-ROMs for the Library," *Special Libraries* 78 (Summer 1987): 191.

Essay, article, or chapter in a collected work

Morgan, E. "Women and the Future." In *Images of the Future: The Twenty-First Century and Beyond,* pp. 143–151. Edited by R. F. Bundy. Buffalo, N.Y.: Prometheus Books, 1976.

[17] E. Morgan, "Women and the Future," in *Images of the Future: The Twenty-First Century and Beyond,* edited by R. F. Bundy (Buffalo, N.Y.: Prometheus Books, 1976), p. 143.

Newspaper—signed and unsigned

Jonas, Jack. "A Visit to a Land of Many Facets." *The Sunday Star* (Washington, D.C.), March 5, 1961, sec. F, p. 1.

[18] Jack Jonas, "A Visit to a Land of Many Facets," *The Sunday Star* (Washington, D.C.), March 5, 1961, sec. F, p. 1.

"Dollar Down: Gold Up." *The Tampa Tribune,* February 25, 1982, sec. B, p. 6.

[19] "Dollar Down: Gold Up," *The Tampa Tribune,* February 25, 1982, sec. B, p. 6.

Book review in a magazine

Morrison, Philip. Review of *The Cosmic Inquirers: Modern Telescopes and Their Makers,* by Wallace Tucker and Karen Tucker. In *Scientific American* 255 (October 1986): 38.

[20] Philip Morrison, review of *The Cosmic Inquirers: Modern Telescopes and Their Makers*, by Wallace Tucker and Karen Tucker, in *Scientific American* 255 (October 1986): 38.

NONBOOK MATERIALS

American Men in Space, The Story of Project Mercury (Phonodisc). Narration by John H. Powers and Fred Hanney. N.p.: CMS Records, CMS 71000, 1964. 2 s, 12 in, 33⅓ rpm, microgroove, stereophonic.

[21] *American Men in Space, the Story of Project Mercury*, Phonodisc, narration by John H. Powers and Fred Hanney (N.p.: CMS Records, CMS 71000, 1964).

The Book Takes Form (Motion Picture). Los Angeles: Department of Cinema, University of Southern California. Released by NET Film Service, 1956. 29 min, sd., b&w, 16 mm. (The Written Word Series.)

[22] *The Book Takes Form*, Motion Picture (Los Angeles: Department of Cinema, University of Southern California, released by NET Film Service, 1956).

Duché, Jacob. *Observations on a Variety of Subjects, Literary, Moral and Religious*. . . . Philadelphia: Printed by John Dunlap, 1764. (Microfilm.)

[23] Jacob Duché, *Observations on a Variety of Subjects, Literary, Moral, and Religious*, Microfilm (Philadelphia: Printed by John Dunlap, 1764).

Hutchins, Robert Maynard. *A Vision of Athens* (Phonotape). Santa Barbara, Calif.: Center for the Study of Democratic Institutions, 1971. 1 reel, 5 in, 3¾ ips, 42 min, 15 sec.

[24] Robert Maynard Hutchins, *A Vision of Athens*, Phonotape (Santa Barbara, Calif.: Center for the Study of Democratic Institutions, 1971).

An Inquiry Into the Future of Mankind: Designing Tomorrow Today (Slide Set). N. p.: Center for the Humanities, 1974. 160 slides, color, 2 × 2 in, and 2 phonodiscs (2 s each), 12 in, 33⅓ rpm, 29 min.

[25] *An Inquiry into the Future of Mankind: Designing Tomorrow Today*, slide set (N. p.: Center for the Humanities, 1974).

Using Library Resources for a Research Paper (Filmstrip). New York: McGraw-Hill Book Company, 1966, 39 fr., color, 35 mm. (The College Library Series.)

[26] *Using Library Resources for a Research Paper*, The College Library Series, Filmstrip (New York: McGraw-Hill Book Company, 1966).

Video

Whales Weep Not. Produced by James R. Donaldson. Directed by Lana Jokel and James R. Donaldson. 26 min. Coronet/MTI Film & Video, 1986. Videocassette.

[27] *Whales Weep Not*, produced by James R. Donaldson; directed by Lana Jokel and James R. Donaldson, 26 min., Coronet/MTI Film & Video, 1986, videocassette.

Television program (or radio program)

PBS: "The Sleeping Beauty," 9 December 1987.

[28] PBS, "The Sleeping Beauty," 9 December, 1987.

Interview (or telephone conversation)

Moore, Fred, interview by author, April 12, 1988.

[29] Fred Moore, interview by author, April 12, 1988.

GOVERNMENT PUBLICATION

United States, Bureau of Labor Statistics, *Jobs for Which a College Education Is Usually Required*. Washington, D.C.: U.S. Department of Labor, Bureau of Labor Statistics, 1976.

[30] United States, Bureau of Labor Statistics, *Jobs for Which a College Education Is Usually Required*. (Washington, D.C.: U.S. Department of Labor, Bureau of Labor Statistics, 1976), p. 16.

Review Questions

CHAPTER 25. THE UNDERGRADUATE RESEARCH PAPER

1. Name and describe the kinds of research papers.
2. List the basic steps in writing a research paper.
3. What kinds of sources will help you restrict your subject for your term paper? In what ways can your topic be limited?
4. List the steps to follow in finding information on your topic. What sources will help you find the correct subject headings to use in your search?

5. What information should you keep about the sources you consult?
6. Describe a bibliography card—or printout, if you use a word processor.
7. What kinds of notes might you take in collecting material? In what form should you take notes?
8. What are the subdivisions in an outline?
9. What items should be included in a bibliographical entry? In a footnote?
10. How do the forms for bibliography and footnotes differ?

Index